MARKETING IS
EVERYBODY'S BUSINESS

D0796630

MARKETING IS EVERYBODY'S BUSINESS

THIRD EDITION

Betsy D. Gelb
University of Houston

Gabriel M. Gelb
Certified Management Consultant
Gelb Consulting Group, Inc.

Goodyear Publishing Company, Inc.
Santa Monica, California

Library of Congress Cataloging in Publication Data

Gelb, Betsy D   1935–
  Marketing is everybody's business.

  Includes bibliographies and index.
  1. Marketing. 2. Marketing—United States—
Case studies. I. Gelb, Gabriel M., 1929–
joint author. II. Title.
HF5415.G3915 1980   658.8   79–26183
ISBN 0–8302–5492–7

Copyright © 1980 by
Goodyear Publishing Company, Inc.
Santa Monica, California

All rights reserved. No part of this book may
be reproduced in any form or by any means
without permission in writing from the
publisher.

Current Printing (last number):
10   9   8   7   6   5   4   3   2   1

ISBN: 0–8302–5492–7
Y–5492–7

Printed in the United States of America.

CONTENTS

6 GOVERNMENT FINGERS IN THE MARKETING PIE / 134

7 WHAT ELSE AFFECTS MARKETING? / 155

8 MARKETERS YOU DIDN'T KNOW WERE MARKETING / 189

ACKNOWLEDGMENTS

A book like this one is the product of several different kinds of work. Fortunately, some top-notch people helped.

Among them are the reporters, writers, and editors who cover marketing activities so capably, and the authors and publishers who gave us permission to reprint copyrighted material. We also include Stacey Maxwell at Goodyear Publishing Company, who untangled the red tape of securing copyright permissions.

For help in unearthing information used in the original articles we thank Robert E. Bergin. We also appreciate the students in marketing management classes, whose comments have led to significant improvements as this book has gone from first to second to third editions.

INTRODUCTION

First the bumper stickers said, "The population explosion is everybody's baby." Then a college campus contributed, "Math is every student's problem."

And now, here's one more: "Marketing is everybody's business."

This book should demonstrate the truth of that statement to the doubters and reconfirm it for those who already know. Our purposes are to inform, to entertain, and—to sell this book. We, after all, are marketing too.

But so is everyone else; that's the point. The marketing dimension of human activities touches state legislatures and solid state electronics, General Motors and Colonel Sanders, T.V. and V.D. That last example is no exaggeration; city and state health departments are trying to promote, and in fact to "market," the idea that young people should know about the prevention and treatment of venereal disease. They are bringing their point of view before people who might accept it, in the same way that insurance companies, fruit stands, tire manufacturers, and hospitals bring to potential customers the opportunity to buy what they have to sell.

Of course, marketing involves more than spot announcements on television and more than selling a message or product. Sometimes marketing activities reach into the research lab; someone says, "Come up with a car that won't pollute." Sometimes marketing requires outguessing the competition; a construction firm submits a bid to build an office building, and has to determine what costs will be in three years and also what the other bidders think they will be.

You don't have to be selling something to be involved in marketing. Anybody who spends his money or his vote or his time reading a borrowed newspaper is touched by a marketing activity that convinced him to make that expenditure. Marketing, in short, takes in all the steps surrounding the production of value and its exchange for other value. So when a candidate trades you his or her promises for your vote, that's marketing, too.

SOME INSIDE STORIES

If all this explanation has led you to believe that marketing is rather grim—relax. Consider the advertising man who was asked to come up with a slogan for the Japanese-made Panasonic tape recorder and cheerfully proposed, "From those wonderful folks who gave you Pearl Harbor . . . " Or consider the national company that changed the name of its gasoline from Enco to Exxon because, among other things, the word "Enco" in Japanese means "stalled car."

And then there was the reported case of a new cigarette developed by Liggett & Myers. The company decided to bring out *Devon*, the first menthol cigarette that also had an activated charcoal filter. *Devon* was test-marketed in Florida; initial sales were good, but there were almost no repeat sales. Investigation brought out complaints from the one-time buyers that the cigarette wasn't really a menthol brand, though advertised to be one. L & M took another look; and finally realized that, yes, a charcoal filter absorbs menthol.

As the *Devon* tale should illustrate, the design of a product or service is thoroughly intertwined with its marketing. Of equal concern in the marketing process are channels of distribution, government agencies, and even the birthrate.

Textbooks on marketing management offer various frameworks for considering topics related to marketing. The selections in this book can profitably be examined using any of these frameworks.

Examples of topics we will explore:

1. *More goods is better:* Whether they're planes, raincoats, or beer.

2. *Services with a smile:* From an air express company . . . to the system that keeps burglars out of your home.

3. *Where marketing happens:* Food retailing, international trade zones . . . and why the milkman wears a sour expression.

4. *The price of success:* Shall it be controlled? Shall it be different for different customers?

5. *Promotion: More than a happy medium.* Ads, packages, personal selling . . . how the prospective buyer can get the message.

6. *Government fingers in the marketing pie:* Some cereal companies prove too successful . . . and Uncle Sam even watches Saturday morning TV.

7. *What else affects marketing?* New life styles? New daydreams? Zero population growth?

8. *Marketers you may not have realized were marketing:* Hospitals, police, museums . . . and very likely your own college.

We have collected articles on all eight topics from publications ranging from *Harper's* to the *Wall Street Journal,* and we have written others. At the end of each section, we've followed up with questions that a marketing manager or a student might ask himself or herself. Alternatively, a marketing instructor might ask them to students.

The articles and questions don't tell the whole marketing story. But among them they do hint at the extent to which (as we said at the beginning) *marketing is everybody's business.*

Cross-Reference Table for *Marketing Is Everybody's Business*	SECT. 1: Goods	SECT. 2: Services	SECT. 3: Channels and Distribution	SECT. 4: Price	SECT. 5: Promotion	SECT. 6: Political/legal environment	SECT. 7: Socio/cultural/technical environment	SECT. 8: Non-business marketers	Readings on research: #'s 1, 4, 11, 35	Readings on segmentation: #'s 3, 8, 25, 47, 52	Readings on international: #'s 2, 4, 21, 50
Enis	Ch. 11, 13	Ch. 11	Ch. 15	Ch. 12	Ch. 14	Ch. 7	Ch. 8		Ch. 10	Ch. 9	
Kotler *Marketing Principles*	Ch. 11, 12	Ch. 22	Ch. 14, 15	Ch. 13	Ch. 16-19	Ch. 23	Ch. 5-7	Ch. 22	Ch. 9	Ch. 8	Ch. 21
Markin	Ch. 7, 8	Ch. 7, 8	Ch. 9-11	Ch. 14-15	Ch. 12-13	Ch. 2	Ch. 2, 5, 17		Ch. 6	Ch. 4	Ch. 16
McCarthy	Ch. 10-12	Ch. 12	Ch. 13-16	Ch. 20-22	Ch. 17-19	Ch. 4	Ch. 4		Ch. 26	Ch. 5, 8	Ch. 25
Boone & Kurtz	Ch. 6, 7	Ch. 6, 7	Ch. 8-10	Ch. 14-15	Ch. 11-13	Ch. 2	Ch. 2, 5, 16		Ch. 3	Ch. 4	
Pride & Ferrell	Ch. 6, 7	Ch. 6, 7	Ch. 9-11	Ch. 8	Ch. 12-14	Ch. 15	Ch. 4, 16, 17	Ch. 19	Ch. 5	Ch. 3	Ch. 20
Rosenberg	Ch. 11-13	Ch. 11, 13	Ch. 20-22	Ch. 14-16	Ch. 17-19	Ch. 3	Ch. 4, 8	Ch. 10	Ch. 23	Ch. 7	Ch. 26
Stanton	Ch. 7-10	Ch. 24	Ch. 15-20	Ch. 11-14	Ch. 21-23	Ch. 30	Ch. 4, 5, 29	Ch. 30	Ch. 26	Ch. 3	Ch. 25

1 MORE GOODS IS BETTER

English teachers see it differently, but consumers around the world have acted for a long time as though "more goods is better." The demand for more housing has provided the foundation for demand in other fields—from disposable diapers to beer.

Furthermore, goods offer fine examples of the product life cycle, in which beer (the product class) flows on while light beer (a product type) emerges and various brands rise and fall within that category. Marketers are particularly interested in new products, and here they range from Italian-flavored ketchup to Cinch, the Procter & Gamble household cleaner that just never caught on.

Not all goods go to households, of course; marketing to organizational buyers is the watchword for Northrop and Tektronix. But they really have the same philosophy, as expressed by a Tektronix vice president: "We found we had to sell a benefit to the customer, not a set of engineering features."

Goods, whether on grocery shelves or in auto showrooms, are what most people first think about when they look at the whole area of marketing. For this look at marketing, goods are a good place to start.

1

COOKING WITH PSYCHOPHYSICS

by Berkeley Rice

> "The leading ketchup tastes like ketchup.
>
> The second leading ketchup tastes like ketchup.
>
> Now there's a delicious Italian alternative:
>
> Introducing Ragú Table Sauce, ketchup's Italian cousin."

You won't recognize this TV commercial unless you live in Boston or Milwaukee, where Ragú Foods' new Italian table sauce is now being test-marketed. Even if you do live in one of those cities, and happen to buy and try the new sauce as the label recommends, on hamburgers, hot dogs, meat loaf, or French fries, you probably won't appreciate its historic significance in the development of food technology.

Ragú Table Sauce may be the first new food product formulated largely by computer, using the science of psychophysics to measure and predict the tastes of consumers. And if two bright young psychophysicists named Howard Moskowitz and David Fishken succeed in their commercial enterprise, this technique may become a standard tool in the development of foods, cosmetics, fabrics, and perhaps even political candidates.

Moskowitz and Fishken have already conducted tests on such products as salad dressing, mayonnaise, coffee, lemonade, candy, yogurt, cereal, pudding, perfume, hand lotion, soap, shampoo, and deodorant.

They also plan an assault on the textile industry, measuring the "feel" of different fabric samples for blue jeans and women's hosiery. While not yet a household word, Moskowitz and Fishken's three-year-old firm, MPi Sensory Testing, has attracted such major clients as Pepsico, Campbell Soup, and Chesebrough-Pond's, and has grown into a business that this year will gross close to $500,000.

It is hard to prove that any new technique in market research is better than any other. None of the new products on which Moskowitz and Fishken have worked has been on the market long enough to prove anything about their techniques. Besides, sales of a new product depend on packaging, advertising, promotion, and marketing strategy as well as on taste. But those in the food industry with whom I discussed Moskowitz and Fishken's work generally agree that it represents a promising new method in a field that has seen little innovation in recent years.

THE HIGH STAKES OF MARKET RESEARCH

Millions of dollars and dozens of careers can depend on the consistency of a sauce or the crispness of a cracker. When food giants like Proctor & Gamble, General Foods, and General Mills bring out a new product, it becomes a major corporate and financial event. Moving a new product through the stages of concept development, market research, prototype development and testing, test-marketing, and the final advertising and promotional binge of national distribution can easily take up to 10 years and from $10 million to $20 million. Industry executives talk like generals about the "launch" or "rollout" of a new entry, speak guardedly about their "strategic research" and the marketing techniques "in our arsenal," and tend to be pretty nervous about talking to outsiders. In fact, of the dozen I spoke with, none was willing to be identified by name. "This is the high roller's ballgame in the U.S. economy," one industry analyst explained. "A lot of heads can roll if these products don't make it, so you can understand the paranoia."

Because of fears of industrial espionage, information about preservatives, stabilizers, sweeteners, and flavoring agents in new products is as closely guarded as the details of a new ballistic missile. Employees involved in new product research are warned against talking about their work to outsiders, and outside consultants are sworn to secrecy. "I've been in companies," says Fishken, "where I wasn't even allowed to go to the bathroom alone."

Of the 4,000 to 5,000 "new" food items that appear each year on supermarket shelves, only a few are truly new ideas, like Pringle's potato chips, Hamburger Helper, Sizzlean bacon, or Stove Top Stuffing. Most are merely new sizes, flavors, or packages of already existing products—often using cheaper or even artificial substitutes for more expensive ingredients.

At many companies, new products are often tested on employees. Senior executives at Post Cereals' offices in Battle Creek, Michigan, used to gather each Thursday morning at 7:30 A.M. for a breakfast test of whatever new product the research department happened to be working on at the time. Other companies traditionally hire free-lance professional tasters, some of whom specialize in such categories as beverages, candies, or baked desserts.

The trouble with experts and employees, however, is that they don't necessarily represent the unsophisticated taste of Mr. and Mrs. America, who are, after all, the ones whose judgment really matters. Many companies therefore hire market-research firms to test their products on panels of "typical consumers"—which usually means housewives, since they do most of the grocery shopping. The tests generally involve only a few samples of the new product and its existing competitors. The taste judgments are usually either sample comparisons ("Which one do you like best?") or simple ratings of the samples on scales of 1 to 5 or 1 to 10. The women are also asked such questions as what they like or don't like about the product; whether they find it too sweet or too tart; whether they think their husbands or children would like it; how often they would serve it to their families.

ESTIMATING TASTE MAGNITUDES

Taste-testing with consumer panels can be long and expensive, requiring repeated trips back to the food labs to formulate dozens of ingredients to achieve a more appealing flavor, color, and consistency within the limits of shelf life and cost. Moskowitz and Fishken claim that their computerized reformulations can reduce the testing process from a few years to a few months.

Their system of "magnitude estimation" avoids the limits of arbitrary taste scales like 1 to 5 or 1 to 10, and lets tasters adopt whatever scale they like, such as a 1 to 100 or even 1 to 1,000, thereby permitting much finer discriminations in judgment. Moskowitz and Fishken use many more product samples than in traditional testing, with each containing a precise variation of the basic ingredients. They also ask tasters to judge as many as a dozen specific product qualities, like flavor, sweetness, color and consistency.

Some industry critics scoff at Moskowitz and Fishken's claim for the sophistication of such procedures. The doubters say that without the training and practice of a professional, an average consumer cannot accurately taste more than a few samples at one session, or rate sensory characteristics meaningfully. Not so, says Moskowitz: "The human being is a phenomenally sensitive instrument, capable of much greater discrimination than has been thought in the past."

Interest in human sensory discrimination is what attracted Moskowitz and Fishken to psychophysics, the study of the relationship between physical stimuli and the human sensations they produce. Essentially, the field began about 1850, with the work of G. T. Fechner, a German philosopher-physicist who devised a tedious method of measuring human sensation in terms of "just noticeable differences." For the next century, academic researchers experimented with Fechner's and other methods, but until the 1950's, with the work of psychologist S. Smith ("Smitty") Stevens, no one had come up with anything that showed much promise of practical application. At Harvard University's psychoacoustics lab, Stevens developed the technique of "magnitude estimation," which allows people to adopt a numerical scaling system of their own choosing to rate their perception of the loudness of a sound, the sweetness of a taste, or the pleasantness of an odor. The ratings can be analyzed to establish the relationship between the subject's perceptions and the physical properties of the stimulus.

TESTING FOR "ITALIAN-NESS"

When Ragú Foods approached MPi Sensory Testing two years ago for help with the recipe for its new Italian table sauce, neither company was starting from scratch. Moskowitz and Fishken had worked on other sauces, and Ragú had already had considerable experience with Italian flavor. Commercials for Ragú's "extra thick and zesty" spaghetti sauce end with the lip-smacking line, "Now *that's* Italian." As one Ragú marketing man brags, "We've played around with the ingredients of Italian flavor for some time now, so it's nothing new for us. We *own* the taste and image of Italian."

To understand what is new about Ragú's new sauce, consider the market for ketchup. Originally a Chinese relish made from the brine of pickled fish, ketchup has also been made over the centuries from oysters, green walnuts, mushrooms, and various fruits, including the tomato. Today it is generally cooked up in large computer-controlled vats in the cavernous factories of H.J. Heinz (which controls nearly half the U.S. ketchup market), Hunt, and Del Monte. Since Heinz produced the first commercial version back in 1875, ketchup sales have grown steadily, to $650 million a year. Today, 97 percent of U.S. households use ketchup regularly, and 44 percent buy a bottle once a month.

Competing head-on with a giant like Heinz (annual sales of nearly $2 billion) would be foolhardy for a company new in the field. But the very similarity of most ketchups on the market led product developers at Ragú Foods to consider a flank attack. From consumer surveys, Ragú's researchers identified a vulnerable "market gap" consisting of those who find ketchup too bland or too sweet, and who would prefer something spicier. Hence the idea for "ketchup's Italian cousin."

The label on Ragú's new table sauce lists the ingredients as water, tomato paste, corn sweeteners, vinegar, salt, onion, and garlic powder, sodium benzoate (a preservative), and various spices and flavorings known only to those intimately involved with the project. MPi's job was to test various combinations of those ingredients to learn which tasted most Italian, and which had the greatest appeal to consumers.

The testing took place early in 1977, with groups of 50 women on the East and

West Coasts each tasting 18 different formulations, and rating them on 10 specific attributes. For "proprietary" reasons, as they put it, neither MPi nor Ragú will reveal any further information about that particular testing. We can, however, follow a similar test that MPi conducted a few months before on a sweet-and-sour sauce.

Consumer panels are customarily recruited by telephone surveys, or by visits to suburban shopping malls. In this case, the test group consisted of 26 women between the ages of 18 and 49 all of whom used sweet-and-sour sauce at home. None had any allergies, nasal congestion, or colds that would dull their palates. For a fee of $37.50, they went through three consecutive days of testing, with each session lasting two hours.

To establish individual rating scales, the women were first given a list of words chosen to elicit the widest possible ranges of likes and dislikes: flower, mud, perfume, murder, cigar, spaghetti, rattlesnake, love, hate, worm, kiss, and bunny. They then rated their like and dislike of the given words, choosing any range of numbers that, in their own judgment, gave them scope to express their gradations of feeling: 1 to 7, 1 to 10, 1 to 100, 1 to 1,000, or anything else. A computer later converted the individual rating systems into a single mathematical scale.

Each day the women tried 24 different formulations of the sauce; samples were made of two tablespoons of sauce on some ground beef. To remove the aftertaste, the women took a bite of cracker after each sample, rinsed their mouths with water, and waited for two minutes.

The women rated each sample first in terms of how much they liked it overall, and then rated 10 of its specific attributes, including flavor, color, sourness, sweetness, and consistency.

Now, if you multiply the 26 women by 24 samples per day, by 10 ratings per sample, by three days of tasting, you get a grand total of 18,720 separate numerical ratings, which helps explain why Moskowitz and Fishkin use a computer.

Once the computer had analyzed the data from the test ratings, it constructed a mathematical model of the relationships among the samples, the ingredients, and the panel's perceptions of different sensory characteristics. It could then answer such questions as how various concentrations of sugar affected the perception of sweetness, or which amount of thickener produced the highest ratings on consistency. Or, by correlating the overall "liking" ratings with those for specific attributes, it could produce an "optimal sensory profile" for the ideal sweet-and-sour sauce, which could then be tried out on other consumer panels.

With Ragú's new sauce, as with other new products, the final challenge takes place during test-marketing. Only one out of 10 products survives. (The survival rate from prototype to test-market is just as low.) If the folks in Boston and Milwaukee fail to respond with sufficient enthusiasm, "ketchup's Italian cousin" could end up among the thousands of casualties discarded each year before they reach the supermarket shelves.

The folks in Boston and Milwaukee are now learning about Ragú's new sauce through TV commercials that have also been pretested on consumer panels for popular appeal. The ads show a close-up of a sauce being poured on hamburgers by a man in a diner, a woman in her kitchen, and a father and son at a picnic. Each takes a bite and exclaims, "Mmmm. That tastes terrific!" Even if such clever dialogue and "visuals" work, however, that alone cannot sell the sauce.

As one industry source puts it, "Advertising may get people to buy a new product once or twice, but if they don't like it, they just won't buy it again."

PH.D.'S IN THE MESS HALL

As Ragú test-market results are being analyzed, no one will be watching the outcome with more interest than Howard Moskowitz and David Fishken. They met at Queens College, where each majored in psychology. Both went on to get Ph.D.'s in psychophysics: Fishken at Northeastern University in Boston, Moskowitz at Harvard, where he studied under the late "Smitty" Stevens.

Moskowitz ended up working at the U.S. Army research lab in Natick, Massachusetts, where, among other problems, he studied boredom with mess-hall menus, using the measuring techniques he had learned at Harvard. In 1975, after several years at the lab, many talks about his work at scientific conferences, and dozens of articles in academic journals, Moskowitz finally convinced MPi Marketing Research, a New York firm, to help him set up shop as MPi Sensory Testing (in which he and MPi share ownership). Fishken joined the firm in 1977. Their average fees for new-product testing now range from $15,000 to $30,000.

HOW NATURAL IS NATURAL?

In addition to relatively specific traits like sweetness, Moskowitz and Fishken are often called upon to measure or increase nebulous qualities like "naturalness," or "old-fashioned" flavor. Those are obviously not readily obtainable flavors that you can simply add to a mixture. To some extent, they are images created by packaging and advertising. But, to a considerable degree, they depend on specific ingredients and sensory characteristics. As one Ragú executive told me, "You can build a product to maximize Italian-ness, the same way you can maximize healthiness or naturalness."

That sort of talk may seem presumptuous to people outside the food industry. But recent advances in food technology have made it possible to achieve (some would say redefine) such qualities as naturalness far more efficiently than by Grandma's methods. Take the old childhood favorite, chocolate pudding. As one food technologist told me, "The real, old-fashioned kind was sort of tan, with lumps in it, and it didn't keep very long. Nobody would buy that stuff today. So you have to put artificial flavoring and coloring in it, and some stabilizer to prevent the lumps from forming, and preservatives to improve the shelf life." In fact, the rising price of the cocoa bean on today's world commodity market has led to the development of "chocolate-flavored" products that contain no real chocolate at all. A spokesman for McCormick & Co., one of the largest suppliers of artificial ingredients to the food industry, boasts that his company's research labs have re-created "almost every flavor known to man: meat, fruit, cheese, wine, vegetables—you name it, we've got it."

That sort of progress doesn't seem to bother Howard Moskowitz. "You see," he explains, "most consumers are not able to articulate their tastes in any meaningful detail. They know nothing about ingredients and their relationship to taste. It's like if you tell me the lights are out on your car, do I change the light bulb, the battery, the alternator, or the voltage regulator? With soft drinks, people often say they want a strong flavor. But, in fact, we've learned that many people want it sweeter when they say 'more flavor.' Some people say they want 'natural' flavor in a fruit-flavored beverage. But how do you make a natural flavor? It's more a matter of the individual's perception."

When they think about the future, Moskowitz and Fishken see unlimited possibilities. They are convinced they can test TV commercials and TV series pilots, treating each simply as a product composed of a number of measurable ingredients designed to elicit a certain response from the viewer. "And what about testing political candidates?" suggests Fishken, with considerable enthusiasm. "After all, a candidate is also a concept or a product. We could optimize or mold the perfect candidate."

That sort of talk bothers me. Just as the selling of a political candidate concentrates on packaging and image rather than on the reality of an actual record of achievement, the brave new computerized world of sensory testing concentrates on consumer perceptions rather than the substance or nutrition of the product.

Of course, such concern presumes that what Moskowitz and Fishken are up to is an accurate science. Howard Moskowitz says that "within the next 10 years we may look forward confidently to that era when sensory analysis fulfills its potential as a powerful science that can accurately assess a consumer's perceptions."

Personally, I'm still not convinced that the prediction of human behavior will ever be an accurate science. And I find that faintly reassuring. As one food-industry source with considerable experience in product-testing told me, "All this computer stuff is supposed to be objective. But people are funny. Their buying behavior is still subjective. The computer may say this is the ideal arrangement of ingredients, but nobody may buy it. It's still a crap shoot until it's out on the market."

From the November 1978 issue of Psychology Today. *Copyright © 1978 by Ziff-Davis Publishing Company. Reprinted with permission.*

2

'EVERYONE AT NORTHROP IS IN MARKETING'

by Louis Kraar

In an era of flourishing world arms trade — U.S. exports will probably hit a record $13 billion this fiscal year—only one American aerospace company relies mainly on its own salesmanship. Northrop, which does more business abroad than at home, had to learn to go it alone. Most military exports are made with Washington's active assistance or by the government itself. Northrop does its own selling. It is thriving as never before by specializing in relatively cheap and simple aircraft—and marketing them as imaginatively as they are designed.

The core of Northrop's successful strategy is not just peddling military hardware, but offering to help solve a customer nation's broader problems. "A customer's economic and political needs," a senior company executive says, "are just as important and interesting to us as the airplane itself." Northrop swings many of its sales by shaping contracts to meet some of these nonmilitary concerns. For instance, the Spanish government, which sought employment opportunities and know-how along with its fighter planes, got the chance to assemble the aircraft it bought.

Northrop leapfrogs its larger U.S. ri-

From the April 10, 1978 issue of Fortune. *Reprinted with the permission of* Fortune *magazine.*

vals with other inventive tactics. Shunning U.S. government-owned plants, which its competitors widely use, Northrop buys its own new manufacturing equipment—which helps boost its annual productivity growth 20 percent above the industry's average. Its sales are about half the size of Lockheed and General Dynamics, but Northrop's return on those sales is among the highest in aerospace. In 1977, its twenty-seventh straight year of profits, the company's earnings jumped 82 percent, to $66 million on sales of $1.6 billion.

A UBIQUITOUS TIGER

Chairman Thomas Jones, fifty-seven, fires up the relentless thrust overseas by telling all his people—from manufacturing supervisors to test pilots—that "everyone at Northrop is in marketing." Aircraft designers—not salesmen—are the first to call on potential customers. Then the engineers develop planes to meet a cost target, rather than the maximum performance possible. By limiting its technical risks from the start, Northrop has always delivered on time and at the promised price. And its planes are built so that they are fairly easy to maintain.

This marketing approach to design has made the F-5 Tiger the most widely deployed U.S. supersonic fighter. So far, Northrop has sold 2,220 of the lightweight jets to twenty-five nations, and the orders keep coming in. Relatively unprovocative because of its limited combat range (300 miles) and firepower, the little Tiger is just the plane for countries like Egypt and Indonesia. The economy-model fighter, priced at about $3 million, suits many nations that cannot afford to pay five times that much for a top-line American tactical plane. The F-5 also gives Northrop a market segment in which there is virtually no competitor except the Soviet MiG-21 jet fighter.

Now Northrop is hotly pursuing customers for its new, more advanced F-18, a fighter developed for its overseas clientele. It lined up the U.S. Navy to buy 800 planes through another special marketing gambit. The company teamed up with McDonnell Douglas, which has had long experience with the Navy and is doing the bulk of production work on the naval F-18's. Northrop will take the dominant role in manufacturing the international model, called the F-18L, which it is marketing exactly like a civilian airliner —by assuming commercial risks that are unprecedented for military exports. The company will modify the naval fighter for land-based use, offer it at a fixed price of about $9 million, and hopes to gain more than enough foreign orders to absorb its substantial front-end expenses. Jones expects the marketing gamble to pay off eventually with overseas sales of 1,500 F-18's.

HOW TO SELL SINGAPORE

The company carries on its search for new business with military precision. Its fourteen overseas offices in such spots as Madrid, Kuala Lumpur, and Riyadh feed superb business intelligence into corporate headquarters at Century City, California. The confidential "business-environment reports" of Northrop operatives vividly track everything from long-term defense plans to satisfied F-5 pilots who gain promotions to jobs that affect procurement decisions. Northrop's reports analyze political and foreign-policy developments more trenchantly than most newspapers and many diplomats.

In the high-security marketing room of its aircraft group in Hawthorne, California, the walls are covered with status boards that outline every development that might influence a possible sale in scores of countries. Welko Gasich, the group's senior vice president, makes frequent trips overseas to get a firsthand feel for market openings. He has just returned from talks with government ministers and air-force chiefs in—among other places—West Germany, a potential F-18 buyer, and Pakistan, which borrowed F-5's from Libya. With considerable understatement, he says, "We're very customer-conscious."

When Singapore indicated keen interest in Northrop's F-5, Gasich immediately dispatched a team that included an engineer, a lawyer, a pricing expert, a test pilot, and a maintenance specialist. In six days, they completely laid out the company's offer, which eventually brought about the sale of twenty-one aircraft. But the marketing effort didn't stop there. Northrop sent photographs of its fighters on the production line, and recently Gasich personally delivered to Singapore's defense minister a plastic paperweight filled with metal chips from the milling machine that turned out part of "his plane."

Jones puts his personal touch on Northrop's promotion by making it a point to meet foreign rulers in the right places. Last year, for instance, he went to great pains to wangle a White House invitation to Jimmy Carter's state dinner for the Shah of Iran, an insatiable buyer of planes. Later in the year, when the Shah's wife spoke at an Asia Society dinner in New York, Jones flew across the country to be there. "A sale," he says, "is the result of a conclusion that the customer reaches after years of work at all levels of the company."

A PEACE HAWK THAT PAYS

Northrop, in fact, anticipated the Shah's growing demands by investing in an exhaustive study of Iran's future needs back in the Sixties. Teams of company specialists lived in various parts of the country for months,

spotting opportunities that led to contracts for a national communications system, aluminum window frames, and other products. But attempts to "get ahead of the power curve," as the marketeers put it, do not always work. A similar effort in Thailand foundered when the Thai military regime was overthrown.

Increasingly, Northrop musters up creative sales tactics to meet the diverse demands of its clientele. In the Middle East, it has leveraged some of its F-5 sales into even larger service contracts to keep the jets flying. The most notable is a $1.4-billion arrangement, called Peace Hawk, with Saudi Arabia. The company is building three Saudi air bases—from taxiways to snack bars—and it is training local workers to maintain their fighter planes. "What we're selling," Northrop President Paine says, "is bringing more and more of their people into the twentieth century."

Peace Hawk makes Northrop practically part of the Royal Saudi Air Force, at least temporarily. Young Saudis "recruited right out of the desert," as Paine says, study English and the fundamentals of technology in Texas, and then return home to work side by side with Northrop maintenance men. Initially, the company's technicians service the planes, gradually turning over the job to their trainees during the three-and-a-half-year program. Eventually, the Saudis are supposed to be self-sufficient in taking care of the planes. Northrop, however, is already discussing a follow-on contract that it expects will be worth more than $1 billion. Paine explains, "You never finish building a modern air force."

By selling its expertise abroad, the company not only gains profits, but cultivates more intimate relationships with nations that buy a lot of planes these days. In Iran, Northrop is running the new Khatami air base near Isfahan, much as it does at several U.S. military installations. "We do practically everything except shoot live ammunition," Paine remarks.

THE DEMANDING SWISS CONNECTION

To nail down a contract in Switzerland for seventy-two F-5's, Northrop has made a unique economic commitment. In effect, it has become a global sales agent for Swiss industrial products, ranging from machine tools to water purifiers. The company has promised to find new business for Swiss manufacturers amounting to at least a third —$150 million—of the fighters' cost over an eight-year period. Most of the Swiss companies that need help are relatively small and lack international experience outside of Europe.

The company's "Swiss offset program," so named because it seeks to offset the order with benefits to the purchaser, is one of the most ambitious of such arrangements. Though other aerospace corporations have agreed to buy products from customers, they have never promoted them around the world. But the meticulous Swiss persuaded the Pentagon, which must approve major military exports, to pledge its "best efforts" to make Northrop deliver the promised marketing assistance. The company is fully aware that its credibility is at stake in its unusual sales campaign for the Swiss.

George Reed, Northrop's offset-program manager, has picked up the know-how of a trading company, he says, "sometimes painfully." Discovering "no reasonable catalogue" that fully presented Swiss industry, he had to compile and distribute a directory listing 800 companies. After fruitlessly dealing by mail and telex with would-be Swiss exporters, Reed opened a Zurich office. "Since there's little that anyone can show Nestlé and Sulzer Brothers about selling abroad," he says, "we end up working with firms that have limited marketing experience."

Taking the most direct route first, Northrop has bought Swiss electric cable, office equipment, and even paper clips. Every division of the corporation, in fact, has a yearly dollar target for buying from Switzerland. Reed placed a $294 order for small versions of the famous Swiss Army knives, which he hands out to promote the offset program. General Electric, which makes the fighter plane's engines, is helping by purchasing precision machinery. In the U.S., the steady rise of the Swiss franc makes it more difficult for Swiss manufacturers to be competitive, a requirement of the offset deal.

WHERE THE "BIG DOLLARS" ARE

But high-quality Swiss products can compete in many of the places where Northrop has good connections. In Saudi Arabia, its Peace Hawk construction work has provided opportunities for Swiss companies to sell steel shelving, walk-in refrigerators, and power generators. In other Third World countries, Northrop representatives are acting as middlemen for Swiss companies. Using both Northrop's contacts and its advice in shaping sales presentations, Pilatus has sold a dozen of its turboprop trainer planes to Bolivia for $6 million. Now the Swiss aircraft manufacturer, which is not a competitor of Northrop, is working on about fifteen other prospects that Northrop spotted for it. Taking a wholesale aproach, Reed is matching Swiss companies with a number of contractors that have large jobs "where the big dollars are," in the Middle East and Africa. For instance, an Italian engineering and architectural firm is putting many Swiss products into hotels in Tripoli and Tehran.

So far, the campaign has brought more than a hundred Swiss companies export orders totaling $50 million, a third of the required minimum. The Swiss government hopes Northrop's continuing effort will offset the entire cost of its planes.

BIGGER PROMISES TO CANADA

The company's help-the-customer strategy may play an even bigger role in selling its new F-18 fighter. The first potential foreign buyer, Canada, is staging a competition for a $2.3-billion contract—the country's largest military order ever. The Canadian government's choice from among six contenders will heavily depend on which aircraft manufacturer can do the most for Canada's sagging economy.

Lee Begin, one of the principal designers of the F-18 and supervisor of its marketing in Canada, says: "Sure, we've got the best military machine. But if we don't have the right industrial and economic solution, then we're not going to win with this airplane." Much of Northrop's formal 4,500-page proposal to Canada, and Begin's sales efforts, focus on a "Canadian Export Expansion" program that would go on for fourteen years. It promises not only to find new markets for manufacturers, but to give Canadian companies subcontracts on the F-18 and technological cooperation for starting new ventures.

If Canada picks the F-18, Jones faces a critical business decision. He must determine how many firm orders warrant spending about $100 million to re-engineer the naval planes for land-based operations. In contrast, rival fighter manufacturers draw development expenses from the Pentagon and pass on any cost escalation to overseas customers. But Jones says confidently, "We're not going to bet the company, though we're prepared to take a calculated marketing risk with our eyes open."

He likens the F-18 marketing gamble to Northrop's decision to invest a third of its net worth gearing up to become the subcontractor for 747 passenger-jet fuselages in 1966, when Boeing had only twenty-five solid orders and limited cash. That plunge eventually brought Northrop more than $1 billion of business, and it is still making 747 fuselages. Today it has the financial strength (including $370 million cash), Jones notes, as well as Washington's blessing, to offer the F-18 to nine countries, including Australia. The company expects to snare enough foreign orders within a year or so of launching the export model to assure its profitability.

CAN JONES BE WRONG?

But Northrop is not wagering everything on the new fighter. Its nearly $2-billion backlog includes work on military electronics, airborne targets, and the guidance system for the U.S. Air Force's proposed intercontinental Missile X. Besides, Jones says, the most likely reason for difficulty in exporting the F-18 would be "an even greater concern about cost, the very thing that would make an advanced version of the F-5 more likely. We have the Chevrolet as well as the Oldsmobile."

Lately, Jones has gained a new kind of prominence and wide respect by speaking out thoughtfully against the huge cost overruns on most U.S. weapons programs. He says, "There's no reason why the defense industry cannot be as efficient as any other sector of the economy." His ideas are credible to congressional committees and professional military forums because Northrop has always applied them to its own operations.

Somewhat surprisingly, he genuinely welcomes President Carter's efforts to control the arms trade. Washington has always been responsible for regulating military exports, he notes, but the Pentagon has often promoted foreign sales of some aircraft in order to reduce its own costs. To Jones's frustration, the Defense Department strongly pushed General Dynamics' lightweight F-16 fighter into half a dozen countries, while long denying him an equal opportunity to offer them his comparable F-18. He only demands a chance to compete in the remaining approved markets. He is finally getting it.

③
HOUSING BUILD-UPS AND DOWNS

Power lawn mowers, carpets, do-it-yourself remodeling equipment, air conditioners, and paint are goods with one thing in common: they boom when the housing industry booms. And the housing industry—homes, apartments, and townhouses—began the seventies explosively as compared with the last decade.

In the first stages of construction, a housing boom brings delight to marketers in basic industries: real estate development, building materials firms, and makers of built-in appliances such as heating and air-conditioning systems, ranges, and dishwashers. Then, as homes are completed and buyers move in, demand increases for the offerings of other businesses: savings and loan companies, grass-seed companies, carpetmakers, even art galleries. An official of the National Association of Home Builders says "a very rough guesstimate" of the size of the market served by basic housing industry suppliers as well as by secondary suppliers will surpass $100 billion in 1977.

In addition, there is the "mover-multiplier" effect, which occurs when a family moves into a new home and that family's old home is taken by another family. Not only do those who move out require new drapes and rugs, but those who move in probably will also. The rug that is to one woman a lively shade of turquoise is to another bilious blue, fortunately for the home-furnishings industry.

And the mover-multiplier effect does not stop with the first refurnishing purchases by the family that moves in. The replacement of the refrigerator reveals worn floor tile underneath; new carpets lead to new drapes to harmonize the color scheme. One thing leads to another, and when both a house and yard are considered, the chain hardly ends before the homeowner is ready to start again at the beginning.

Even companies that at first glance aren't thought to benefit directly from a housing boom may be doing so. For example, if a company makes textile machinery, carpet manufacturers are among its customers; and they share in the prosperity created by more housing starts. Even the chemical division of Borden, Inc., which makes adhesives for floor materials and wall coverings, anticipated a 10 percent to 15 percent gain in business in one year at the height of the housing boom.

A relatively new boomlet which resulted from the 1971-72 housing boom is the home-security business. Many firms are manufacturing and installing basic 24-hour alarm protection against intrusion into the home, and the homeowner can also add to the basic system automatic alarms for fire, smoke, and potential humidity damage; and connection to a central switchboard at police headquarters or a private security guard company.

The do-it-yourself home-improvement industry flourishes along with a housing boom. Americans spend about $9 million annually to improve, remodel, and repair their homes on a do-it-yourself basis. A spokesman for the National Home Improvement Council, a trade association of manufacturers, suppliers, and contractors, estimates that the industry has grown at an average of 6 to 10 percent a year for the past five years and

may boom along at 10 percent or better for the next five years.

To meet this demand, manufacturers turn out some 50,000 easy-to-install products such as sinks, ceiling tile, and doors. And retailers in this industry have developed vast supermarkets called "home centers" to join hardware stores in marketing these products. There are already 4,000 to 5,000 such centers across the nation, and their numbers are rising at an annual rate of 20 to 25 percent. To encourage novice do-it-yourselfers, salesmen in the large retail centers frequently tell people just how to go about building a darkroom in the basement or warn customers not to panel over a window or an electrical outlet. Easy-to-follow instruction booklets—and even short courses—are also available.

Unfortunately, the same massive economic consequences occur in reverse as the housing boom slows. And to understand the build-ups and downs requires a thoughtful look at this industry:

WHAT'S HOUSING?

Walking up and down the aisle of a supermarket it's easy to see that the cans and boxes on both sides of that aisle make up products we call "groceries." The same idea applies outside the store if you're walking up and down the street: the townhouses, apartments, and single-family homes on both sides of that street make up the products we call "housing."

But marketing a home and a hot dog differ dramatically. Credit, rarely an issue in the supermarket, often an issue in the furniture or appliance store, is all-important to the seller and buyer of housing. First, builders must borrow in order to build, and their interest costs are one factor that pushes up home prices. They must sell quickly; it is estimated that every day's delay in the completion of a $30,000 house costs the eventual buyer $14 in inflation, overhead and land-holding costs—more than $5000 for a delay of a whole year.

Second, the prospective buyer must borrow—probably an amount twice his or her annual income, but at an interest rate that expands enormously the amount actually paid out over the years of the mortgage. Furthermore, he must find a lender—and those costly delays run on while he does so.

ONE HELP: THE NO-FRILLS HOME

With all these factors raising single-family home costs, early 1976 saw the median price of a new home reach $41,700 —nearly three times the median U.S. family income and beyond the reach of 80 percent of U.S. families. The result, in many areas, was a 1976 newcomer—the no-frills home.

Money magazine called this new housing product a Minihouse—missing many frills from previous years, but priced between $20,000 and $40,000. Says *Money's* reporter, Jeremy Main:

> Reminiscent of cheap structures put up in the post-World War II building boom, these so-called basic houses, confined to developments, are unlikely to win any architectural awards. If well built and designed, however, they can be comfortable, serviceable and surprisingly cheap. As a prime example, Fox & Jacobs Inc., the largest house builder in Dallas, is producing a ranch house called the "Today," with three bedrooms, two baths and a one-car garage, for $20,450. The house crowds its seventh-of-an-acre lot and has a rather cramped "family" room—a living room, dining room and kitchen all in one. But it is centrally air conditioned and shag carpeted wall to wall in the family room, master bedroom and hall.

Builders don't like to use the word basic or any other term that implies cheapness. They insist there is no sacrifice of quality. They prefer to talk of "affordable" or "young family" houses. Basic houses are, in fact, "starters"—usually the first house purchased by a young family. While the market for over-$40,000 houses still flourished, builders virtually ceased making starter houses. But now they are beginning to realize that the customers they had been ignoring are precisely the people who still want to buy. People who already own houses may postpone shopping for bigger houses in hard times, but new families must find something to live in.

Business Week, eyeing the disappearance of housing "frills," found regional differences in where the cuts were made. Atlanta builder William R. Probst, they reported, plans homes with only 1,200 sq. ft. to 1,400 sq. ft. of space. Deltona Corp. in Miami eliminates garages, carports, and screened porches, and lowers ceilings by six inches. Los Angeles-based Kaufman & Broad, Inc., scratches dishwashers, refrigerators, and other extras, and shaves space from both house and basement. Other builders eliminate sod, leave some space unfinished, or use cheaper materials.

Massachusetts builders never offered much in the way of frills to begin with, says Sanford Kaplan, president of Sanford Construction Co. in Needham, Mass. "There is little we can cut except the size of the house."

In Massachusetts and elsewhere, *Business Week* notes, zoning and environmental requirements actually work against the idea of the compact house. The trend in recent years has been to increase minimum lot and house size and to require builders to install roads and sewers, adding to price.

SCHOOL KIDS PICKET

Environmental requirements in general
have become a growing issue to builders.
One company in La Jolla, California, for example, found itself in a 1975 confrontation
with school children protesting a new subdivision. Their solution was reported in
House and Home as follows:

> "We had just moved our grading
> equipment onto the site," says project
> manager Bob Buie, "when 15 children
> appeared carrying homemade picket
> signs."

The pickets were pupils from a school across
the street who were protesting because two
natural ridges and a canyon were going to be
graded.

The bad guys: Avco Community Developers Inc. and the Marine Builders Co.

Buie, an Avco vice president, explained
that new landscaping would turn the
scraggly canyon and ridges into a park with
picnic and recreation areas and bike and jogging paths. Apparently impressed, the children dropped their signs and returned to
class. But Buie didn't drop the matter.

> "These kids obviously had a pretty
> bad impression of builders," he says.
> "And we thought it should be
> changed."

Working through the San Diego Unified
School District, Avco and Marine Builders
put together a six-week series of 20-minute
lessons for a special summer school course
aimed at elementary school children. Teachers were design and marketing people connected with the project. Lessons were house
design, land planning and landscape design,
interior design, advertising and public relations. They included a project tour so that
the children could better understand some of
the ideas they had learned.

Community fears of a return of the
ticky-tacky house also stir resistance, to new
building in general, but to the no-frills house
in particular. In Georgia's DeKalb County,
however, a recent zoning change allowed a
drop in minimum requirements from 1,400
sq. ft. to 1,200 sq. ft. in most residential
areas, but permits only two-thirds of the
units in a development to be this small.

Most of the shoppers for the new
cheaper type of home seem to be young mar-
rieds, says *Business Week,* trying to escape
the soaring bills of all-electric apartments.
Soaring energy rates, however, appear to be
fueling prosperity for at least one small sector of the opposite end of the housing market. Homes in the private Ocean Reef Club in
Key Largo, Fla., are moving "better than expected, considering the economic climate,"
says developer Harper Sibley, Jr. "We've
sold five units to top executives in the coal
industry in the last 30 days."

SOURCES

1. Main, Jeremy, "Here Comes the Minihouse,"
   Money, February, 1976, pp. 56-60.
2. "School Kids Picket Builders, So Builders
   Move into the Classroom," *House and Home,*
   November, 1975.
3. Slom, Stanley, "The Business Booms At 'Home
   Centers' As More Home Owners Do Own
   Chores," *Wall Street Journal,* March 13, 1973,
   p. 22.
4. "The No Frills American Dream," *Business
   Week,* June 16, 1975, pp. 17-18.
5. Wong, William, "When Housing Booms, So Do
   Grass Seed, Art, Toilets, Rugs, and Frit," *Wall
   Street Journal,* May 25, 1972, pp. 1, 17.

4

MARKETING RESEARCH AIDS DEVELOPMENT OF STRAWBERRY SOY MILK

by Robert V. Caruso
(Project Director
Meals for Millions Foundation
Guayaquil, Ecuador)

The Meals for Millions Foundation, Santa Monica, Calif., believes that marketing research is necessary to develop high-nutrition foods that poor people in developing countries not only will eat but also that they can and will buy and that can and will be made and marketed locally at a profit.

In the past, little or no marketing research has been employed in this field and, as a result, a substantial number of food products have been developed which were unacceptable in the countries where they were introduced. But conducting such marketing research in Guayaquil, Ecuador, isn't easy.

I know because I recently directed such a $50,000 marketing research study aimed at developing a cheap soybean-based food product for young (0-6 years old) children which could be marketed commercially. In addition to test marketing food products, the study also looked at the advertising, pricing, packaging, and distribution that should be used for the products.

The foundation believes that soy technology has advanced to the point where soy-based food products can be sold on their own merit—the true test of consumer acceptability. Results of the study showed that a strawberry-flavored powdered soy milk would be most acceptable and marketable.

In finding that out, we also discovered several other facts as we encountered and worked to solve problems related to the questionnaire, sampling, methodology, personnel, politics, and data analysis. Among these facts and problems, which may be of help to other researchers in Latin America or elsewhere, are:

—In Ecuador (as in other developing countries), researchers must conduct direct interviews although they are costly. Few people, especially those who need high-nutrition soy products, can afford phones. Mail service is either nonexistent or unreliable, depending on the part of the country. And literacy rates are low.

—Retailers are reluctant to cooperate with interviewers, suspecting they may be tax inspectors.

—Interviewers not only must know the native language, but must also know the local and regional popular expressions.

—In Ecuador, there is little census data available. Researchers had to make their own maps of blocks, buildings on the blocks, and households in the buildings.

—Before designing and conducting a study, researchers must understand and learn to deal with the social and class structure of the society being studied. Interviewers are likely to feel "out of place" in certain neighborhoods.

From Robert V. Caruso, "Marketing Research Aids Development of Strawberry Soy Milk to Help Feed Ecuador's Poor . . . At A Profit," Marketing News, December 5, 1975. Reprinted from Marketing News, published by the American Marketing Association.

In Guayaquil, some employees thought certain activities (training interviewers, tabulation, etc.) were for lower-status employees, not for them. It is important, researchers found, to explain job descriptions carefully before hiring people and beginning a study.

—Besides a colloquial knowledge of the language and class structure, researchers must understand local labor laws and know what packaging, processing machinery, computers, etc. are available.

—Researchers must let local politicians know what the study is about to avoid their interference on the belief that it might be subversive and should be stopped or hindered.

After coping with all this, we found that low-income respondents moved so frequently that longitudinal study data analysis was difficult. Fortunately, the sample size was large enough to offset some of the "respondent mortality."

We conducted the study in six stages— the first a household consumer survey to determine the demographics of the 0-6-year-old market.

Creative exploration panels of five to eight mothers of young children were used to develop the questionnaire. From a random sample of 378 households drawn from the entire city (Ecuador's largest) 183 households with young children were chosen.

After surveying these households, we found 70 percent have incomes of less than $200 a month; strawberry and natural milk are preferred flavors in this market; and people buy food for young children on the basis of confidence in brand names and taste, not quality and nutrition.

Of the responding families with young children, 56 percent own TV sets. Most popu-

lar programs among mothers in this group are soap operas. Family members making purchasing decisions usually go to corner stores and open markets, rarely to supermarkets.

For the second stage of the study, we questioned a random sample of 290 retailers. This stage determined the most popular brand of milk, that it is stocked because customers prefer it, not because of price or credit arrangements, and that the store owner usually buys for the store.

In the third stage, manufacturers of foods consumed by young children were asked about product distribution, sales volumes, production costs, ad techniques, pricing, etc.

At the fourth stage, we reviewed the data to develop foods for test marketing comparable to those pinpointed in the first stage. We decided to test powdered soy milk with chocolate, coffee, banana, orange, strawberry, and milk flavors, beef-flavored textured vegetable protein, soy flakes, and precooked whole soybeans.

Members of three consumer panels learned to prepare the soy-based foods at the fifth stage and tested them at their homes. We also determined the panel members' reactions to the products, labels, and promotions. The products that survived these tests were strawberry and milk flavored soy milks, soy flakes, and textured vegetable protein.

The in-home use survey was repeated with the 183 households, which had participated in the first stage, using only the products favored by the consumer panels. Members of these households found the strawberry-flavored soy milk most acceptable.

At the sixth stage, respondents from the first and fifth stages were exposed to promotional materials to determine which ones best fit their favorite product.

Next step for the foundation is to help

form an enterprise to produce strawberry-flavored soy milk, then to help design production facilities, provide processing equipment, train people to operate it, and design a marketing plan for the product, which can be produced entirely from local ingredients, except for the strawberry flavoring.

By producing the soy-based food products in-country, the foundation believes two goals will be accomplished: 1. Ecuador will not become dependent upon a foreign source to supply this type of food product and 2. it will contribute to the further development of food processing technology in the country.

This enterprise would never have succeeded without systematic marketing research, plus feasibility studies of costs and production requirements.

P&G'S SECRET INGREDIENT

by Peter Vanderwicken

Ask almost anybody in the world of business to characterize Procter & Gamble, and chances are you'll get a familiar answer—"it's a marketing company." The cliché implies that only by puffing them up with great gales of advertising can P&G sell its products in such huge quantities. Now, it certainly is true that P&G is very big in marketing—the nation's No. 1 advertiser, in fact. The $200 million that the company spent on TV in its last fiscal year provided one-tenth of the networks' total revenues. And P&G is certainly very *good* at marketing. A company that ranks No. 1 in the U.S. in laundry detergent (Tide), shampoo (Head and Shoulders), toothpaste (Crest), shortening (Crisco), disposable diapers (Pampers), toilet paper (Charmin), and several other consumer products as well has to be doing some very effective marketing. But to repeat that "marketing company" stereotype is to miss the true secret of Procter & Gamble's success.

That secret, in a word, is thoroughness. Procter & Gamble manages every element of its business with a painstaking precision that most organizations fail to approach. Thoroughness extends to the careful and tenacious recruitment of employees, the development of a much-admired executive

From Peter Vanderwicken, "P&G's Secret Ingredient," Fortune *(July 1974).* © *1974 Time Inc.*

corps, the design of manufacturing facilities, and the creation and testing of products. By the time a product gets to the marketing stage, the thorough preparation through all the prior stages has already endowed it with an edge on competitors.

Before Chairman Edward Harness will allow a new product to be put on the market, he insists that its superiority (meaning consumer preference for it) be demonstrated by actual tests. "Some people suggest that product differences in our field are minimal or infinitesimal," he says. "I can't agree. When you find a significant body of women who believe the characteristics of what they want are found in a product—this is the essence of consumerism, giving them what they want."

One of the less obvious benefits of the P&G approach is that it helps employee morale. People who work for P&G believe the products they make and market *are* better. As they see it, they're engaged in something fundamentally worthwhile. The high morale accounts in part for the legendary competitive enthusiasm of the company's salesmen. "They eat, sleep,and dream P&G," says a vice president of a supermarket chain who sees a lot of them. A campus radical of the Sixties who went to work for P&G and then quit to run an arts foundation says of the company as he recalls it: "Their integrity and fairness permeate every dimension of what they do."

THE DIFFERENCE 4 CENTS MADE

And then, of course, there's that famous marketing. P&G tests its marketing methods as painstakingly as its products. In some cities with cable TV, one sample commercial goes to homes on one side of a block and another to homes across the street. Researchers will then ask residents whether and how well they remember what they saw.

Before a new product is introduced nationwide, P&G tests it in one or more cities that are demographically representative of the nation. The company sets up an initial production line, backs the product with a massive barrage of advertising, and puts it on sale in supermarkets. If a product fails this test, it is normally dropped. But occasionally one gets a second chance.

One product that was not discarded after initial failure went on to become a huge success: Pampers, which now rivals Tide as P&G's bestselling brand. On its first market test, Pampers bombed. The product was priced too high—about 10 cents each, which was more than the cost of buying a cloth diaper and washing it. By simplifying the package, speeding up the assembly lines, and using less costly components, the company gradually got the price down to 6 cents.

As the price dropped, each of three subsequent tests over four years indicated a bigger potential market. So management progressively reduced the profit-margin target and raised the volume target. By the fourth test, the price was right and Pampers took off.

Prior research is supposed to prevent P&G from flopping in its test markets. "My boss said years ago," Harness recalls, "that when you go to test market you should be 90 percent sure. That's our approach." According to one survey, 112 of 204 brands put into test markets in the U.S. in 1971 failed to make it to nationwide distribution. P&G's success ratio has been better, but nowhere near 90 percent. Of sixteen brands test marketed in the last decade, seven failed to win general distribution.

THE MISSING MAGIC

The expansion of a new brand nationwide is reminiscent of a military campaign in its complexity and intensity. Generally, distribution is extended outward from the test markets as production capacity becomes available, until after six months or a year, the brand is sold throughout the country. P&G may spend $25 million or more promoting a brand in its first year on the market, and the company continues to run tests to discover the least expensive combination of ways to reach potential consumers. Surprisingly, giving out samples door-to-door can be the cheapest method of introducing a new brand, especially if it is delivered with samples of another brand that shares the cost.

In the last ten years, P&G failed in an attempt to extend a brand beyond its test market on three occasions. Hidden Magic, a hair spray, turned out to have no magic at all. Stardust, a dry bleach, failed to convert housewives from the customary liquid. Cinch, a spray household cleaner, just never caught on, and the men at Procter & Gamble still haven't figured out why.

On any brand that flies, P&G expects to recover development and marketing costs and begin earning a profit within three years. Getting into the black, though, is only the beginning of an endless process of trying to hold and expand market share. A typical brand budget provides for a promotion of some kind—a "3 cents off" offer, a coupon, or a premium—about every three months.

Contrary to what might be expected, P&G runs its most attractive promotions not to lure customers when a brand's sales are falling off, but when the demand is highest. Cake mixes sell best before Thanksgiving and Christmas, for example, while soaps and detergents move fastest in the late spring and summer. Promotions are aimed at building market share, and it is easier to increase penetration when the total market is growing. If the product can expand its share then, it may be able to hold some or most of the gain as sales fall off seasonally during the rest of the year.

Similarly, P&G and other manufactur-ers increase advertising expenditures on their fast-selling brands and reduce them on brands that are doing less well. They figure that a dollar spent advertising a high-volume item will return a greater profit than a dollar spent on a brand with lower volume or a smaller market share.

Daytime television is still the most efficient means of selling soap (and Pampers, too), and Procter owns, produces, and sponsors six long-running TV soap operas, which get the attention of housewives as their predecessors on radio did for almost half a century. Products such as deodorants and hair sprays, which also appeal to working women and to men, are more efficiently advertised on evening TV.

Once a brand is established, P&G changes it in some major or minor way twice a year. The company recently changed the formulation of its dishwasher detergent, Cascade, to prevent the granules from caking. It added a new ingredient to Downy fabric softener to help minimize the buildup of lint-catching static on clothes in a dryer.

There is a lot of show biz in the soap biz, to be sure, and a good many of the changes seem trivial. A supermarket executive laments: "One year they'll add blue dots to a detergent and say, 'new blue improved,' and the next year they'll take them out." Ed Harness, though, claims there's a good deal less straining for superficial novelty than there was a couple of decades ago, when the industry was more flamboyant.

UP AGAINST THE LIFE CYCLE

All the attention P&G gives its existing products represents an effort to cope with an inescapable challenge facing consumer-goods manufacturers. Left unchanged, a packaged product will tend to increase its market share for a few years after it is introduced, hit a peak, and then sink into decline. Though no one knows for sure, many marketing men believe these product life cycles are becoming shorter. A study by the A. C. Nielsen Co. concludes that 85 percent of all new brands can expect less than three years of success before their market shares start declining rapidly. While manufacturers can try to lengthen the life cycle by launching a new advertising campaign or redesigning a package, they don't always succeed. And when they do succeed, the study says, they revive the brand for only an average of fifteen months before it sinks once again.

Procter & Gamble's strategy of frequent, regular improvements, accompanied by unceasing barrage of advertising, has in most cases virtually overridden the life cycle. Several P&G products introduced long ago are still very much around. Crisco was first sold back in 1912. Ivory soap made its debut in 1879 and is now the most venerable brand sold in American grocery stores. No established P&G product has died in the last ten years.

This stability pays valuable dividends. P&G sells only forty-nine branded consumer products (plus some industrial bulk chemicals and variations of its domestic brands abroad), and that is a rather small number for a $5-billion company. It means that the average P&G brand sold in the U.S. is in itself a sizable business, permitting many economies of scale. And since the company's established products aren't dying off, the sales and profits contributed by newly introduced brands are net gains for the company's growth.

POISED FOR A LEAP FORWARD

For the last 125 years, Procter & Gamble has been growing at an average rate of 8 percent a year, compounded—one of the most splendid long-run performances in the annals of business. For the last two decades, the company has increased sales, profits, *and dividends* every year without a miss.

Its prospects, moreover, seem pretty bright. After a relatively quiet period of introducing few new products, P&G has seven in test markets, including a fabric softener, a paper towel in a countertop dispenser, a liquid laundry detergent, and a tampon that the company began developing thirteen years ago. Hopes run high in Cincinnati that the tampon, named Rely, will take a major share of the market from Tampax and Kotex. Demonstrating the new product, P&G executives plunk Rely and Tampax into separate beakers of water to demonstrate their own product's superiority. They are confident enough about the outcome to make an explicit claim on the package: "Rely absorbs twice as much as the tampon you're probably using now."

BUT WILL THOROUGHNESS WORK ANYMORE?

To all appearances, the company has great potential for growth abroad. Right now, foreign business accounts for a quarter of its sales and, owing to the recent price controls in the U.S., a somewhat larger portion of earnings. Recently sales have been growing faster abroad than in the U.S.—about 35 percent a year—but the president of the international division, William Gurganus, says that he expects foreign sales "to remain one-quarter of our total business."

This statement suggests that Gurganus, at least, believes domestic business is poised for a leap forward. The burst of new brands could well keep sales rising briskly for several years. P&G took 119 years to reach its first billion dollars in sales, nine years for its second, five years for its third, three years for its fourth, and little more than a year for its fifth. At the recent rate of growth, sales could more than double by 1980. If history is a guide, profits would keep pace.

Some analysts on Wall Street, however, express serious doubts whether Procter & Gamble can sustain its remarkable pace. One big question concerns the time-consuming process of testing that is a crucial element in the P&G system. As the life cycles of packaged goods grow shorter, manufacturers are compressing the time they spend in developing new products. A new shampoo is introduced about every three months now, for instance, and each new one threatens the market shares of all those on the shelves. Under such conditions, can P&G continue to spend years developing and testing its products? Can P&G still count on thoroughness?

Harness and Howard Morgen, Harness's predecessor as chief executive, seem unworried about predictions that their company will have to change its ways. Morgen, indeed, maintains that some trends at work in the society favor the Procter & Gamble style. "The development cycle may be longer in the future," he says, "because of the consumer and environmental movements and the red tape of government. It can take the FDA a year and a half to clear a product, and this is after it's ready to go to market. All this benefits a company like ours which does its research well."

6
SHEDDING A ONE-PRODUCT IMAGE

Business Week

Wall Street's rating of Tektronix Inc.'s financial potential has long been an embarrassment to the Beaverton (Ore.) company that dominates the $300 million worldwide market for oscilloscopes, one of the most widely used of electronic instruments. While the stock of Hewlett-Packard Co., Tektronix' archrival in electronic instruments, regularly sells at a price-earnings ratio in the 30s, Tektronix' stock drags along at half that rate. The problem is that Tektronix, despite its $344 million sales volume in the past fiscal year, has the image of a conservative, one-product, engineering-oriented company with little marketing savvy.

More important to Tektronix President Earl Wantland than either the image or the stock price is the questionable viability of a company that stays in just one business. Wantland has been laboring for the past five years to push Tektronix expertise into new fields, and now his efforts seem to be paying off. By setting up a separate, marketing-oriented organization, Wantland has helped to create a new market worth $100 million a year—with Tektronix holding almost a 50 percent share. As a result, the once-monolithic company is beginning to split up

Reprinted from the February 16, 1976 issue of Business Week *by special permission. © 1976 by McGraw-Hill, Inc.*

into divisions with considerable autonomy, and old-line executives are learning that even engineers must focus on markets if they are to break away from dependence on a single product line.

"We needed to develop the financial and operational structures that would allow us to look separately at a product line or business," Wantland explains. "This had never been done before at Tek, but I felt we had to do it to get a realistic appraisal of our market opportunities."

FASTER PACE

The new business is built around graphic terminals, devices that display computer-generated maps, charts, and drawings on a TV-like screen. Tektronix' sales of the terminals have more than doubled to $49 million, or 15 percent of the company's total business, in the last fiscal year. And the growth rate of the market for these specialized terminals promises much more. That rate eased to 20 percent late last year because of the recession, but now it is moving back to its earlier pace of 35 percent to 40 percent annually.

At Ford Motor Co. the graphic terminals are helping to calibrate distributors for auto engines. At Phillips Petroleum Co. they are taking drudgery out of mechanical drawing. At Houston Natural Gas Corp. they are helping produce maps of underground piping. Says Lawrence L. Mayhew, vice-president in charge of Tektronix' Information Display Group, the independent organization within the company set up to develop and market the terminals: "What it boils down to is that graphics has the potential to substantially improve the efficiency of man's interface with machine."

Tektronix made its first tentative move toward the new business in 1964 when its researchers found a way to maintain an image on a cathode ray tube for 15 minutes. In a conventional CRT the phosphor coating on the screen glows for only a split second when it is hit by a beam of electrons. Images must be constantly rewritten or "refreshed" if they are to remain visible. In a computer application this calls for costly memory devices to store the position of each point in the graph or drawing being displayed.

A COMPLETE BUST

Tektronix was interested in the new technology mainly for its oscilloscopes, TV-like instruments that display the electrical characteristics of electronic circuits for testing and analysis. But in 1969 the company decided to sell a CRT terminal based on the new storage tube. It went about the task in its old, engineering-oriented way. "We made the assumption that if we could sell oscilloscopes, we should be able to sell anything," says William D. Walker, group vice-president for engineering. The new product was not backed up with a marketing plan. It was designed by engineers used to building products for other engineers and was priced at $10,000, which turned out to be a lot more than even a limited market was willing to pay. As a business and a path toward diversification, the new product was a bust.

Wantland, then newly elected executive vice-president, realized that the company had to devise a whole new strategy and try again. In 1970 he set up the Information Display Group and put Mayhew, a 37-year-old former design engineer, in charge. Mayhew proceeded to revise many of the company's cherished habits.

He sent the terminal design back to engineering with orders to take out as much cost as possible. Until then, Tektronix had always been more interested in turning out high-quality products than in shaving prices. That approach had worked as long as its markets consisted chiefly of other engineers. When the redesigned terminals emerged, the price tag was cut by more than half, to $4,000.

But the biggest wrench was in marketing. Says Mayhew: "We found we had to sell a benefit to the customer, not a set of engineering features. Market development was a new term for us. Our strength had always been in product innovation, and we felt comfortable with a product-oriented organization." Organizing around customer groups was "unstabilizing" he admits.

TIMING HELPED

Mayhew's strategy was to couple product dominance—guaranteed initially by its new storage tube—with promotional assaults on key markets. Concentrating at first on original-equipment manufacturer customers, he lined up all the major producers of computer-aided-design systems, several top minicomputer producers, and a variety of other companies making specialized equipment.

Timing helped him, too. A rapid decline in hardware costs was moving computing out of the cloistered corporate data processing centers and into individual offices and to the factory floor. In these environments, new techniques for tapping the computer's power have become essential, and Tektronix' terminal provides an economical way for computers to draw graphs, maps, and even their own circuitry.

Customers were quick to respond. "The Tektronix equipment gives us the best cost-performance trade-off," says Lucien C. Coenen Jr., staff marketing manager for Auto-Trol Corp., which uses the Tektronix terminal in its automated drafting system.

Tektronix has apparently learned its lesson. Heavy emphasis is still on marketing. Recently the company has taken more interest in specialized markets such as petroleum

exploration, publishing, and medical diagnosis, assembling teams to study each field and come up with the hardware and the software for each application. "We are looking at areas where our technology is applicable and where there is money to spend on it," says Jerry Ramey, a Tektronix engineering manager. The most successful of these efforts is one aimed at seismic data mapping.

NEW CHALLENGE

But competition is heating up for the Tektronix terminal. The cost advantage of its storage tube is being eroded by rapidly falling prices of semiconductor memories. Says Robert Benders, president of Calma Co., a Tektronix customer: "When it gets to cost equivalence with the storage tube, I believe 'refresh' technology—using memory devices to store the image—will take over because it is a more versatile approach."

Digital Equipment Corp. has introduced such a terminal selling for $2,500, or $500 under Tektronix' lowest price. But because of the DEC terminal's limited resolution, it cannot do the intricate three-dimensional plotting that Tektronix models can.

Tektronix, meanwhile, has pushed into DEC's territory by introducing a microprocessor-based "smart" terminal that provides graphics without having to tie into a computer. Wantland insists that his company has no intention of getting into the computer business, but he adds, "Everybody is going to make good use of the microprocessor (the so-called computer on a chip)."

The success of Mayhew's autonomous approach to the information display market has not been lost on other Tektronix managers. "What we hadn't fully appreciated," says Walker, the engineering vice-president, "was the role of your customer base in trying to diversify." Tektronix has now set up separate divisons for its communications and big-systems customers. And it recently split the remaining test and measurement group into two units—one for laboratory instruments, the other for service gear.

"Now decisions can be made at a lower level," Walker says. "The planning and budgeting processes are already much improved." Also much improved is Tektronix' chance of becoming a diversified company.

7

THE FAMILY BEHIND LONDON FOG

by Thomas Goldwasser

ELDERSBURG, Md.—"What we want," says Jonathan Myers, "is for every person in this country to walk into a store and say 'I want a London Fog' instead of 'I want a raincoat.'"

Mr. Myers is the president of the Londontown Corporation, maker of world-famous London Fog raincoats. Some might view his desire as excessive, given that Londontown already sells eight times as many men's raincoats as its nearest domestic competitor. In fact the company, with sales of $90 million in 1977, sells six out of every 10 raincoats bought in the United States. And, within its own high-quality price range, Londontown has even a larger share of the market. This suburban Baltimore company also is the nation's largest seller of women's rainwear, with 34 percent of the market.

Not only is Londontown the biggest in the business, it is also the oldest. In an industry that has lost more than 70 percent of its manufacturers in the past decade, with fewer than 28 of 100 remaining, Londontown has survived and prospered for more than

© 1978 by The New York Times Company. Reprinted by permission.

half a century because, Mr. Myers says, it makes a quality product. To ensure that its prosperity continues, Londontown of late has embarked on two major ventures. It is licensing its name for use by makers of umbrellas, shoes, rainhats and other products. And it's manufacturing outerwear, including gear for campers.

"That's where the demand is," says Mr. Myers. "Each year, there are 5 million units of men's rainwear sold in this country and 30 million of outerwear. For women, the numbers are two-and-a-half times that." Londontown's outerwear lines run the gamut from lightwear golf jackets and camping jackets to heavy car coats, competing with such established brands as Zero King, Mighty Mac and others.

According to Herschel Langenthal, vice president for financial administration, "We're moving into the licensing business, using our name in all kinds of shoes, dress to jogging, in Florida. And we require that the manufacturer live up to our high quality. We can't afford to lose our reputation."

Among the companies that pay to use the London Fog trademark on their goods are the Gold Star Hat Corporation of New York, Miller Brothers Industries of Dallas, Schertz Umbrellas Inc. of New York, the Bowen Shoe Company, and Fashion Rite, makers of rainwear for boys and girls.

Israel Myers is Londontown's 72-year-old chairman and patriarch. As a 16-year-old law student, he took a part-time job with the year-old business in 1923, and has been there ever since. His 39-year-old son Jonathan joined the concern in 1961, while Mr. Langenthal, his Harvard-educated son-in-law, came aboard ten years ago.

Under the elder Myers's leadership, London Fog has been the major innovator in designing, manufacturing and selling lightweight stylish rainwear in the United States. Company firsts include: machine-washable coats, use of the Dacron-cotton material that can withstand the manufacturing process without melting, full zip-in linings and double-knits for raincoats.

Early in 1976 Interco, the St. Louis-based manufacturing and retail outlet conglomerate whose products include Florsheim Shoes, acquired a majority interest in Londontown. Jonathan Myers, together with his father, wife, sister and brother-in-law, still owns—in Interco stock—the equivalent of 42 percent of Londontown. He says the family agreed to the sale primarily to improve shareholders' positions.

When the merger was announced—an exchange of six shares of Interco for 10 of Londontown—the price of Londontown's stock jumped two-and-a-half times on the New York Stock Exchange. Since then, dividends have doubled, and sales, which totaled $69 million in 1974, will exceed $100 million this year.

Jonathan Myers maintains that his company's autonomy did not diminish when it was bought by Interco. Edward P. Grace, treasurer of the St. Louis-based giant, with 440,000 employees and annual sales exceeding $1.6 billion, concurs.

"We bought London Fog for the same reasons we buy any company: a superior name in its field, a long historical profit growth performance and a new field for us. London Fog couldn't be doing better, and we leave them alone."

Does that autonomy extend to pricing? Last summer, the Federal Trade Commission issued a consent order accusing Londontown and its parent company of resale price maintenance, or price fixing. According to E. Perry Johnson, the F.T.C.'s assistant director of regional operations, "London Fog and Interco did not admit any violations of law. For settlement purposes only, they agreed they wouldn't dictate the retail price to their customers."

Jonathan Myers comments, "For years

we had a suggested retail price on our product for our customers, and we've agreed not to do that anymore. We don't sell to discount houses, and everybody has always paid the same wholesale price to us."

The rainwear industry, Jonathan Myers explains, "is a cheap industry to get into. All you need is a loft, a few machines and labor. It's very labor intensive. And many of these fly-by-night people thought that there was a sure bet for a quick buck. What they really did was cut corners, which meant an inferior end product. They got out of it exactly what they put in. You just can't operate that way in the long run."

London Fog has always studied the market carefully and reacted accordingly. "We've tried to stay ahead of the customers, to set the trend," he says.

But the company made a serious error in failing to see where the women's market was headed in the late 1960's. And it paid dearly for its mistake. From 1968 to 1970, its sales plunged from $42.5 million to $30 million, precipitated by a 65 percent drop in its women's division.

"You might say," observes Mr. Myers, "that up to that 1968 period, we just took the women's market for granted. That is, we thought what was good for men was also good for women."

The drop in sales led Jonathan Myers, who in 1968 at the age of 29 was the nation's youngest president of a New York Stock Exchange-listed company, to unload a large amount of inventory. He sold 100,000 women's raincoats—out of fashion stock that normally is just taken off the market when the new lines come out—and used the cash to cover the drop in sales. The stock price slid as well, from $41 at the end of 1968 to a low of $5½ in 1970. "We really took a bath on the stock then, but we felt that there was no other choice." In 1970, as the company's recovery began, the stock price rebounded to

a trading range of $11 to $13, which it maintained until the Interco purchase.

As London Fog changed with the times, it regained its strong, 34 percent share of the women's market. In fact, it sells more raincoats to women in America than anybody else. Its closest competitor is Forecaster of Boston, followed by Misty Harbor and a host of imports. Among the imports, Burberry and Aquascutum, long-standing high-quality British lines for men and women, lead the field. However, with their $300-plus price tags, London Fog does not consider them direct competitors.

"Sure," Israel Myers says, "any raincoat that isn't ours could be considered a competitor. But our most expensive coats cost $85 to $140."

Spanish imports, like Cortefiel and Induyco, make some dent in the market; also, designer products, including Calvin Klein and Diane Von Furstenburg, lend their names to designer rainwear for women. Ironically, these coats are made in Hong Kong and countries with cheap labor costs.

If fashion is the watchword for women in rainwear, utility fills the bill for men. "Our market surveys show us," says Jonathan Myers, "that we have a 94 percent, unaided recognition factor." That means when the word raincoat is mentioned to the American male, 94 out of 100 think of London Fog; truly, a merchandiser's dream come true. In fact, sales of its men's division dwarf those of Glen Eagles, undoubtedly its nearest competitor. Glen Eagles, also a Baltimore company, is a division of Hart, Schaffner & Marx.

When law student Israel Myers went to work at Londontown in 1923, the Baltimore manufacturer made naval officers' uniforms, but not rainwear.

"In those days," the elder Myers says, "if you really wanted to criticize someone, you said he made raincoats. They were considered the bastards of the industry." Alligator of St. Louis was making $10 raincoats, and some New York firms were turning out goods at one-third that price.

The Depression, of course, devastated most manufacturers, but Mr. Myers, who by then headed Londontown, hung on. "There certainly weren't any other jobs, so my two associates and I stuck it out."

Londontown's prospects picked up appreciably near the end of the 1930's. By the early 1940's, Mr. Myers began to think seriously of trying to fill the new demand for lightweight coats.

Mr. Myers's first endeavor involved the Army, which gave him a contract for 10,000 raincoats. "Rubber was in short supply," he recalls, "so I made it synthetically on a sheet of cotton." The demand grew, but the shortage of materials continued. "By the end of the war, I was buying up dirigibles, cutting them up, and selling shopping bags," he says. Later, as supplies became more plentiful, Londontown began selling raincoats to Sears Roebuck and J. C. Penney.

By 1951, the company employed more than 200 people and had all the business it could handle. That year, in conjunction with Wamsutta Mills and Du Pont, Londontown started using a new fabric, Dacron, in its rainwear. It looked good, didn't wrinkle and repelled water. Yet the revolutionary material wasn't perfect—it tended to melt during the sewing process. But in 1953, Du Pont came up with a lubricant that put an end to that problem.

In March 1954, Saks Fifth Avenue ran a major advertisement in The New York Times singing the praises of the new Dacron and cotton raincoats for men. Mr. Myers, who had paid $6,000 for the ad, had sold Saks exclusive rights to the coat for 30 days. Selling for $29.95 retail, demand exceeded even Mr. Myers's optimistic predictions. This year, he says, the company expects to regis- ter more than $100 million in sales, with 500 workers employed at Londontown's new 515,000-square-foot distribution center here.

8

SEGMENTATION—A HEADY BREW

How much of America's beverage dollar goes to buy beer? The brewers say it's about 18 cents—and climbing. That adds up to an $8 billion exchange, in which consumers hand over an increasingly larger share of their beverage dollar to a shrinking number of breweries.

What this all means is that beer consumption is moving ahead of coffee and milk to take an expected second place in the stomachs of Americans by 1990. Soft drinks will retain their hold as the most popular beverage category.

Here are market readings and projections from *Impact,* a beer, wine, and spirits newsletter:

	MARKET RANKINGS	
	1978	1990
Soft drinks	28.4%	35.7
Milk	19.5	12.5
Coffee	18.6	11.9
Beer	17.7	19.7
Tea	9.4	11.8
Juice	3.2	3.5
Distilled spirits	1.6	1.8
Wine	1.5	3.1

These consumption estimates, reported by *Advertising Age,* indicate that by 1990 soft drinks and beer will, between them, capture 55% of the total beverage market. Not including tea, coffee, and milk, the 1977 revenues of this market were put at $35 billion.

Beer today is an $8 billion market, dominated more and more by large companies. In 1977, Anheuser-Busch, for example, reported sales equal to Coca-Cola's—both were slightly over $2 billion.

The stakes in the beer marketing battles are, thus, enormous. And the casualties, as you might imagine, are many. For example, in 1933, after Prohibition was lifted, the U.S. had 750 independent breweries. Today only 47 remain.

MORE BRANDS OF BEER

Yet your supermarket shelves are crowded with different brands, even more than existed five years ago. What accounts for this? Simply that the brewers have recently discovered segmentation, the targeting of different products to different socio-economic or psychographic groups in the population.

In 1979, more than 250 brands of beer were available on a national or regional basis. Thus, while breweries have declined in number, brands marketed by those 47 brewers have proliferated.

However, while most of the national business publications write about the battles among the major brands, many a story can be told about how the smaller breweries are surviving. Lone Star Brewery, in San Antonio, has built a loyal following by promoting its Texas heritage in elaborate museums on its brewery site not far from the Alamo and in television advertising that promotes tongue-in-cheek sporting events such as chili cookoffs and armadillo races.

Joseph Huber Brewing Co., in Monroe, Wisconsin, keeps afloat by changing the label on its beer cans 24 times a year. This policy makes each can a target for acquisition by one of the 14,000 members of the Beer Can Collectors of America and the 80,000 persons who collect cans but are non-members.

August Schell Brewing Co. of New Ulm Minnesota, sells its beer under seven brand names, including such seasonal specialities as Hunter Beer (sold only during hunting season) and Xmas Beer (sold, guess when?).

PICKING THE SEGMENTS

But the battle royal is confined to the majors. And what they've learned is that no one beer can capture all beer drinkers.

Pabst Brewing Co. feels it has a winning approach by targeting itself to "upscale" young adults—those with above average income. Pabst buys space in 280 college newspapers and on college radio stations. "We feel the quality message is especially important with the college-age beer drinker . . ." comments Pabst's vice president of advertising.

In the 1978 period, the beer company rankings were: first, Anheuser-Busch; second, Miller Brewing Company; third, Joseph Schlitz Brewing Company; fourth, Pabst Brewing Company; and fifth, Adolph Coors Company.

MILLER'S SURGE

The big news of the industry has been the resurgence of Miller. A subsidiary of Philip Morris, "Miller turned the industry on its ear," commented *Fortune* magazine, with "hell-for-leather marketing and shrewd advertising, combined with efficient manufacturing methods."

Miller's hard-fought battle with A-B during the late 1970s is not the first threat to the dominance of A-B. Schlitz was the talk of the industry in the late 1960s when it built highly efficient breweries. But by 1978 its pace had faltered, and 1978 sales actually declined from the level of 1977.

BEER BOMBSHELL IN 1975

Miller's basic weapon was the introduction of a light beer in 1975. The appeal of a beer with fewer calories captivated many drinkers who switched from other brands. A-B, the industry leader, appeared to sit out the challenge: "We didn't take Miller seriously, but we do now," said a top A-B executive to a *Forbes* magazine interviewer in mid-1978.

"Anheuser had always concentrated its marketing fire on Joe Sixpack: male, a heavy beer user, blue-collar," said *Forbes*. "Meanwhile, Miller's Murphy [John A. Murphy, president], recognizing that the beer market could be segmented like other markets, brought out Miller Lite and domestically made Lowenbrau."

Miller started buying top television network sports shows, all highly rated, and began its advertising barrage. "We were perfectly aware of when they (Miller) bought the Monday Night Football package," August Busch II later admitted. "We [had] looked at the cost of that on a total dollar basis, but not on a cost-per-thousand-beer-drinkers' basis. That's where we missed the boat. We were simply outsmarted." So Miller gained 65% of the light beer market, and its sales soared.

From a base of 5.4 million barrels of beer sold by Miller in 1972 (to A-B's 26.5 million), the gap kept narrowing. By 1978, the estimated score: 32 million barrels for Miller, to A-B's 41 million. Miller's gain in 1978 over 1977 was 33%, compared to A-B's 12%.

By then, August Busch, who took over the company from his father, Gussie, now retired, had beefed up his staff and begun his counter-attack. In 1977, he hired 100 executives from such founts of marketing expertise as J. Walter Thompson (the big ad agency), Coca-Cola, General Foods, and Procter and Gamble.

TWO "LIGHTS" FROM A-B

Anheuser's advertising was geared up to support two light beers: Natural and Michelob Light. It aimed special campaigns at ethnic groups it had previously ignored. To reach the sports fans, A-B really went all out. It now sponsors nearly 200 professional and college teams, including such esoteric sports as hydroplane racing, hot-air ballooning, and touch football.

Meanwhile, while Miller got the headlines for marketing savvy, A-B lost none of its profits. In 1978, A-B sales and profits were both at record levels; the industry leader wasn't hurt except in its pride. It appears that the growth of the top two companies had been carved out of the sales of the next tier of beer manufacturers.

For example, Coors had been on top in California, the nation's biggest single market. But in 1978, Anheuser displaced Coors in California, and Coors' earnings dropped 11%.

So now Coors is on the marketing bandwagon after a humiliating decline from its "high" of five years ago when demand was so great it actually had to ration its beer.

Bill Coors in early 1979 told the *Wall Street Journal:* "We're going to lick this thing. We don't intend to become a dead giant." What Coors was referring to was the onslaught of Miller and A-B, which led to Coors' dropping in California from a 41% share of the market to a 23% share.

Coors had only one product, which said right on the label: "America's fine light beer." For years that one product propelled Coors ahead. But that growth was stopped, and Coors was in deep trouble.

NO MORE MYSTIQUE

Prior to the new marketing thrust of Miller, Coors almost sold itself. It had a mystique that led to an annual growth gain of 10%. Many drinkers used to ask their friends to "bring back a case of Coors" when they ventured into one of the 16 states where Coors is sold.

"The engineers at Coors thought quality production would overcome sophisticated marketing," reported the *Wall Street Journal.* But, after all, "quality" is in the eye of the beholder.

"We had great arguments about whether to try to sell our banquet beer [regular Coors] as a light beer," recalled Peter Coors, the senior vice president for sales. "A year ago I was the only one who wanted a light beer. We'd been kicked in the teeth a couple of times and I was tired of spitting out teeth."

Finally, in the summer of 1978, the company brass agreed with Peter and introduced Coors Light. At the same time, the company announced plans to become a national marketer of beer. Admits Bill Coors: "We'd certainly be better off if we'd started earlier."

THE "BLACK ARTS" ARRIVE

And now, "the dreaded outsiders—practitioners of such black arts as marketing, promotion, consumer research and new product development—are lurking about Coors' stark concrete headquarters," is the colorful way one business writer phrased the new feeling at Coors.

In summary, then, market segmentation—and new products to reach different segments—has been brought to the beer industry by Philip Morris, the company that uses this approach in its cigarette marketing. And Anheuser-Busch, and the rest of the pack, have responded.

What the future holds, according to Anheuser-Busch's advertising agency, D'Arcy-

MacManus & Masius, "is in the area of market segmentation. Increasing segmentation and product differentiation in the industry are already evident. . . . more brands will appear and these brands will be aimed towards blacks, females, Hispanics, etc."

"The sudden development and growth of the light beer category is tangible proof of successful product and marketing innovation," says another agency spokesman. "The introduction of light beer injected a new vitality into a long-dormant industry in terms of new consumer-oriented marketing and advertising practice."

SOURCES

1. "A-B Aims to Win by Segmenting Light Beer." *The Marketing News,* publication of the American Marketing Association, December 29, 1978.
2. Cappo, Joe, "Take Away Label, Beer Tastes Change." Chicago *Daily News* Service, carried in the Houston *Chronicle,* November 21, 1976.
3. Flaherty, Robert J., "We Missed the Boat. . . We Were Outsmarted." *Forbes,* August 7, 1978.
4. Huey, John, "Over a Barrel: Men at Coors Beer Find the Old Ways Don't Work Anymore." *Wall Street Journal,* January 19, 1979.
5. Ingrassia, Lawrence, "Some Breweries Find New Market to Tap When Sales Are Flat." *Wall Street Journal,* November 24, 1978, p.1.
6. O'Hanlon, Thomas, "August Busch Brews Up a New Spirit in St. Louis." *Fortune,* January 15, 1978.
7. "Study Projects Major Soft Drink, Beer Gains." *Advertising Age,* January 8, 1979, p. 82.

SECTION FOLLOW-UP
MORE GOODS IS BETTER

Ketchup, airplanes, houses, beer—all down the list of goods, marketing management has similar questions to ask:

1. Who influences the purchase of this product? Just the individuals who pull a ketchup bottle off the shelf or sign a purchase memorandum? If not just those people—who else?

2. What affects their choice to buy or not, and then, their choice of brand or supplier? Does an industrial specifier take into account a chance remark by the company president for or against some possible supplier? Does a home-buying adult consider the reaction of a mother or father hundreds of miles away? How about the interest rate?

3. Where do people expect to find out about the product? Where do they expect to buy it? What do they expect to get with these "goods"? Expert help for their own maintenance crews in learning to service aircraft? A subtle label on the raincoat to show it's a prestige brand? A recipe on the ketchup bottle label or the cake mix box?

2 SERVICES WITH A SMILE

If you can't touch the product you're about to buy, it's a service. Transportation as opposed to airplanes; communication, not wires; security as opposed to a stronger lock: those are services. Goods may be included as part of the service, of course; most of us would rather not buy the service of flying in the absence of a plane. But marketing services is something more than marketing goods, and it's often more difficult.

How do you market the promise to pay for car repair if, but only if, the buyer smashes up his automobile? How do you market safety for a home or a business? Telephone service? The services of an architect?

We can offer only one answer: you hire someone who's selling a service called "marketing."

9

FEDERAL EXPRESS AGGRESSIVELY PURSUES SMALL PACKAGE MARKET

Interview with Heinz Adam,
director of marketing
Federal Express Corp.

The young and aggressive management of the Federal Express Corp. have built guaranteed one-day delivery service for small packages into a $150 million business in five short years, according to Heinz Adam, director of marketing. Continued growth seems assured.

This is John Hicks for Direct Marketing *magazine. Today (January 16, 1978) I'm in New York City talking with Mr. Heinz Adam, director of marketing for Federal Express delivery service, located in Memphis, Tennessee. Heinz, let's go back over the history of Federal Express. How did the company get started and why?*

A. It was the brain child of our 34 year old chairman of the board, Frederick Smith who started the company five years ago. Our first month of operation was in April of 1973. Fred had the idea that there was a need in the business community to provide a service that would guarantee overnight delivery of small, highly time sensitive packages or documents. He had spent some time in the Marine Air Force and came up with the idea of starting an airline for packages only. From that concept to the place where we are

today is quite a jump but needless to say it took quite a bit of effort and some $80 million of capital that was required to keep the company going.

Q. You have, as you said, this hole in the market. Is there nobody really servicing the small package market?

A. That's right. The problem with commercial airlines is that they fly where people need to go rather than where packages need to go. Our system is designed from the ground up to handle packages and we are non-discriminatory. In other words, we will provide the same level of service from Macon, Georgia or Jackson, Mississippi as we do for Chicago, Los Angeles, or New York. There are businesses, hospitals, and lawyers all over the country that have a need for overnight delivery of parcels and they are spread all across the country not just the main population centers.

Q. How many communities do you service?

A. We serve about 10,000 communities in the United States and that represents just about 80% of the population.

Q. When you say small packages, what size are talking about?

A. We are talking about a weight maximum of 70 pounds. We are not really in the containerized large freight business.

Q. If I wanted to send a parcel to Seattle, Washington, would I need a contract with Federal Express?

A. No, all you do is look in the Yellow Pages, get the number of our nearest office and call for a pick-up. In the afternoon one of our couriers will come by and pick up your package and it will be delivered to your consignee before noon the next day.

Q. As long as we are on the subject Heinz, tell me exactly how this system works. Do you own these trucks?

A. We own at least 800 trucks and we also own 32 fan jets. We employ about 3,000 people. Federal Express just received the authorization to fly larger airplanes. For two years now we have been working to get legislation passed that would allow us to fly larger airplanes because our system has grown so much. We've just put our first one into service. I believe we will be getting six or seven of those jets. I figure that we'll soon have close to 40 airplanes, carrying about 30,000 packages a night.

Q. What is the cost for delivery of a package?

A. To give you an idea, we have a service called "Courier Pak" that is basically a document delivery service. The cost to use the "Courier Pak" in which you can get up to two pounds of printed material picked up and delivered before noon the next day is $14, which is extremely reasonable.

Q. Nobody can complain about that. How do these packages get to their destinations? Let's say I'm in Los Angeles and I want to send a package to New York, how do you do it?

A. We have a unique system. Our own couriers would pick up the package as they are making their rounds in the afternoon. Then at night, your package would be put on an airplane departing let's say from New York. It would fly to Memphis where all our airplanes fly and arrive around midnight. They are all unloaded and then the packages are sorted in a large sorting operation and within about two to three hours all the planes are re-loaded going back to their destination cities. They arrive before sunrise the next day and then the packages are unloaded off the airplane, re-loaded on trucks and delivered to your door before noon.

Q. That's a pretty fancy system.

A. It's virtually fool proof. Our reliability rate is very extraordinary for this industry. It's primarily due to the fact that we have minimized handling. There is no need to transfer a package from one airline to another to get it to its destination point.

Q. How many packages do you carry in a night now?

A. Right now we are carrying about 30,000 packages a night. On that first day when we started back in April of '73, we carried six— three were ours and three were empty boxes. That was quite an auspicious start.

Q. How many customers do you currently have?

A. We currently have about 80,000 customers. We issue what we call customer numbers and we have about 80,000 assigned. I can't tell you exactly how many total customers we have because there are a lot of customers who will pay by cash or consignee type billing.

Q. You mentioned before we started to make this recording that your company is totally vertically integrated. Tell us what you mean by that?

A. It means that your package never leaves our hands. We have our own trucks. We have our own airplanes. In fact, we could be considered one of the largest airlines in the United States by virtue of the equipment we have. We handle a package from beginning to end. I guess our climb really started about three years ago when it was decided this company was in either a go, or no go situation. We went to the board of directors and requested $1 million to go on television to advertise Federal Express.

Q. That was an unusual move.

A. Absolutely, but it turned out to be the best possible thing we could have done. It created a broad based awareness because we knew there was a latent need for the kind of service we were providing. It was just a question of getting people to know that this service existed and was available to them. Television has certain benefits to it. There is a credibility associated with TV because you're on with Procter & Gamble and General Motors. Credibility is important, especially when you're talking about the kind of business we are in where it's literally somebody's job on the line if the package isn't delivered.

Q. Do you think it was an unusual move to use the mass medium to reach what some people might consider a very segmented market?

A. At that time it was an unusual move because our knowledge of the market and our target for Federal Express's growth was predicated on isolating the heavy freight users. We could identify those pretty well. There were 2,400 companies. I think the reason for going on was to give a credibility to the Federal Express concept. From what we know today it was a very wise move because we've learned as we've become more expert, and have gotten more research data available that *everybody* and *nobody* wants to make shipping decisions. So virtually anybody who's in business, whether it be a secretary, a mail room clerk, an executive vice president, is a potential user and a demander of Federal Express service.

Q. It's not just the head man you are aiming at then?

A. Absolutely not.

Q. In other words any company can have many decision makers in it when shipping decisions are made?

A. For our services, yes.

Q. What did that first TV Commercial say?

A. The first one was basically an announcement type ad. We called ourselves the "new airline." It was just an announcement to the universe out there that there is a company called Federal Express and we don't move people we move packages.

Q. There was nothing the customer could refer to for information?

A. No, it was strictly an awareness program. In fact all of our television commercials have not had any specific reference number. We've felt that using a telephone number on the tube in the 30 second commercial just

doesn't make a lot of sense. People don't always have a pencil and paper handy.

Q. How did you go about contacting companies after the commercial?

A. We didn't really follow up with an extensive direct mail campaign. The television concept was strictly to create awareness. It wasn't part of an overall defined marketing program.

Q. As your sophistication grew and you got to know your market a little bit better Heinz, what happened? Did you continue to use television?

A. We started to use it to communicate a specific story. We said to ourselves, in eyes of the potential user Emery Air Freight is the standard carrier of the industry. There was an independent research company called Opinion Research in Princeton, New Jersey which did a survey for us that indicated we were about twice as efficient in delivering packages overnight than Emery. We felt that was very strong stuff and we decided to do a television commercial about it.

Q. This was a comparative?

A. Actual name identification with competition going after the leading competitor. Needless to say that commercial also worked very well, but we also found there was a credibility gap. People asked how we can perform this kind of service and be that reliable. They just don't believe you can do that. As an outgrowth of that we created three commercials about our services—overnight reliable, overnight and fleet and they ran in '76. Basically, those commercials were designed to reinforce the Federal Express system and to tell people that we have our own planes, our own trucks and that is why you can rely on Federal Express to get the job done. Another thing you should keep in mind while we are talking about television is we are not on network but rather strictly spot television. Our current campaign runs in about 15 markets

A million dollar deal shouldn't go down the drain over a 2 lb. package.

You blew it.
You had everybody lined up in Atlanta to close the deal.

The only problem was, the contract was out in Portland.

And it's almost impossible to get *yourself* from Portland to Atlanta overnight, much less a document.

Too bad you didn't know about Federal Express COURIER PAK.®

For only $12.50, we'll deliver up to 2 lbs. of documents, tapes, blueprints, contracts, and so forth practically anyplace in the country overnight.

We come to your office, pick up the package, fly it overnight in our own planes, and deliver it before noon the next day.

You don't have to do anything except pick up the phone and call our toll-free Hotline: 800-238-5355, or call our local office listed under Air Cargo in your Yellow Pages.

It's the simplest, most efficient, and most reliable document delivery system around because the package *never* leaves our hands.

We pick up and deliver not only in big cities like New York, Chicago, and Los Angeles, but also in smaller cities like Peoria, Macon, and Rochester, and over 10,000 other communities.

So the next time you need something sent from one city to another overnight, you now know it's not impossible.

In fact, with Federal Express Courier Pak, it's easy.

FEDERAL EXPRESS COURIER PAK.®
When it absolutely, positively has to be there overnight.

COURIER PAK® is a registered trademark of Federal Express Corporation.
U.S. postal regulations specify that if you include any first class (letter) material in the Courier Pak, proper postage must be applied and canceled.

only. We're not advertising in every market that we serve.

Q. Have you ever used direct mail advertising?

A. In '77 we had used direct mail advertising quite successfully. What we did was take a list of our customers who use our service the most and give those names to Dun & Bradstreet. D & B then passed them through their listings and matched them according to SIC codes. Once we had done that we could see which of those businesses were using our service the most, according to SIC codes.

Q. How many SIC numbers did you come up with in that initial research?

A. About 34 SIC codes. By combining that identification with the research we had that *everybody* and *nobody* makes shipping decisions. The next problem we encountered was how to merge those and get an efficient mailing program together. The solution to this can be seen in the program we just completed in which we mailed to 49,000 companies in those specific SIC codes. The unique thing about it is that rather than just mail to the mail room supervisor at the company, we mailed the same piece to five or six different job categories within the same company. We only mailed to 49,000 companies, but we mailed a total of 184,000 pieces.

Q. You addressed by job title?

A. Yes, not by individual names. Now the interesting thing that came out of this was the phenomenal results we achieved. We mailed this piece at the end of September '77 and as of a couple of days ago, we got about 14½% company response. If you are talking in terms of the 184,000 pieces we mailed out, we got about 8,000 BRC's back requesting information which is about a 4.3% response. To me the most pertinent thing about this whole direct mail program is the attitude of the sales department because we were dedicated to provide our sales people with bonafide leads.

Q. While we are on this subject Heinz, how many sales people do you have?

A. We have about 140 sales people. Originally, whenever we had done a direct mail program of any sort and we provided the sales department with leads, we often heard gripes from our sales people that we weren't providing bonafide leads. Through this new program we were able to achieve much greater penetration into companies than we had been able to before. It also, more importantly, elicited confidence in the marketing department that wasn't there. Our sales people felt good about the fact that we were doing a good job providing them with leads to people who actually wanted to talk with them.

Q. What does that letter say that you mailed to these 49,000 companies?

A. It's an offer to send them our "Overnight" kit. It tells them how to get a package delivered tomorrow morning. The reason we sent an "Overnight" kit is because in our 1978 advertising our tag line is,"When it absolutely, positively has to be there overnight, (use) Federal Express." What we did was we timed the direct mail campaign to coincide with the high point of reach and frequency of our television advertising. We hit them with the direct mail but also built a bridge between our commercials and our print advertising. If you see the fulfillment package, you'll note that it tries to conform to the style of our print advertising. They are almost identical to the graphics used on our TV ads too.

Q. What's in the kit?

A. Contained in the package is our service guide that's basically the bible of Federal Express. It contains all the information you really need to know about Federal Express: our rates; areas we serve; and how to do business with the company. It also contains some small brochures for our specific services such as "Priority One," which is our overnight parcel delivery service and a "Courier Pak," our overnight document delivery service.

Q. Are there any other advertising programs that Federal Express is engaged in?

A. We have a correspondent sales unit, which fills requests for specific information, either by mail or when people call up our 800 number. When an inquiry comes in our customer service agents have a form that they fill out. They capture the caller's name, company name, address, and then check off certain areas that that caller might be interested in. Let us assume that the customer heard that we are putting together a co-operative venture with Swiss Air to enable a European company to ship a package and have it delivered anywhere in the United States the next day. We utilize an IBM System 6 ink jet printer where we will then personalize letters to people who have called in or asked for information. Each letter is individually addressed and typed on one of those ink jet printers. Then we put into that letter one of our brochures giving the specific information on what they are looking for.

Q. Is there any outstanding group in an SIC grouping that tends to use Federal Express more than another?

A. I would say that there is a symbiotic relationship between new industries that have developed in the last ten or twenty years and their need for expedited delivery. They seem to have greater open-mindedness to use or to build into their business mix the need for overnight deliveries. The computer industry, electronic industry and medical industry are heavy users of Federal Express.

Q. What's in store for Federal Express now? You've come a long way in five years.

A. The big excitement right now is that the 727 legislation has been passed. I just saw the first 727 take off last Sunday on its first flight from Memphis out to the West Coast. A 727 can carry about 40,000 pounds of freight compared to a Falcon jet which can carry about 6,000 pounds.

Q. Are there any other new programs that you will be engaging in?

A. We will be opening what we call convenience centers, which will allow the Federal Express customers later access to our system. If somebody is working late and he has to get a package out after 6 PM, we will have strategically located convenience centers in the major metropolitan areas where a potential user will be able to drop that package off as late as 9 PM and still have it delivered before noon the next day. Those convenience centers are designed to accommodate business in a particular geographic location rather than a city in its entirety. The marketing tool that we will employ to create the awareness of this service will probably be direct mail advertising because of its ability to pinpoint a market. For example, we might do a saturation mailing of a zip code coverage area within a fifteen block radius of a convenience center in New York City.

Q. Will you be using your TV advertising program as a follow-up to a mail program such as this?

A. We will probably do some of that. One thing I haven't told you about is that we are working closely with TV stations that are carrying our advertising. We have a sales person at each of the 76 stations we're advertising on. They are responsible for providing us with mailing lists and from these we are putting together station support programs.

Q. In the local station situation Heinz, would you provide mailing pieces to these stations for mailing to prospects in the area?

A. We would use the latest technology like the IBM jet printing system located at our Memphis office. We would try to personalize letters.

From the January 1978 issue of Direct Marketing. *Reprinted with permission.*

10

DOWN HOME BANK WINS UPTOWN BRAND OF SUCCESS

by Alan B. Eirinberg

Texas is noted for its big stories . . . and its big banks. There's the Dallas-based First International Bankshares with $9 billion in assets, the Houston Texas Commerce Bankshares boasting $6.9 billion and the $1.6 billion Allied Bankshares.

But, according to *Forbes* (Sept. 4) none of the bank holding companies has more than 8% of the state's banking business. Texas is one of the few states that has no branch banking. There are more than 1,300 banks in the state.

This here story is about one of these banks. It's not in a big city. In fact, it's not even in a big town. And, the bank's assets don't approach anywhere near the $100,000,000 figure.

But, pardner, the First State Bank of Rio Vista, Tex., which proudly refers to itself as the Cow Pasture Bank (you got it right. pardner—The Cow Pasture Bank), is a case study in successful marketing. Once again, it proves that you don't have to be the biggest to be both innovative and creative.

While Rio Vista isn't far from "Big D"

Reprinted with permission from the September 18, 1978 issue of Advertising Age. *Copyright © 1978 by Crain Communications, Inc.*

(about 60 miles), no oil wells dot the landscape. About 200 farmers and ranchers live in the area.

In all fairness, the town has grown. Its population now numbers all of 400, but more than ten banks operate in the county.

Cow Pasture deposits have grown from just over $5,000,000 in 1965 to $11,000,000 in 1970 and almost $27,000,000 in 1975. By June 30 of this year deposits exceeded $40,000,000—a far cry from $2,000,000-plus the bank reported at the end of 1960.

Obviously, this growth hasn't come just from the immediate area. Cow Pasture draws customers from the Dallas-Fort Worth metroplex and from surrounding small towns, and is even able to retain a high percentage of customers who relocate to other cities and states.

FLY-IN SUCCESS

Now, what could a small bank like this, with an in-house agency, possibly do to build such customer loyalty? Sit back, pardners, while I spin the tale of the Cow Pasture Bank. Many a big city "dude" would give his eye teeth to credit himself with a comparable success story.

All of you know about drive-in and walk-up banking, but I'll bet you haven't heard about ride-in and fly-in banking. At Cow Pasture Bank the ranchers can ride their horses right up to the teller's window to cash checks and make deposits. Just behind the bank is a mowed landing strip bordered by white painted tires. First State stakes its claim as the world's first fly-in bank. Private pilots fly in regularly to conduct their banking business.

Since the repossessd cattle were fenced off so that the back pasture could be used as a landing field, more than 250 persons have been sworn into its "Cow Pasture Squadron." Any pilot who legally lands his plane on the strip is eligible for membership. Bill Jones, vice-president, and lending officer, doubles as Squadron Leader. Bill presents new members with the following certificate:

> Mary Jones has cleared the top wire, braved the elements, successfully dodged the cows and mesquites, and has landed at the Cow Pasture Bank. The Cow Pasture has been duly inspected and all the fences of the back forty are still intact, and the plane's landing gear is still attached. Henceforth the above inscribed is hereby recorded as a member in good standing of the Cow Pasture Squadron.

New members are given yellow flying caps with patches carrying a humorous cartoon of an aviator riding an eagle. Student pilots from the Dallas-Fort Worth area often take their solo flights to the Cow Pasture Bank. Although the "Squadron" club is limited, its reputation and strong association with the bank is known throughout the vicinity.

Another first for the fly-in bank came when one of its customers, Al Bascom, parachuted down to the landing strip to make his deposit.

Cow Pasture's advertising takes the form of tongue-in-cheek cartoons which make light of many of the problems faced by farmers and ranchers in the area. This approach is followed through in all its sales promotion materials.

BARBED WIRE CHECKS

First State Bank's checks carry a humorous cartoon of a cowboy lassoing a skinny bronco. The check is outlined with barbed wire. The look is an integral part of Cow Pasture's letterheads and brochures. Pamela Smith, business development, says, "Our check is not just another pretty bit of artwork. It is the reason customers have fun banking by mail thousands of miles away."

Also, she points to their employe relations program which accounts in great part for the bank's progress. Notes Ms. Smith, "This is where folks come when they want to do their banking business in a relaxed, friendly fashion."

Every customer is invited to pause for a refreshment in the bank's coffee shop, and special guests join the staff for lunch. Therein lies another story. Jessie Fantroy is Cow Pasture's cook. Her typical homestyle lunch might be ham and candied yams, barbeque and potato salad, or turkey and dressing. Jessie isn't just another good cook. She devoted 16 years to a very special family— the First Family—when she cooked for President and Mrs. Lyndon B. Johnson at their lake house near Marble Falls, Tex. She was like a member of the family. L.B.J. wanted her to move to Washington, D.C. with him, but Jessie just couldn't tolerate the Secret Service men testing her cooking.

The bank printed a cookbook called "Cow Pasture Cooking," based on Jessie's cooking, with over 600 recipes contributed by friends and customers, as well as special selections devoted to Mrs. Fantroy's kitchen. The cover carries the line, "Over 56 years of home made bank services." The cookbook covers everything from hot wassail served at the bank during the Christmas season to Texas-style enchiladas and Jeff Davis pie.

The Santa Fe Railway provides the bank with numerous customers and friends, so it was natural for Cow Pasture to sponsor "Santa Fe Appreciation 1975" as a salute to the railroad for its economic, civic and "good neighbor" approach to Rio Vista. Legend has it that a railroad worker took a look over the Nolan River Valley in 1880 and said the words Rio Vista which are Spanish for "view of the river." That became the official name of the little settlement started when the railroad came into the territory.

Cow Pasture printed thousands of Santa Fe Appreciation booklets carrying

First State Bank of Rio Vista, Texas, customers are invited to "drive-in, walk-in or fly-in" to do business at the Cow Pasture Bank. *(Advertisements courtesy of First State Bank of Rio Vista, Texas.)*

cartoons depicting various railroad scenes. Both local papers published special sections honoring the largest income producer in the area. The bank exhibited unusual photographs, models and other memorabilia telling the Santa Fe story. Officials lunched at the bank, and Cow Pasture organized tours through Santa Fe's shops. Santa Fe Appreciation Day drew fantastic attention to the bank, but the approach was low-key and designed to show Cow Pasture's appreciation to this large sector of the community—without overcommercializing the effort.

To recognize cattlemen in the area, the Cow Pasture Bank designed a special 8½ x11 giveaway. The first three pages of the piece are devoted to a detailed history of cattle brands. The fourth covers the heraldry of the branding iron and the final page traces the main cattle trails used to drive the cattle north from their home breeding grounds in Texas.

FAMILY ALBUM

Cow Pasture's annual report, "Fifty-six years on the prairie," is dedicated to its founder, Lowell Niles Smith Jr., who founded the bank in 1920. He passed away in 1975 and was active to the time of his passing. Keeping with its historic tradition, four pages of the report are devoted to the "Family Album" which depicts the bank's staff, officers and directors dressed in turn-of-the-century attire. A sizable part of the publication covers the history of the area and the bank's progress during the 56 years since its founding accompanied by some wonderful old photos. One column carries excerpts from the *International Herald Tribune, National Enquirer, Chicago Tribune, London Daily Mail* and other newspapers commenting on the world's first fly-in bank.

The report salutes Carlos Lee "Pop" Myres, public relations manager for First State Bank starting in 1967. (During the 1936 Texas Centennial, he was credited with giving Dallas the name "Big D.") Pop died in 1972 following a career as a singer, radio announcer, tv commercial star and Texas prairie philosopher. One day Pop said, "The name First State Bank of Rio Vista is too long. Why don't we call it the bank in the cow pasture?" And, so it became the Cow Pasture Bank.

A short look at the bank's advertising budget for last year will give you a better idea of how it allocates its money. About $14,000 goes to radio and newspaper advertising, $6,000 to caps, pens, calendars and other giveaways, $5,000 to free soft drinks, candy, gum, etc., $8,000 to lobby projects and special sales promotion materials, $2,000 to flowers for customers who are in the hospital, graduate, marry or die and $1,000 for Thanksgiving-Christmas cards. The above doesn't include football schedules, pillows for ten surrounding towns, agricultural printouts, uniforms for baseball teams and many other supportive efforts covering community needs.

Well, pardners, that about spins out the tale of the Cow Pasture Bank; a truly innovative financial institution.

11

LIKE A GOOD NEIGHBOR, RESEARCH WAS THERE

by Blair Vedder
President, Needham, Harper & Steers Inc.,
Chicago

I am going to give you a 20-year history of one company and I intend to make only one point: that the real value of research in building productive marketing and advertising stragtegies is never—repeat, never—a one-time thing.

The greatest value of communication strategy research, I am convinced, lies in its continuous application to a company's life—as people change, as competition changes, and as the company itself changes. The idea of a once-in-a-lifetime blinding insight from research can be a snare and a delusion.

The relatonship between the State Farm Insurance Co. and our company began in 1939. The most recent 20 years of that association is in part testimony to the contribution that continuous and sound consumer research can play in guiding and sharpening communication strategies.

To an outside observer, State Farm's advertising moves over the past two decades may appear as a series of changes for the pure sake of keeping the communication fresh and different from competition. Not so. Each change was a determined response to a new understanding of the consumer's perception of State Farm—carefully tracked over time.

During the 1940s, State Farm became the country's leading auto insurance underwriter. It was known for its low rates—lower than any of the companies who sell their policies through agents who represent more than one company.

However, in the early 1950s a major competitor, who also had exclusive agents and a low-rate advantage, began to rapidly close on State Farm's lead. That competitor was Allstate, backed by the full resources of Sears, Roebuck & Co.

Moreover, State Farm was still perceived by many as a rural company, specializing in insuring cars of farmers, which was not surprising, because the company, indeed, was founded in Bloomington, Ill., in 1922 to serve the farm market.

Sales projections in 1953 indicated that, at their comparative rates of growth, Allstate would pass State Farm in number of policies by 1957 or 1958. A major change in State Farm's advertising direction was in order. The question was: To what?

A national study of prospect attitudes was fielded in 1954—the first of its kind ever undertaken for or by State Farm. Like much research, it tended to confirm many things that State Farm had already suspected:

—State Farm was acknowledged to offer low rates, in fact, a significant number of prospects and policyholders were convinced that State Farm offered the lowest rates in the industry.

—State Farm, with its central Illinois heritage was perceived as a solid company, but not a giant.

From Blair Vedder, "Like a Good Neighbor, Research Was There," Marketing News, *February 27, 1976. Reprinted from* Marketing News, *published by the American Marketing Association.*

While both of these attributes were expected and could be counted as positive, they had certain negative overtones in the prospect's mind:

—Low rates suggested inferior claim service. In a world where there is no free lunch, prospects concluded that something had to be missing in State Farm's benefit structure for it to sell insurance at such low cost.

—Second, if State Farm was indeed a small company, it may not have the resources, to stand behind and fully cover its policyholders.

A new ad direction was set for State Farm, the keystone of which was the first multi-page insert to appear in *Life* magazine. In five consecutive pages, the ad detailed a full story of the company—its size, rate of growth, how it was able to sell auto insurance at low rates, and its claim service practices.

The impact of this communication was a bit startling (understatement). State Farm's share of the auto insurance business began to accelerate rapidly. And consumer attitude research had a new advocate.

Three years later, State Farm repeated its consumer probe. The effectiveness of the new communication direction was confirmed: Prospects and policyholders clearly acknowledged State Farm's rate advantage, and now there was no longer doubt about the size of the company or its resources.

However, an unexpected and undesirable side effect had been created—one that, over time, could undo much of the progress that was being made. People equated corporate size with corporate disinterest.

A big company was, per se, cold, impersonal, and insensitive. Yet, if you have an automobile accident, you want to be treated with tender loving care, not as another number among millions of policyholders.

This presented a far more delicate communications problem. Could State Farm, through advertising, preserve its growing identity as a giant in its industry, selling insurance at low rates, and still assure the prospect that it was, indeed, a company with a genuine and personal interest in its policyholders' well being?

By luck or by genius, the answer was found in the personality of the most human penny pincher of our time: Jack Benny. The world's most careful buyer (he still drove a Maxwell) became the spokesman for the careful drivers' car insurance company.

It was an ideal marriage; fun for the audience and for the people in the Benny show. It worked quite well. And, in print, the saving and service story was presented with a light touch.

Yet, the world would not stand still. Competition would not let it. Allstate was not about to give up its challenge and, with Ed Reimers' hands, consistently outspent State Farm in advertising by margins of up to 50 percent a year.

State Farm went back to its prospects and customers to find out how Allstate's continued pressure was affecting their perception of State Farm. What Allstate was doing had not influenced the relative sales position of the two companies, but it undoubtedly was having some effect that could presage an eventual sales shift.

One effect of Allstate's effort was to accelerate a strong element of confusion; you can play endless anagrams with the names Allstate and State Farm. And that's what was happening in the customer's head.

Again, the communication goal changed—now it became one of minimizing the confusion while continuing to stress savings, still with a warm and friendly tone. Audio identification in radio commercials helped distinguish more clearly State Farm from Allstate.

Ten years had now passed since the *Life* insert. State Farm's lead over Allstate was approximately $200 million in earned premiums, equal to Allstate's size 10 years before, when the race between the two began. State Farm had altered its stance several times during that period for one and only one reason. Consumers' perceptions kept changing.

These perception shifts were caused in part by the actions of competition, in part by changes in the marketplace, but—and perhaps this is the significant point—they were also caused by unexpected side effects of State Farm's own communications tactics.

In 1969, the automobile insurance world suddenly turned upside down, not for competitive, but for economic reasons. Underwriting losses skyrocketed as they are skyrocketing today. And most auto insurance companies sharply curtailed their new business activities.

However, most automobile insurance policies are written for six months or a year and, when economic conditions turn sour, no insurance company wants to lose its best policyholders at renewal time. The task of advertising at such times is not to bring new policyholders to the agents' offices but to retain the better policyholders by keeping the company's name clearly in the front of their minds. It requires a neat balance between low-key sell and high identification.

Radio was the vehicle State Farm chose to use, and their spokesmen were such wags as Al Capp, Jackie Vernon, Phil Foster, Henry Morgan, and Don Adams.

Slowly, early in the '70s, the automobile insurance industry moved out of its constricted situation and into a more aggressive sales posture. But the period of economic squeeze had changed the industry and State Farm's relationship to it.

In many areas the company's histori-

cally strong rate advantage over competition had narrowed or disappeared. More important, the concern of policyholders had begun to turn away from the issue of cost to one of service.

New research showed that people's primary interest was in buying insurance from an agent who was knowledgeable, who was available, and on whom they could count when they needed help. With 10,000 full-time, exclusive agents, State Farm was in a better position to meet this expectation than anyone else.

So, in 1971 a promise that continues today to identify State Farm was born: "Like A Good Neighbor, State Farm Is There." That promise has been expressed with a good amount of film drama and more recently with the agent as both the star and the spokesman of the message.

Today State Farm is the undisputed leader in car insurance. It is also the largest homeowners' insurance company and one of the fastest growing major life insurance companies.

The close interplay of research and creativity has unquestionably contributed to the effectiveness of State Farm's ads. That advertising in turn has played a role in the company's success.

But all of us who work with State Farm know that the greatness of the company is traceable only in a small way to its ads. State Farm offers a superb product and absolute commitment to fully serve its policyholders through its unequaled network of agents. State Farm's advertising has been the vehicle for making people more conscious of these attributes as people's concern about the attributes has changed over time.

Without continuous tracking of these shifts, I am convinced that State Farm's advertising would have contributed far less than it has contributed over the past 20 years. Instead, it has been research guiding almost every major change in direction that has greatly enhanced the results from the advertising.

To come back to the beginning, research in the development of productive advertising and marketing can never be a one-time thing. The radical and constant changes that occur in companies, in people, and in products simply won't allow it.

12
SELLING BELL: ITS MONOPOLY ERODING, AT&T BEGINS TO LEARN THE ART OF MARKETING

by Georgette Jasen

NEW YORK—American Telephone & Telegraph Co. was the host of giant birthday party last month—for Mickey Mouse.

More than a thousand guests crowded into the Broadway Theater here, where Mickey's first film opened in 1928. Some wore Mickey Mouse ears. There were Mickey Mouse T-shirts, yo-yos and balloons, plus an enormous birthday cake.

Actress Stephanie Mills of The Wiz, which is playing at the Broadway, led the singing of "Happy Birthday" and the Mickey Mouse Club song. Mickey beamed. Then he and Minnie Mouse led guests into the theater lobby for the unveiling of a newly installed Mickey Mouse telephone.

So goes Ma Bell's big new marketing campaign. Last spring AT&T held a shipboard party to launch three new phones, one featuring the comic strip character Snoopy. A professional publicist travels the country

Reprinted by permission of The Wall Street Journal, © *Dow Jones & Company, Inc., 1978. All rights reserved.*

promoting decorator telephones at women's club meetings and on television talk shows. There are plans for the phones to appear in a new Farrah Fawcett-Majors movie.

SEEKING OUT CUSTOMERS

Meantime, advertising budgets are increasing geometrically. Salesmen are going out to visit customers instead of waiting for them to call. Researchers try to determine future customer needs and develop products and services to meet them.

"We're doing things that everyone that's had to sell has been doing all along," says Edwin Langsam, a media-relations manager who works with the marketing department. But it's a big change for the Bell System, which for nearly 100 years was unchallenged as a monopoly. Says Leonard Hyman, an analyst with Merrill Lynch, Pierce, Fenner & Smith, "The attitude used to be, 'Here's the service, and if you don't like it use a carrier pigeon.' "

That attitude had to change. As a result of regulatory and court decisions, customers now can go elsewhere for their telecommunications equipment and services. With advanced technology, more products and services are available than ever before. What's more, the nation's phone companies need new areas of growth now that 96% of American homes have basic telephone service.

This year, the Bell System expects to spend $2.1 billion on marketing, up from $1.8 billion in 1977 and more than twice the amount spent in 1973, the year the marketing department was created.

"VERY BUSINESSLIKE"

The competition has been watching. "They're going about it in a very business-like manner," says Walter Seuren, vice president for commercial marketing and distribution of RCA Service Co., an RCA Corp. unit that designs and installs telephone sytems. Mr. Seuren adds, "That the Bell System is more aggressive is helpful to everybody. It encourages the customer to look at what he's got and how he can upgrade it."

Some other observers are impressed, too. Just a few years ago, AT&T "had neither the organization nor much consumer-marketing skill. They've done a lot in a relatively short period of time," says Martin Bell, a professor of marketing at Washington University in St. Louis. But he adds, "They still have a long way to go."

Harry Newton, a consultant with the Telecom Marketing Group in New York, is more critical. "The telephone industry couldn't market its way out of a paper bag," he says. He agrees, though, that "they're learning."

There's little urgency, Mr. Newton says, because much of the phone companies' growth comes from rate increases—$885 million for the Bell System last year, when total revenue rose $3.7 billion. "It's the only industry where 100% of the participants are profitable," he states, "and they still have over 90% of the market, so what do they care?"

A NUMBER OF OBSTACLES

It isn't easy to change a century-old company with nearly one million employees. Plans conceived by marketing experts at AT&T headquarters aren't binding on the 23 operating companies, and not everyone is enthusiastic. "They create the mold and then fit everybody into it," says a marketing manager at one operating company. "What works in Manhattan won't necessarily work in Dubuque."

There are other problems, too. Some

regulatory commissions limit advertising. Pricing, too, is regulated. Equipment has to be approved in every state for nationwide advertising to be effective. And, says Mr. Bell, the marketing professor, "They have an image problem. They have to make sure that attitudes toward the telephone company don't get confused with attitudes toward specific products and services."

In addition, AT&T continues to lease equipment, while competitors offer the option of buying it. The phone company owns the equipment even when the customer pays in a lump sum rather than monthly. And when an AT&T customer "purchases" a decorator phone he actually buys only the plastic shell; the company owns the mechanism.

Yet there have been significant changes in the way AT&T and its operating companies conduct their business. AT&T recently announced a complete restructuring of the corporation into residence, business and network segments, and the operating companies are following suit. "It's a profound change," John D. deButts, AT&T chairman, said in a recent speech, "not just a reshuffling of boxes on our organization chart."

As an example of the new structure, the executive vice pesident responsible for the business segment, Thomas E. Bolger, is concerned only with services and equipment for business and government. It's the first time a top-level executive's responsibilities have been limited that way.

Other changes are just as profound. For the first time, AT&T is bringing in top-level people from outside the company. The best known of these, Archie J. McGill, vice president for business-market management and development, is a former vice president of International Business Machines Corp. He joined AT&T in 1973. Now, about half his staff is from outside the Bell System.

Mr. McGill laughs when he's asked whether he encountered any resistance to his plans. "I'm a change agent, I came here swinging the bat," he says. "There's bound to be an element of friction. But the help from the top has been extraordinary."

MARKET PLANS

Using the IBM approach to marketing, Mr. McGill has divided the business market into three groups: industrial; commercial; and government, education and medical. The groups are further subdivided into specific industries, making about 70 segments in all, with a market plan for each. The market plan, which may be several hundred pages long, profiles the industry, explains its communications needs, sets marketing goals and describes a sales-action program, to be carried out by a "marketing team."

Mr. McGill defends such specialization. "If we're going to design a system to solve a customer's problems," he says, "we have to understand his objectives, where he's trying to go and what he's trying to accomplish."

The Bell System also is experimenting with business-sales centers, where a customer can see and try some of the sophisticated equipment available and have a system designed to fit his needs. In another experiment, which AT&T officials expect to be expanded, Illinois Bell Telephone Co. is paying commissions to its business-marketing staff. This is a first for the Bell System.

TELEPHONE STORES

On the residence side, the market has been divided into mobile and nonmobile segments. To reach the residential customers who rarely move and have little occasion to get in touch with the phone company, Bell has PhoneCenter Stores. There customers cen select a telephone and in some cases take it home and plug it in themselves. Some of the stores are in shopping malls, to attract impulse buyers.

Bell companies also are using the mail, usually in the form of inserts in the monthly bill, to advise customers of new products and services.

In an experiment in Columbus, Ind., Indiana Bell Telephone Co. let some customers have certain services free for trial periods of 30 or 60 days. Known as custom calling, the services permit conference calls and forwarding to another number and provide a signal when another call is waiting. Together, the services usually cost about $5 a month.

Advertising to residential customers has increased enormously. AT&T expects to spend $12.5 million on it this year, compared with less than $2 million in 1977. The money is going into nationwide television and magazine ads that tout the variety and quality of Bell telephones and urge customers to "be choosy."

BUSINESS ADS INCREASE

More money is going for business advertising, too. The budget this year is $11 million, up from $7.5 million in 1977. Ads in trade and general-business publications promote a Bell system as the solution to business problems.

In addition, operating companies are spending more to advertise. New York Telephone, for instance, expects to spend $4.6 million this year, compared with $3.5 million in 1977. Some of its advertising is more aggressive than the parent company's, such as ads using testimonials from customers who tried the competition and came back to Bell.

Employes are feeling the effects of all these changes. Now that there are marketing experts, employes getting experience in various specialties are moving around less. Internal measurement systems have changed, too. Instead of the number of customer contacts, the emphasis now is on total revenue. Sales people now have to deal with customers face to face instead of by phone.

But there already are signs that the Bell Marketing System, as it is called, is working. Bell Telephone Co. of Pennsylvania, which tried the new system is its hospital segment, says it won 50% more customers and had a 300% greater revenue gain than when using traditional methods.

LEARNING ABOUT HOGS

Many customers seem happy. Bruce Burkland, marketing manager of Farmers Hybrid Co., a Des Moines-based unit of Monsanto Co. that sells pigs for breeding, was impressed with the service he got from Bell System representatives. "They really learned our business," he says. "They got out into the field and worked with the hogs and with the customers." When they made their pitch, Mr. Burkland says, they knew what they were talking about.

To be sure, some customers are going to the competition. The Citicorp Center in New York and the MGM Grand Hotel in Reno are among those with non-Bell telephone systems.

That's a fact of competitive life, says Mr. Bolger, the executive vice president for the business segment. "We're not going to have 100% of the marketplace, that's just not in the cards," he says. "But I think we stack up well, very well, indeed."

There's one very definite advantage AT&T has over the competition, says James Nations, a marketing manager at Southwestern Bell Telephone Co. "Marketing is a lot like warfare," he says, "and the largest army usually wins."

13
WE SELL SECURITY

Worried about burglars creeping into your home? About bad-check artists bankrupting your business? About credit card thieves? If so, you're in good company—and a good company to own these days is one selling the service called "security."

The field includes everything from a computerized credit-card-checking system to a full protection setup for a residential subdivision. Security is a multi-billion-dollar business, and behind its growth is another growth industry: crime. Not only are criminals increasing their dollar volume, but they are spreading out the locus of their operations: in the 1970s, crime was reported to be increasing faster in the suburbs of the United States than in its central cities.

What marketing opportunities has all this lawlessness provided? Pinpointing a few may indicate the range of services that constitute the security field. In the suburbs, subdivisions and individual homeowners are buying antiburglary systems. In the retailing world, computers are foiling both the credit card thief and the "paperhanger," the professional passer of bad checks.

FORTRESS SUBURBIA

A graphic illustration of the security bonanza awaits the visitor to a subdivision developed by a crime-conscious marketer. Certainly the subdivision is surrounded by a brick wall. At the gate stands a guard provided by a security service; and if the subdivi-

sion advertises its homes as castles, the guard at the gate may be colorfully garbed and hold a musket. The subdivision may even go to the extreme of one development on an island in the Colorado River: the island has no car access, and property owners reach their homes by over-the-water cable car. They leave their cars in a fence-enclosed parking area on the mainland, where there is an attendant on duty 24 hours a day.

What may well be the nation's most sophisticated security system, however, has been installed in a 100-acre Texas community near Houston. The community, Sugar Creek, requires buyers to tie in to a central computer for security purposes. Instead of opening their doors with conventional keys, homeowners punch their own particular combination on a set of buttons to open it.

What if someone punches the wrong combination? The computer will activate an alarm at the central office and summon a guard to the home. Furthermore, the mistake will trigger an alarm bell at the home and turn on outside flood lights. As a serendipitous side effect, a fire at the home will set in motion the same series of alarms.

Of course, not every subdivision's security service purchases approach the Sugar Creek scale. But each development that buys a guard service, a cruising patrolman, walls and gates, two-way radios, or even stickers for the windshields of its residents' cars is surely making crime prevention pay—for some supplier.

"Private street patrol and private guard protection were once the hallmark of exclusive residential enclaves, but now they are being supported by middle and low-income residential areas as well as by the largest and smallest business enterprises," says attorney Sydney C. Cooper, a senior criminal justice researcher for the New York City Rand Institute and a former police officer. However, Charles Barnard, a *Satur-*

day Review author, profiles the typical buyer of electronic home protection as a fictional "Sam Mills," who boasts a $200,000 house complete with original paintings, a 1931 Pierce Arrow to complement his new Buick, and a bejeweled wife.

"Sam," Barnard reports, "was not the type to stint when it came to fortifying his castle."

> For $4000 Sam had installed one of the best electronic alarm systems available. Attached to every possible point of entry into the house were sensors that could detect the first vibrations of a burglar's jimmy and trigger the alarm. A howling siren would then go off in the house, and, simultaneously, a light would flash on a central switchboard miles away where the alarm company's ever-ready personnel would pick up the phone and alert the local police. This tie-in to "central security" was via the telephone wires. To guard against the possibility that some enterprising thief might think to cut the wires before attempting a burglary, the phone lines were buried.
>
> Inside the house ultrasonic Intruder Alarms disguised as dictionaries were installed in all the downstairs rooms. If a sizeable, unidentified shape crossed the room and disturbed their high-frequency waves, spotlights would flash on and a second alarm, independent of the central house alarm, would begin to wail. More electronic sensors were hidden behind the nineteenth-century painting and under the jewelry chest; they were plugged into the main alarm. For additional protection, a photoelectric unit was set up to beam its nearly invisible infrared light across the garage door opening. Anyone who rolled the Pierce Arrow from the safety of its shelter would cut the beam and set off the main alarm....
>
> When the alarm installation was completed, the salesman suggested that Sam throw a party for his neighbors to show off the new system.

"Then, if they hear your alarm go off some night, they will know what it is," he said. What he didn't say was that the party would also be a splendid free advertisement for his wares.

By 1979, however, homeowners in more modest income brackets were swelling demand, bringing total installations of burglar alarms to an estimated 1.4 million homes. One security company owner says most people who order alarm systems give the same reason: a burglary at their own home or that of a neighbor. Industry spokesmen note, however, that the growth in burglar alarm purchases also may be a spinoff of smoke and fire alarm sales. Once a homeowner gets the idea that he can buy a machine to protect against some threat, it is only logical that he or she begins to think about threats other than fire.

BUSINESSES BUY, TOO

A field like home alarms that can sell nearly a half-million units in a year is surely nothing to sneeze at. But dwarfing the expenditures of individual homeowners on security services are the expenditures of businesses; adding them in makes security more than a $10 billion industry.

What are the problems that industrial security is purchased to solve? Originally, they were the same ones that plague the residential security buyers: the threat of burglary and fear for the personal safety of employees. Now, however, more problems have been added. Two which are unique to businesses are the bad-check artist and the credit card thief.

Computers are adding sophistication to the security designed to foil both. For the bad-check writer, often called a "paperhanger," the service being marketed is designed to catch him or her in the act—the only way, according to United Press International, that such a person is in any real danger of going to jail. The procedure is to store in a computer's memory a detailed file of known offenders, including driver's license numbers, real or fake, and information on the way they operate. Then when the supermarket courtesy booth staff member or the bank teller punches pertinent information into a terminal on an individual who is trying to cash a check, the computer instantly offers a signal if something is amiss.

Business reporter Leroy Pope cites one Telecredit success: when two women tried to cash payroll checks at a Los Angeles supermarket, a Telecredit check revealed that the paychecks were drawn on an account that had been closed for months. In another case, says Pope, "when a paperhanger realized he had been caught, he grabbed the bad check from the store cashier and swallowed it. He was convicted because the judge allowed as evidence the printout from the Telecredit computer showing the check to have been bad."

Meanwhile, another branch of the security-by-computer industry has decidedly gone national. The field is credit card security, which translates into letting a retailer know instantly if that nice gentleman who handed him a Bank Americard or Master Charge card just happens to have stolen it.

The security service can also print out from its computer a file on criminal patterns; Interbank, the security organization handling Master Charge, is doing so already. Thus, "We can see how much fraud each merchant has, both in dollars and as a percentage of sales volume," says Interbank's Robert Dodge. "We can see where each missing card has been used, and how it's been lost."

Dodge explains how the data is used. If one merchant shows a consistently high incidence of fraud he says, "the bank which signed him up is advised of it."

Merchant collaboration in fraud schemes is rare, but "it does happen," Dodge notes, adding, "I think this is one of the greatest risks in the credit card business. We keep very close track on merchants. Very close track."

Printouts showing how cards are lost also have specific applications. If most cards in a certain region are being stolen from mailboxes, for example, it can lead to changes in mailing and card registration procedures. Furthermore, printouts tracing the geographic progress of a stolen card can be used to alert local police and security officers.

All in all, business is prospering whether in home electronic alarms or industrial-security electronic computer services. A spokesman for the U.S. Department of Justice points out, for example, that more money is spent on private security than on police. For those in sales who seek a job in a growth industry, the future promises, of course, "security."

14
FOUR MYTHS ABOUT ARCHITECTS

A profession offers, by definition, a service: legal advice, medical advice, tax advice; or advice on how to design a garden, building, or whole shopping center, for example. Architects, like most professionals, have a group-imposed restriction on advertising. John Doe, Architect, does not authorize a television spot showing pictures of his successful building, and concluding, "Would you like a prizewinner, too? Call Doe!" But for the architect association, advertising is perfectly ethical, and the *Wall Street Journal* markets to such advertisers the service of putting their message in front of a large group of readers.

Four myths about architects.

"To the architect, time is no object."

The truth is that in the new science of fast construction, it is *architects* who are the pioneers. Using new techniques like "Fast Track" and "Critical Path," they are meeting and even beating some murderous deadlines. At the site for Memorex's huge new headquarters in Santa Clara, California, architects had steelwork up in 3 weeks, the first products rolling off assembly lines within 9 months, and the entire complex (4 buildings, which won awards for their good looks) finished inside of 2 years!

"He loves to spend your money because his fee is a percentage."

The truth is that architects today will often negotiate a *fixed fee* before they begin work. But the architect who did Cities Service Oil's headquarters in Tulsa was working for the traditional percentage. He found a way to use the outer walls as a truss, thus reducing the cost of the building by $1,000,000 and–incidentally–clipping a sizable sum off his own fee!

"His estimate is an under-estimate."

The truth is that despite the dizzying impact of inflation, architects' estimates have proved to be surprisingly realistic. A random sampling of 25 architectural projects in North Carolina last year showed that final construction costs were $3,195,843 *under* the architects' original estimates. And there's no reason to believe that North Carolina's architects are any shrewder than the rest.

"He cares more about the way it looks than the way it works."

Ten businessmen who've dealt with architects recently have taken the trouble to demolish *this* myth. They describe how their architects gave them buildings that work in ways they would never have thought of themselves, and we've put their stories into a booklet. We'll send you a copy, free: Just drop a card to American Institute of Architects, 1785 Massachusetts Avenue, N.W., Washington, D.C. 20036. (It happens to be a good-looking booklet, as well.)

("Four Myths About Architects," advertisement in the *Wall Street Journal*, September 12, 1972, by the American Institute of Architects. Reprinted by permission of the publisher and the advertiser.)

SECTION FOLLOW-UP
SERVICES WITH A SMILE

—Services are the fastest-growing sector of the economy—and as we run out of raw materials, they'll grow even faster.

—Services need to be explained more thoroughly than goods, which buyers can see.

—Services are people, so everybody connected with the delivery of a service is in marketing.

The three statements above raise questions for the managers who market each service described in this section—from package transport to voice transport to protection of money or homes. They also raise questions about possible new products for many marketers who will decide to grow by "joining the service":

1. How do buyers compare products that they can't hold next to each other and evaluate?

2. Isn't every service really a "package" of goods and people for rent together in a system? If so, the creation of new service ideas is mostly a matter of assembling the goods and the people that will prevent or solve a problem. Can you list two problems you had in the last week (you got caught in the rain; you stepped in chewing gum) and design a service to forestall the problem or cope with it?

3. How does an organization train package handlers, alarm or phone installers, bank tellers, architects, and claims adjusters to be consciously skillful marketers? What would each do differently if he or she understood marketing and considered it part of the job?

3 WHERE MARKETING HAPPENS

—Among department store displays . . .
—At lunch, with a food broker picking up the check . . .
—At a grocery store . . .
—Or at the door of your apartment . . .

These places are "where marketing happens." The Sears catalog, the milkman at the back door, and the newspaper ad promoting bicycles from overseas all deliver the same message: marketing happens all over.

Moving goods to buyers can be innovative: if you leave an order, vitamin pills will appear next to your cottage cheese. The stores who sell to you are half the picture; the marketers who sell to the stores are the other half. The whole picture is properly called "channels of distribution"—the kind of channels where new ideas are dredged up every day.

15

MODERN MILKMEN SELL SOME PRODUCTS MORE THAN UDDERS

Associated Press

SAN FRANCISCO—Like the hard-riding peddlers of frontier times, today's milkman must offer a wide range of goods—from pens to panty-hose—to survive.

And for most the tough competition of the local supermarket is as hazardous for business as hostile Indians and desperadoes.

"We had 20,000 home delivery customers in the city of San Francisco in 1948," said Buzz Korn, sales manager for Foremost Dairy Products.

"Today we have 6,500 customers."

Home-delivered milk is more costly than supermarket milk—primarily because of labor costs—sometimes by as much as 15 cents a half gallon.

"It's simply a question of money," said an industry spokesman. "People don't want to pay the price."

To counteract their competitive disadvantage, Korn's drivers began selling a wide range of hardware items.

"We started this about a year and a half ago," he said recently. "In the first 19 months our milk routemen sold $125,000 worth of cookware in the Bay Area.

"In the month of December we sold $46,000 worth of nondairy merchandise from our trucks."

Products carried by the drivers include pantyhose, garbage pails, laundry detergent, toys and candy, said Korn.

"Many of our drivers each carry a case of 48 pairs of pantyhose," he said, " . . . We even have a white poodle dog with a built-in transistor radio."

Home delivery, which at one time accounted for 50 to 80 percent of milk sales, has fallen off to about 15 percent nationally, industry sources say.

For those milkmen lucky enough to survive the sharp drop in business, tradition and loyalty can play a large part in keeping customers.

"These people trust me and consider me their friend," said Al Leiss, 54, who has driven routes in Oakland and Contra Costa County for more than 25 years. "I have the keys to a lot of their doors.

"We can't offer price any more. We can only offer convenience and the promise of truly fresh milk."

Leiss, who earns $44 per day, estimates that he has lost some 150 customers on his three routes during the past five years. He now services about 100 customers on each route, he said.

The milkman can still occupy an important place for those who remain, however. Leiss stopped his van outside a home in Concord. The occupant was not in.

"I have the use of the key to the house," he said.

"I just go in, open up the refrigerator and see what she needs. She never even leaves me a note. It's all built on integrity and trust."

From "Modern Milkmen Sell Some Products More Than Udders," The Associated Press, carried in the Houston Post February 16, 1973. Reprinted by permission of The Associated Press Newsfeatures.

16

WHERE MIDDLE AMERICA SHOPS

Every business asks itself a question that may seem almost philosophical in nature: "What kind of company do we want to be?" And even if the question is *not* asked, the company answers it anyway: "We want to be the kind of company we've always been."

Sears, Roebuck and company, the nation's largest retailer and tenth largest U.S. corporation, recently asked itself that question and somewhat to its chagrin, found that its answer was printed on the front pages of several business publications. ("Leak Splashes Sears' Top-Secret Five-Year Plan Over Retail World" was the headline in late 1978.) But having Sears' internal business exposed to public view was probably an instructive lesson in marketing planning for hundreds of other consumer-oriented companies.

Sears sells so many products and services in so many stores that whenever the retail giant makes even a minor change, the retail—and business—world listens. And when the chain whose sales amount to one percent of the U.S. gross national product goes through a painful analysis of its strengths and faults, then the reverberations—exposed to public view—are highly instructive.

Here is the net conclusion of the five-year plan, as printed in *Crain's Chicago Business*, a business weekly in Sears' home city:

Sears is a family store for middle-class, hometown Americans. We are the premier distributor of durable goods for these families, their homes and their automobiles.

We are the premier distributor of non-durable goods that have their acceptance base in function rather than fashion. We are valued by middle-class America for our integrity, our reputation for fair-dealing and our guarantee.

We are not a fashion store. We are not a store for the whimsical, nor the affluent. We are not a discounter, nor an avant-garde department store . . .

We are not a store that anticipates. We reflect the world of Middle America, and all of its desires and concerns and problems and faults.

Sears has thus taken the middle ground in the marketing battles that lie ahead. But what was the background for this statement of marketing strategy? And doesn't this strategy go back in time?

Yes, admitted Sears chairman Edward R. Telling. He admitted that the new blueprint "takes us back closer to where we were 15 years ago."

During those 15 years, Sears had taken some steps that lowered its margins of profitability while a number of other chains had increased their profits.

In hindsight, Sears' problems started in 1967. It began a strategy to lure higher-income shoppers by upgrading product lines and adding more goods at the top end of the price spectrum. The new merchandise sold at higher gross margins and for a time contributed to some nice gains. But while Sears was pursuing the affluent shopper, other chains were chipping at its prime market. Still its overall share of market remained stable until 1974, when inflation became rampant. Then many retailers ran into trouble, but Sears most of all, as shoppers began to concentrate on values and bargains while Sears had blurred its image of purveyor of values to Middle America. So in 1975, Sears began self-examination, hiring the consulting firm of McKinsey & Co. to overhaul its far-flung management structure. More and more buying decisions were made at Sears Tower, its Chicago headquarters, as opposed to its buying offices in New York City.

Then in 1977 Sears ran into more difficulty. Its strategy was to become more "promotional," that is, cut prices and keep sales going for longer periods. Sears spent $518 million on advertising in 1977 compared to $419 million in 1976. While the plan appeared to work for the first half of 1977, profits in the third quarter declined while sales went up. Then in the fourth quarter sales increased by 13% but profits dropped a dismal 36%. That nosedive contrasted with rising profits of competitors.

Part of the problem was that Sears had installed an incentive plan that promised store managers bonuses based on volume. And store buyers were so carried away with increasing volume that at the end of 1977, inventories were almost $200 million higher than expected.

What are some of the specifics in the five-year plan? The report says that many of Sears' product lines are in a mature stage of growth. To add vigor, the report calls for expansion of the $3.5 billion home improvements group to increase repair and installation services; sale of Sears' own brand of home computers, a potential multi-billion dollar market; reduction in the advertising-to-sales ratio starting in 1979 and continuing thereafter—advertising was cut by 7% in 1979, to $482 million; expansion of Sears' $3.5 billion catalog business; dropping the ill-fated incentive compensation plan; and moving the 2,000-person buying staff in New York to Chicago. Other changes call for increased emphasis on basic product lines and less emphasis on some areas where competition has proven more effective.

17
GASTRIC MEASURES LIKELY, FOR WAR IS SELL

by Carl Hiassen
Knight-Ridder Newspapers

America's hamburger giants are struggling tooth-and-bun for supremacy in a marketplace fueled by the grandest of all traditions: gluttony. The prize: a juicier share of the $20 billion fast-food market. The stakes: simply gastronomical.

All three big burger companies—McDonald's, Burger King and Wendy's—raid each other's executive pantries, engage in onion espionage and recipe reconnaisance, recruit informants to leak secret documents, even set aside "combat funds" to blitz the opposition.

The armaments are slogans, promotions, commercials, new products and free premiums: balloons, whistles, *Star Wars* glasses, puzzles, prizes and comic books. For example, Burger King officials estimate that every two weeks for the last 12 months, the company has given away 6 million such premiums to kids as "a reward for coming to Burger King."

At its seven-story corporate headquarters in Miami, the Burger King Corp. has kicked off its second year of Operation Grand Slam with a direct challenge to Ray Kroc's seemingly invincible McDonald's empire.

From the Houston Post, *January 28, 1979. Reprinted with permission of Knight-Ridder Newspapers.*

"THE SMALL GUYS"

"The small guys have dropped by the wayside," reported one market analyst. "Now, it's the battle of the giants."

Slogan-for-slogan, burger-for-burger, clown-for-clown, the battle cries incessantly ring across the land.

"You, you're the one. Hot 'n' juicy hamburgers, 256 ways. Have it your way. We do it all for you. Who's got the best darn burger in the whole wide world?"

Not very pretty, is it? And this is only what the public sees.

A price war would be something Americans are accustomed to, but the cost of hamburger meat simply is too high and the profits already too marginal for that. So, behind the scenes, burger bosses scheme in other ways to seduce you away from the competition and expand the already vast fast-food market beyond its traditional mainstay of the lunchtime stopover.

"It's not a question of *whether* Americans are going to eat hamburgers but *where* they are going to eat hamburgers," said Burger King marketing vice president Chris Schoenleb.

In coming months, Americans will be pelted unmercifully with high-powered pattie propaganda. Hold the pickles, hold the lettuce and send in the clowns.

If the burger barons have it their way, stopping at a hamburger joint won't be just something sacramental. They want you for breakfast, for dinner, for snacks. They want you for birthdays, holidays, weekends. They want you when Mom doesn't want to cook or when Dad doesn't want to eat Mom's cooking, or when Dad himself threatens to cook. They want you to become—in market lexicon—a heavy user, the hamburger eater who stops in at least once a week.

Schoenleb figures, "If every customer made one additional visit per month, that would get us an additional $100,000 per store annually.

They want you so bad they'll spend millions for your business, bribe your kids with toys and do everything humanly possible to make you believe their hamburger is really different—tastier, bigger, faster and more fun to eat than anyone else's.

WHOPPER PROBLEM

Picture a somber predawn conclave of top Burger King field commanders at an empty Miami Burger King where the main topic of discussion is "that damn Whopper problem." It is November 1978, and Whopper patties being packaged in new cardboard containers at a temperature of 95 to 105 degrees are often clammy by the time a customer bites into them. Why, demands a Burger King vice president, aren't the Whoppers being packaged at 135 degrees and delivered hot? "We're not leaving here until we find out," he announces coldly as he and his colleagues gather around the broiler, flipping burgers.

The early rumblings of war began when a top McDonald's executive, 37-year-old Don Smith, defected to become president of Burger King in February 1977. It didn't take long to see what he had in mind: to outMcDonald McDonald's.

"Before Don's arrival, I think we were resigned to our No. 2 position. Don doesn't accept that philosophy. He believes it's possible to be No. 1," said Jerry Ruenheck, Burger King's vice president in charge of operations.

Smith mounted a Big Mac Counterattack by increasing the size of the standard Burger King hamburger from 1.6 ounces to 2 ounces. Then he introduced new cheddar cheese and implemented a computerized french-fry system that turns out a product virtually indistinguishable from the famed McDonald's golden fries.

MAGICAL BURGER KING

Next came the debut of the Magical Burger King, a mincing magician whose avowed mission is to beat the buns off Ronald McDonald. Analysts say the auburn-bearded King could conceivably shake McDonald's traditional grip on America's kidvid hamburger market, and Burger King insiders are optimistic that it won't be long before the Golden Arches start sagging.

"Don Smith has done a remarkable job," said investment analyst Thomas Postek of Chicago. "He's trying to go right after the kid's market, which has been so important to McDonald's. No one has really gone after the heart of McDonald's business until now."

If this wasn't enough, McDonald's recently has been plagued by costly and totally unfounded rumors. One, propagated by a misinformed preacher, said Ray Kroc was tithing a percentage of the McDonald's fortune to something called the Church of Satan. Another rumor, equally ludicrous but expensive in terms of customers, suggested McDonald's in Southern states were making hamburgers out of earthworms.

Kroc's organization sizzled, staged press conferences with nutrition experts and recouped by doing what it does best: uncorking its boundless advertising resources to drown its challengers in commercials.

"Their whole approach to the business is one of war," says Burger King's Chris Schoenleb. "They are paranoid. It's phenomenal what they try to do to us. We like to stay above all that, but there are times around here when it gets down and dirty."

Burger King itself is under siege from the flank position and cannot afford to take its No. 2 status for granted. An Ohio-based company called Wendy's Old Fashioned Hamburgers has become the fastest growing resturant chain in U.S. history by aiming for a young adult market that traditionally has dined at the Home of the Whopper.

Six years ago, there were only nine Wendy's hamburger spots in the country. Today, there are 1,400. And what's more worrisome, according to industry sales figures, the average Wendy's is showing larger per-store revenues and profit margins than Burger King. "We want to be bigger than General Motors," said R. David Thomas, the beefy founder and chairman of Wendy's International.

Some investment analysts prefer to describe the tightening competition as the "maturing" of the fast-food hamburger business. Others bluntly call it a "shakeout" that will produce big winners and big losers. "It certainly is an all-out assault," said one.

The Big Cheeseburger is, of course, McDonald's Systems Inc. The Illinois-based conglomerate is the largest food processor in the United States, surpassing on dollar volume both the U.S. Army and the Department of Agriculture. Last year, the company sold $3.7 billion worth of Big Macs, Quarter Pounders, fries, Egg McMuffins and hot apple pies. In December, the company opened its 5,000th restaurant, in Japan. Investment analyst Carl DeBiase has predicted that by the year 2000, McDonald's will be doing $23 billion worth of business annually. The price of one hamburger: now about 35 cents.

Next in line is the Burger King Corp., owned by Pillsbury and based in Miami, where it was founded in 1954 by James W. McLamore. After purchasing the company in 1967, Pillsbury invested about $20 million and enlarged the chain from 274 stores to 2,500.

Last year, Burger King fed America $1.1 billion worth of Whoppers, Whalers, Yumbos, fries and shakes. A hamburger there sells for about 40 cents and last year Burger King served 825 million of them. In fiscal 1978, the company enjoyed a healthy 26 percent growth in sales.

Finally comes the challenger, Wendy's International, which is opening new restaurants at the rate of 500 every year. In 1977, Wendy's total sales exceeded $425 million—a startling 127 percent increase over 1976. A plain Wendy's hamburger, bigger than the competition's, sells for 93 cents.

During 1979, these three hamburger giants will cut the ribbon on approximately 1,300 new restaurants, spend about $215 million on advertising and serve millions of hamburgers to customers all over the world.

Publicly, none of these companies likes to talk in militaristic terms, and all courteously profess the highest respect for the competition. Each one, they say, has its own market and isn't really worried about the others. Which is more baloney and insect remnants than you'll find in a hundred tons of USDA hamburger meat.

THE MEASURE OF VICTORY

Victory is not measured so much by how many stores you have (no one is even close to McDonald's in that category), but by how much one unit, or restaurant, earns over its competitor across the street. That's why old flappy-footed Ronald is running a bit scared from Burger King and Wendy's.

"Given the tremendous lead McDonald's has in sheer numbers, it would be ridiculous to say we can overtake them in total sales," Don Smith said. But he feels Burger King can gun for McDonald's in the store vs. store showdowns that are so important to franchisees, investors and market hawks.

In August, some Wall Street analysts temporarily downgraded McDonald's stock to "hold" instead of "buy" after second-quarter figures showed sales volume had leveled off with price hikes. Meanwhile Wendy's was rolling up a 7 percent volume increase and Burger King was showing a 5 percent gain.

McDonald's executives publicly shrugged off the scare, and with good reason. The average McDonald's restaurant takes in $845,000 in annual sales (more than 1,000 earn in excess of $1 million), compared with $572,000 for Burger King and $609,000 for Wendy's.

Yet in recent months, the gap between the leader and the challengers has narrowed. New Burger King franchises are racking up about $735,000 in annual sales and have gone head-to-head against McDonald's in Canada, traditional Ronald country.

Ray Kroc, relates one acquaintance, "is truly paranoid about competition." Years ago when a Burger King opened across the street from the flagship McDonald's restaurant in Oak Brook, Ill., Kroc is said to have looked out his office window and muttered, "I'll see those sons of bitches in hell."

There are some differences between a Burger King burger and a McDonald's burger. Both are made from pure beef, but Burger King makes eight burgers out of every pound of meat while McDonald's gets 10. Both are pre-frozen, pre-formed patties. One is cooked on a grill and the other on a broiler. Burger King advertises a choice of styles; McDonald's pre-cooks and packages its burgers.

Another area of competition is restaurant ambiance. Gone are the days when hamburger joints have all the charm of a downtown bus station. Today all camps are striving for "the total eating experience" with motifs ranging from early Disney World (for the kiddies) to Bourbon Street blues.

The recent concern over atmosphere reflects a widespread industry worry the American public will get tired of going to hamburger joints long before it gets tired of hamburgers. "The boredom factor," one hamburger honcho calls it.

MORE POPULAR THAN EVER

With more women working and more of the family's food dollar being spent outside the home, the hamburger is more popular than ever. Its success is not strictly an American aberration, for there is a burgeoning global grease glut. In Canada, the Big Three burger companies are slugging it out, with each franchise selling more sandwiches than its American counterpart. Burger King has 51 foreign outlets from Spain to Denmark and is actively looking for more; with 586 foreign units, McDonald's is everywhere—from Guam to Costa Rica to New Zealand. Its Japanese division even went worldwide recently when it opened a San Francisco franchise.

There are problems of course (McDonald's found out belatedly that the French translation of "Big Mac" is "Big Pimp") but all three companies are looking longingly at European and Asian markets where hamburgers are still a much-sought novelty.

For Burger King, the immediate problem is cutting into McDonald's domestic domination and repelling Wendy's charges. The two-year goal set by Don Smith is to increase by $100,000 the annual sales of each store, and to sustain the 25-30 percent growth rate Burger King has enjoyed over the past three years.

Saturation, decline and ultimate public revulsion at the mere sight of a hamburger —even haughty gourmets don't predict such a scenario. Americans, a nation of heavy users in every other vice, are loyally addicted to hamburgers. Thirty years from now, decrepit old Ronald probably will still be around, gumming his Big Mac and honking his prosthetic nose on Saturday mornings.

"Remember, there are six or seven thousand small towns in the U.S. that have never seen a fast-food restaurant," Schoenleb said hungrily.

"Look at it like this," said Burger King spokesman Paul Reinhard. "There are 235 billion eating occasions every year in the United States. We get that figure by taking the population, multiplying it by three meals a day and multiplying that by 365 days.

"Now only about 12 percent of these eating occasions occur outside the home. That means there's 88 percent still there. We can't say there's saturation until we get a lot more of that 88 percent."

Burger King President Don Smith is more blunt. "There's no such thing as saturation," he says.

Market analyst Tom Czech was incredulous at the suggestion that America's tastebuds might someday tire of hamburgers. "We've grown up on grease, and we're gonna stick with grease," he said. "It's part of our life."

18
EX-COKE, PEPSI EXECUTIVES JOIN TO FORM FIRM

by Mark Potts
AP Business Writer

NEW YORK—Watch out Coke and Pepsi. Stand back Royal Crown and Shasta. The over-the-hill gang is in the cola business.

Vowing to have the best-selling soft-drink within a decade, a group of former Coca-Cola and Pepsi-Cola executives has banded together to form King-Cola Corp.—a company whose leaders average 62 years of age and total 188 years in the soft drink business.

Their senior member, at a chipper 82, is Walter S. Mack. He was the first president of Pepsi-Cola, ran the Nedick's hot dog chain and has headed several other companies. Building on what he learned at Pepsi, Mack says he thinks he can revolutionize the soft-drink business—and put the now-fledgling company on top.

"I hope to be No. 1 within 10 years," he says. "There's no reason I shouldn't be. Because what we're doing is giving the public the best cola drink at the lowest price."

Whether King-Cola will be the best-tasting is a subjective thing, but its pedigree is impeccable. The man who came up with the drink's formula is Thomas Elmezzi, a former chief chemist and 43-year veteran at Pepsi. Emezzi is 63.

Whether it will be cheaper is to judge. Mack says he can undercut other soft-drink makers by using modern marketing techniques.

The key is dispensing with the traditional system of making the drink at hundreds of bottling plants throughout the country. Franchised for a particular geographical area, these bottling plants generally deliver finished product directly to stores—a distribution system Mack thinks is a waste of money.

What he wants to do is make the King-Cola at 29 bottling plants, each assigned to a particular region—a Kingdom, of course—then distribute the drinks to centralized warehouses of grocery chains and let the chain bring the soda to individual stores.

"What I am doing is going to bring the cola industry up to date," says Mack. "What I'm simply going to do is deliver King-Cola at minimum cost, the way Campbell's soup and Heinz ketchup do—deliver it in truckloads to grocery warehouses."

According to Mack, that will result in a hefty saving to consumers. He says a six-pack of King-Cola will cost between $1.09 and $1.19, compared to the $1.59 to $1.89 consumers pay for Coke, Pepsi, Royal Crown, Seven-Up, and other brands which, because of perpetuating agreements with their bottlers, are locked in the old system.

About the only large competitor not distributing product that way is C&C Cola—a regional brand in the East. C&C doesn't use that system because Mack founded it about 15 years ago as a test of the concept he's using to market King-Cola. He later sold C&C.

The market Mack sees for King-Cola is about as far away from the Pepsi Generation as Mack himself. He refers to prospective customers repeatedly as "our families." Defining that further, he says, "Our people, the people we're going to cater to, isn't the wild surfing crowd. The American family, the people who are the backbone of this country—they're our public."

King-Cola already is signing up distributors, and Mack says there have been 200 applicants for the 29 Kingdoms. The drink already has been test marketed in Indianapolis. National distribution of both King-Cola and Slim-King, a diet version, is set for January 1979. The introduction will be heralded with an advertising campaign using the slogan "Twice as Nice! Less in Price!"

Copyright © 1978 by the Associated Press. Reprinted with permission.

19
A QUICK LOOK AT OPTICAL SCANNING

Genuine innovations are rare in the business world, but two characteristics they seem to share are:

—They take much longer to become accepted than their developers had planned.

—Their impact extends far beyond what their developers had envisioned.

For instance, technology familiarly called "the scanner" is slowly but powerfully making its way into the $125 billion food marketing industry. By mid-1979, major chains were finally beginning to learn its awesome potential.

The movement started in 1972 when food manufacturers agreed to cooperate in a massive plan to speed up the checkout process at your neighborhood supermarket. Here was the concept: Each item in the store would be coded so that it could be "read" by an optical scanner that would transmit the information to a computer. The computer identifies the product by its code, "rings" it up, and prints the price and item on the receipt.

The parallel lines on each package are called the Universal Product Code (UPC). With its use, the computer keeps track of what's in the store's inventory, what's been sold, and when it's time to reorder. Scanning gives the customer a more complete list of items than he or she received before UPC, and the store receives important information about what's going on on a daily or even an hourly basis.

In 1973 the UPC bar codes to be "read" by optical scanners began to appear on an experimental basis. By 1978, more than 90% of all frozen foods and dry groceries were marked with a code, as were 60% of health and beauty aids.

In the meantime, the flood of orders for the automated checkout stands failed to materialize. Several major electronic manufacturers dropped out of the competition to supply the supermarkets with the automated machines. By 1979, only five major manufacturers were left, headed by I.B.M., with over half of the business.

UNION FEARS

The problems were diverse. For one thing, labor was upset. The Retail Clerks International Union feared that many of its members would lose their jobs. Their opposition faded, and by 1979 they decided not to oppose the march to checkout automation.

Several leaders in the consumer movement were upset, fearing that supermarkets would no longer list the prices on each individual item and would simply post the price on the shelf. This change would reduce the amount of information available, they felt. They won the support of a number of states and cities, which passed laws making individualized price markings mandatory.

The food industry had maintained that the consumer would benefit if the supermarkets could reduce the labor costs involved in individual price postings. However, they agreed to go along and still keep the cans and boxes marked, even in an automated supermarket.

A major hurdle was—and remains—the cost of installing the machines: from $110,000 to $275,000, depending on the type of cash registers already in the stores and other factors.

By 1978 many of the major chains had experimented with at least one automated store. Yet altogether, only 415 of the nation's 33,000 supermarkets had been automated as of September 1978.

The results of these experimental stores were heartening to grocery chains seeking to boost what they felt were very slim profits. The Food Marketing Institute reported that most supermarket operators planned to introduce scanning systems within the next several years.

What had caused the turnaround? Hard facts from several of the leading chains; their results went far beyond what the original developers had anticipated.

UNFORESEEN ADVANTAGES

The originators had trumpeted the savings of labor both at the checkout counter and in the price-marking process. But, as stated above, price marking was difficult to avoid given the restrictions placed by legislative fiat.

Here are the real-world advantages reported by food chains that have set up the scanner systems:

1. Higher sales. "Consumers . . . have fallen in love with scanners," reported *Fortune* magazine. Sales gains of up to 25% were cited.
2. "Hard" savings, those actual tangible gains in day-to-day operations. Giant Food Inc., a publicly-held chain, reported savings of $5,529 per month at a typical store with a volume of $560,000 a month. The savings came from reduced cashier labor plus fewer

price breaks accidentally given to customers by fallible checkers.

3. Less "shrink"—fewer losses from theft and honest errors by deliverymen. Ralphs Grocery Co. on the west coast said that shrink control could save $33,000 per store per year.

4. Faster reaction to promotional winners and losers. This can mean more finely tuned pricing and product mix, said Ralphs, such as better reporting on "dog" (slow-moving) items.

5. A new profit center in marketing research. Using the fast data captured by the computer, Super Value Stores, a $2.6 billion wholesale food giant, has set up a subsidiary called Testmark to sell information on movement of food items through the 1,971 retail stores it services plus many others. Giant Food has also received Federal Trade Commission approval to sell data from its scanner-equipped stores.

Now that the combined impact of UPC and the scanner have been proven, the rush is on to adopt the expensive system that hard-headed chain management believes can save even more money than originally expected.

Giant has placed a big new order with I.B.M. and hopes to have two-thirds of its stores on the system by 1980 or 1981.

NCR Corporation, a leading manufacturer of the equipment, has cut its prices by 20% and sees a big boom ahead.

Four out of the top twenty food chains in the U.S. had at least one automated store by early 1979. Rapid movement toward the scanner is predicted for another reason: about 50,000 supermarkets have advanced electronic checkout systems that are upgradable to the scanner for about half the $11,000-per-lane cost for the full system price.

PROFITS MAY RISE AGAIN

What the big chains now see is a way out of the declining profit they've experienced in the 1970's. Over the years, their after-tax profits have been about one penny on each sales dollar. This ratio dropped to two-thirds of a cent in 1977–78, leading to a number of major bankruptcies and mergers.

But some observers of the huge industry are worrying about the effect of scanners on independent chains. Independents account for half of all U.S. grocery sales. Their local flexibility in their marketplace has enabled them to compete with the chains.

With the scanners, the chains would finally have a technologically-based cost advantage over the independents. In an industry with razor-thin profit margins, such an advantage could propel the industry into price wars, which would put pressure on the small retailer.

But other experts are not so concerned. Profitable independents could adopt the scanners also, and perhaps at a later date the cost of the new systems may decline. Besides, consumers don't always shop *en masse* at the store with the lowest prices. Consider the convenience food stores, with their limited assortments and relatively higher prices. They are the fastest-growing segment of the food business.

SOURCES

1. Cook, Louise, "Little Lines on Boxes and Cans Being Used at More Supermarkets." Associated Press, published in the Houston *Chronicle*, December 3, 1978, Section 3, p. 3.
2. Coyle, Joseph S., "Scanning Lights Up a Dark World for Grocers." *Fortune*, March 27, 1978.
3. "A Creaky, Costly System." *Time*, July 28, 1975.

4. Honomichl, Jack M., "Retailers Move to Set
    Up Independent Research Units." *Advertising
    Age*, October 30, 1978.

20
GROCERY SHELF PSYCHOLOGY

Los Angeles Times

Ever wonder how a particular brand of frozen peas or canned punch you'd never seen before suddenly finds its way to a prominent place on your grocer's shelf?

Or why clothing and hardware are often displayed next to baby food and pet food?

Or why certain products always seem so conveniently located—on a big table at the end of an aisle or at eye level in the center of the aisle—while others are well beyond your field of vision, if not your reach?

All this is the work of food brokers.

There are 2000 food brokers nationally . . . and each has a staff of salesmen who regularly visit grocers, representing food manufacturers. . . .

The brokers, whose commissions from manufacturers average about 5 percent, use everything from computer analysis to bribery to convince grocers what products to stock and where to display them. . . .

One broker . . . woos supermarket executives by taking them out for long weekends on his yacht—with an abundance of food, liquor and accommodating young ladies.

Still another has been known to leave the keys to a new Cadillac on a market buyer's desk during product negotiations.

"I call it entertainment grease," says Jerry Driscoll, national sales manager for Hunt-Wesson frozen foods.

It can be anything from a pen with the company name on it to a broad for a week in the Caribbean. That's the name of the game —finding ways to get the buyer to buy your goods."

Though Driscoll readily admits these practices exist, most brokers and grocers insist they are rarely used anymore.

Tom Field, grocery merchandiser for Alpha Beta Acme markets, says his firm has such strict rules on broker relations that "We won't even go to lunch with one."

Broker Ted Rosenfield says the computer has rendered entertainment grease virtually obsolete.

"In the days before widespread computerization, a market owner didn't always know how a given product was selling at a specific time," Rosenfield says.

"You could con him a little, wine and dine him and get him to carry your product.

"Now he gets a regular IBM printout on exactly what's selling in his store and the other stores and how every product is doing against its competition.

"You can't get to first base with him unless you've got a product that sells, no matter what you offer him on the side."

But suppose there are several competing products that sell well?

How does the broker convince the buyer for a big market chain that his product deserves shelf space?

"You try the obvious argument first," says D.V. Brown, a Pasadena, Calif., food broker and former president of the National Food Brokers Association.

"You say your product is better or cheaper than its competitors, and maybe you let the buyer know you're planning a big advertising campaign on the product . . . ," Brown says.

If conventional blandishments fail . . . he can offer free labor—stocking the grocer's shelves if he'll agree to display the product. . . .

Or he can also offer the buyer a discount or advertising allowance—a refund of, say 50 cents or one dollar a case or a choice between that and a new television or washing machine for his home.

Federal law requires that such enticements be offered equally. . . . But there is no limit on the discount. Nor is there a prohibition against other incentives.

Getting a product into a market is only half the battle. The other half is placement within the market in a prominent or appropriate location.

This is a science in itself—a blend of salesmanship and psychology.

One broker who represents the No. 2 selling product in his field has convinced markets to place the No. 3 seller between his product and No. 1 on the display shelves.

"If the housewife sees our product, and looks next to it to a make a comparison we want the choice to be between us and No. 3, not us and No. 1," he says.

Another broker, who represents the manufacturer of a relatively new spray-can spot cleaner, conducted a survey which showed his product to be "an impulse item— you don't put it on a shopping list; you just buy it if you happen to see it.

"That," the broker says, "is my job—to make sure the housewife sees it."

To do that, he convinced grocers they should display his spot cleaner next to the coffee—a big volume seller—instead of with the other cleaning compounds.

Result?

His product has already captured 85 percent of the spot cleaner market.

Baby food and pet food also are big sellers, and markets ration space adjacent to them with miserly care.

Markets operate on a smaller margin of profit than any other industry—less than 1 percent after taxes—and anything they can do to increase volume however slightly, makes that tenuously thin margin more bearable.

There's far more profit in commodities other than food. That's why markets are carrying more and more paper goods, clothing, hardware, housewares, sundries and the like —particularly on displays near big food sellers and in prominent locations at aisle-ends, at eye-level and near checkstands.

"Before long," says broker Robert Zinn, "the markets will be like the old-time general store. You'll be able to buy anything there from a steak to a stove."

The average broker today represents 23 principals. What happens when he has two competing products—two brands of catsup or two cookie principals?

PARTICULAR PROBLEMS

Brokers customarily avoid these situations, though they occasionally are unavoidable— as when a longtime account introduces a new product or acquires a subsidiary that specializes in something already produced by another long-time account.

Brokers insist that they give equal service to all principals—competitors or not. But the principals, like the brokers and the grocers, maneuver for every edge they can get.

Hunt-Wesson Foods recently offered free trips to Alaska for the salesmen in its brokerage firm who sold the most frozen food.

Wouldn't that tempt the broker's salesmen to concentrate on Hunt-Wesson products to the neglect of his other principals, a Hunt-Wesson executive was asked.

"What the hell do you think we run the contests for?" the executive shot back. "You're in competition for your broker's time. It's up to you to devise ways of getting a greater percentage of that time than you actually contribute to him in dollar volume."

DIFFERENT EMPHASIS

Brokers downplay these contests—just as they minimize the "entertainment grease" and eschew the term "middle man" as descriptive of their profession.

These terms, they believe, contribute to the image of the broker as a wheeler-dealer whose function raises prices and costs the consumer money.

"You start talking about giving buyers a weekend in Vegas and giving brokers a week in Alaska, and the consumer knows she has to pay for it in the end," one broker says. "That makes us look bad."

MANY SERVICES

The food broker performs many services other than negotiating for shelf space in a market, and these services reduce operating expenses for the manufacturer and the grocer. Their savings, in turn, are passed on to the consumer.

When Van de Kamp's officials decided to package their foods and sell them frozen in the market, it was broker Robert Sloan who conducted the market studies that determined their potential for success. It was also Sloan who pioneered the sale of the first frozen chives.

SOPHISTICATION GROWING

As videotaping and computerization become even more widely used, the transition from bribery to service and sophistication will be complete.

"We take video tapes of commercials for out principals' products out to the markets," says another broker. "We show the grocer what to expect, give him an idea how we're going to promote the product in his area.

"We give him suggestions on coordinated displays, check his shelves and make sure he's got the right products out with the right prices on them. We even show him computer printouts on how a product sold in the test markets."

Broker reliance on "friendship" and "rapport" and "entertainment grease"—already on the wane; the exception now, not the rule—will all but vanish.

"Look," says one broker, "if you can buy a customer off with bribes, so can your competitor. It becomes self-defeating."

"If the product doesn't sell, payola only works temporarily," says marketing consultant Don Odesskey. "Then the grocer's in trouble. He can't afford to carry a product that loses money, and he can't accept the broker's money, then not carry it. He loses, and no one really wins.

"Everyone's finally getting wise to that now."

From David Shaw, "Grocery Shelf Psychology—It Aims to Please," Los Angeles Times, *August 18, 1970. Copyright 1970, Los Angeles Times. Reprinted by permission.*

21
DUTY-FREE TRADE ZONES GAIN POPULARITY AS FIRMS, CITIES REALIZE THEIR BENEFITS

by David P. Garino
The Wall Street Journal

KANSAS CITY, MO.—In one simple move last year, Fischer Manufacturing Co. improved cash flow, reduced costs and increased foreign sales.

What did the pool-table manufacturer do? It became a tenant of the foreign trade zone operated here by Great Midwest Corp.

The basic advantage of a foreign trade zone is that imports may be stored, processed, or assembled without duties being paid until the goods are physically moved out of the zone to elsewhere in the U.S. Moreover, if imported goods are later exported, no customs duties are paid at all.

Fischer, a division of Questor Corp., uses imports extensively: slate from Italy, pool balls from Belgium, cues from Japan and rubber materials from Taiwan and South Korea.

Before moving to the foreign trade zone, Fischer paid duties at once on imports, and pool tables for both domestic and foreign sale were assembled at its Tipton, Mo., plant.

AN AID IN COMPETING

Now imports are stored here until needed, and cash flow—profit after taxes but before depreciation—is improved because of the deferral of duties. Pool tables headed abroad are assembled in the trade zone, and thus duties are avoided. The cost-saving has made Fischer's products more competitive in foreign markets, and "the export business has been better than domestic sales," Edgar DeMeyer, director of marketing, says. He adds, however, that both domestic and foreign customers "are buying like the devil" after a slackening in demand last year.

"There is definitely a growing interest in foreign trade zones," says John J. Da-Ponte Jr., executive secretary of the Foreign-Trade Zones Board, a federal agency that must approve zone sites.

Seventeen U.S. cities now have foreign trade zones; more than half have been approved since 1970. The Foreign-Trade Zones Board is processing an application for Chicago, and Mr. DaPonte estimates that 17 other cities are seriously considering setting up a zone. Applications are expected soon from Atlanta, Buffalo, St. Louis and the Wilkes-Barre-Scranton area of Pennsylvania, he says.

In the fiscal year ended June 30, 1974, U.S. zones handled $205 million of merchandise, up 25 prcent from the year before. Although fiscal 1975 figures aren't complete, Mr. DaPonte estimates there was "at least a 25 percent to 30 percent increase" despite the world-wide recession. "Even larger gains should be recorded as the newer trade zones come into operation," he predicts. (The zones' volume is just a tiny fraction of U.S. trade, of course; in calendar 1974, U.S. merchandise exports totaled $98.27 billion and imports $103.53 billion, government figures show.)

IT'S AN OLD IDEA

The concept of a foreign trade zone, or free port, isn't new. In fact, a portion of ancient Carthage functioned as a free port, and in ancient Greece a stone wall surrounded a harbor plot in which goods in transit were guarded, exempt from duties.

Enabling legislation for establishment of foreign trade zones in the U.S. was passed by Congress in 1934.

In recent years inland ports, such as Kansas City, have become foreign trade zones. "In an era of jumbo jets, containerized ships, trains, trucks and barges, major international trading centers no longer must be tied to deepwater ports," says Marshall V. Miller, secretary and general counsel of the Greater Kansas City Foreign Trade Zone.

Moreover, Mr. DaPonte notes that a foreign trade zone "is one element of total economic development" that communities can use to attract capital. In most instances, approval for the zones is granted to a city agency, which in turn may license a company to actually conduct operations.

For companies, the advantages extend far beyone duty deferral.

Companies can "play the tariff game," processing imports within the zone to qualify for lower duties. For example, assembly of bicycles in a zone saves money because the duty on a completed bicycle is only 5½ percent, while duties on bicycle parts range from 6 percent to 15 percent; thus a U.S. bicycle-parts importer that does the assembly work outside a zone would pay the higher tariff levied on parts.

Customs duties can be avoided by not paying duties on substandard or damaged materials.

If the importer has ordered unwisely and the goods don't sell in the U.S., they can be removed duty-free and shipped abroad.

Theft losses are negligible. The zones have their own security arrangements, and merchandise also comes under the protection of the U.S. Customs Service.

Seasonal goods can be stored, duty-free, to assure availability. For instance, waiting in Great Midwest's zone is a recent shipment of 60,000 boxes of Christmas lights from Japan.

And buyers can conveniently inspect goods before purchasing them, sometimes in attractive showrooms. For example, in Great Midwest's trade zone, which is situated underground in a former limestone mine, Fischer has not only a storage area but also a showroom with Tiffany-style lights over pool tables. As a marketing ploy, Fischer has hired Dorothy Wise, a former billiards champion widely known as "Cool Hand Dottie," to show trick shots and entertain customers, Mr. DeMeyer says.

INQUIRIES "LIVELY"

Foreign trade zones are being aided by the improving economic climate. "Inquiries are very, very lively," James E. Burke, vice president of Great Midwest, says. In nearby Kansas City, Kans., activity also is brisk at the underground, 405,000 square-foot zone operated by Inland Distribution Center, a division of Beatrice Foods Co. Victor Mersten, general manager, says, "In the last few months, inquiries have gone from two a month to 100."

Mr. Miller at the Kansas City Zone Board believes the recession has taught companies the need for "pinching pennies." He adds: "A few years ago, some companies were going full blast, so they said, 'We don't want to bother over a lousy 10 percent to 15 percent, which could be saved in duty deferral.' Now they're saying, 'We'd like to study the advantages of foreign trade zones.'"

Morgan Maxfield, president of Great Midwest, maintains that "Kansas City will become the Panama of North America" (Co-

lon, Panama's foreign trade zone, this year is expected to handle more than $1 billion in merchandise). Great Midwest, which at 2.8 million square feet is the largest enclosed zone in the U.S., has been trying to attract a foreign car maker, for either manufacture or assembly puposes.

"It makes economic sense for them," Mr. Maxfield says. He notes that while the duty on an imported car is 3 percent, it is 15 percent on an air conditioner. Thus, "on a $300 air conditioner, the duty is $45, but installed it's $9. When you're talking about many thousand cars, that's a lot of money," he adds.

OTHER ZONES PROSPER

Some other recently approved zones are also prospering.

At McAllen, Texas, for instance, the only zone on the U.S.-Mexico border is enjoying such booming demand that 20,000 additional square feet of warehousing is under construction. A major customer is the Republic of Mexico, which stores and displays a broad array of goods, including sugar, cotton cloth, lamps and brooms. In addition, the zone's industrial park houses a produce importer and medical equipment manufacturer.

Of course, not all companies would benefit from a foreign trade zone. In most cases, large volume or high value products are required. Nor is success automatically guaranteed for a trade zone operator. Little Rock, for example, was granted a zone in October 1972, but it still is hunting for its first customer.

From David P. Garino, "Duty-Free Trade Zones Gain Popularity as Firms, Cities Realize Their Benefits," Wall Street Journal *(September 26, 1975). Reprinted with permission of* Wall Street Journal. © *1975 Dow Jones & Co. All rights reserved.*

22

JUST A MINUTE, MARSHALL McLUHAN

by Cynthia Saltzman

If Manhattan Island tomorrow were submerged under lava, archaeologists of the future might conclude we were a society of literati. Pocketed in the concrete, steel and glass, they would discover hundreds of miles of bookshelves (530 miles at the New York Public Library alone) lined with millions of books. In one square mile of mid-Manhattan, they would find 36 bookstores. In a ten-block stretch along Fifth Avenue they would uncover enough palatial book establishments to build a case for literary addiction: Brentano's, Barnes & Noble, Scribner's, Doubleday, Rizzoli.

Of course, Manhattan is the most highly saturated book market in the country, but the rest of the U.S. has also witnessed a bookstore rampage. In the last two decades the number of bookstores in America has quadrupled from 2,885 to 12,000. This year Americans will spend $5.5 billion on books—72% more than in 1972. Book publishing, with revenues of $4.3 billion, is approximately 23% larger than network television, nemesis and reputed assassin of the printed word.

Add to that the $14.6-billion newspaper industry (up 50% in total revenues since 1972) and the over $4 billion magazine industry (ad revenues up 62.4% since 1972), and printed communications seem far from moribund, Marshall McLuhan notwithstanding.

But don't write off Dr. McLuhan. With all the activity in publishing, Americans as a whole are not reading more books—just spending more. The total number of books sold in the U.S. this year will be about 1.41 billion, less than the 1.47 billion of 1974. Although magazine circulation is at an alltime high of 263 million, per capita circulation is still below the 1969 record. Newspapers may be flooded with advertising revenues, but circulation has remained level for a decade. Library circulation per capita fell 6% from 1965 to 1974.

Most telling of all, according to a study by the University of Texas, nearly one-fifth of the population can barely read. This 19% of the country is "functionally" illiterate: They cannot even read labels on medicine bottles, much less *The Great Gatsby*.

Why have book sales grown so? Higher prices, of course. Much higher prices. You can't get a best-seller for under $8.95, and textbooks can run to $40. A decade ago the best-selling *The Day of the Dolphin* sold for $5.95. Book prices outpaced inflation by a margin of 20% from 1972 to 1976.

And the good news is this: "The people who read are reading more," says Martin Levin, president of the book publishing group for the Times-Mirror Co. True, the total number of books sold today does not match the number sold four years ago, but books sold to *individuals* have increased by a third in the last five years and now total over 1 billion books a year. While schools and libraries buy fewer books, book-reading individuals buy more. "There is a long-term trend," says industry statistician John Dessauer, "toward the consumer and away from institutions. The sales proportion to the consumer is increasing all the time and at the moment it seems to be strong in bookstores." Last year libraries purchased 11 million fewer books than they did five years ago; for schools the drop was 50 million.

As publishing becomes more and more a consumer products industry, marketing becomes more important. "Alfred Knopf once said the only way a book is sold is by word of mouth," says Andrew H. Neilly Jr., president of John Wiley & Sons, the professional-and-textbook publisher. "That may have been true when he published H.L. Mencken, but it's certainly not true of most books today. You have to have a pipeline through which these things find their way to where the customer is."

Witness the rise of the nation's two major bookstore chains: Dayton-Hudson's B. Dalton and Carter Hawley Hale's Waldenbooks. Dozens of smaller chains, like Marboro in New York and Crown Books in Washington, have appeared in cities across the country. Like fast food, the two big chains followed the middle class to the suburbs. (Dalton claims its customers are predominantly 25-to-35-year-old college-educated professionals and managers with incomes over $15,000.) In just 12 years, B. Dalton has captured about 10% of the retail market. This year it has opened new stores at the rate of one a week. And in November it will open a 100,000-title store, one of the largest in the country, in the midst of Manhattan's book-selling fray, which it estimates is a $95 million market. Dalton's 328 outlets will sell some 45 million books this year and its revenues will be about $178 million, 25% above last year's. In terms of outlets, not revenues, Waldenbooks is even bigger: It now has 400 stores in 40 states.

These two bookstores have brought contemporary chain-store controls to the traditionally low-margin, high-inventory bookshop. "Our computerized inventory system tells us every book that is sold in every store every day, by title and by vendor," says Floyd Hall, Dalton's 40-year-old president—who came to books through Montgomery Ward's retailing ranks, rather than through seminars on English literature.

The computer, says Hall, enables Dalton to spot trends immediately and re-stock titles—typically 30,000 in a store. It simplifies the major difficulty of book selling: the vast number of titles.

A bookstore has to sort through some 418,000 books in print in the U.S., 42,000 new titles this year and 3,400 vendors with a variety of discount schedules. Even with Dalton's system, it took four years to make money. Last year pretax earnings, about $14 million on the $178 million in sales, were some 40% above 1976. This year they are expected to rise 20%. (Hall claims that postage increases will cost $1 million.)

"One of the inhibiting factors in the consumer book industry has been the lack of distribution outside of the major metropolitan areas," says E. Wayne Nordberg, of Prescott, Ball & Turben, a consultant to the industry. "The chains are overcoming some of that."

Book clubs were the first hardcover distribution pipeline to less populated parts of the country. They, too, are thriving. In 1958 there were 56 book clubs in the U.S.; now there are 198, some highly specialized like Doubleday's Mystery Guild and Science Fiction Book Club. Book clubs identify their readers by magazine or direct mail advertising and connect publishers to them.

Today publishing houses themselves, like Wiley, increasingly are using direct mail, pioneered by publishers like Time-Life in the 1950s. This year some 151 million books will be sold by direct mail.

Perhaps the most successful form of book distribution has brought the mass market paperback to drug stores, supermarkets, airports and newsstands. Paperbacks have proliferated since the 1930s, when Simon & Schuster brought out Pocketbooks. Now some 12 paperback publishers sell about 512 million books a year in the U.S. Consider that the *Immigrants*, a mass market bestseller, has sold 1.6 million copies and *Thurs-*

day the Rabbi Walked Out, a hardback best-seller, has sold 60,000. Significantly, many of these paperback publishers, like Dell Publishing, were started by magazine publishers—distributors, in short, as well as publishers. Mass market paperbacks sell well not only because they cost a fraction of the price of a hardback but also because they are available in so many places.

Yet Martin Levin of Times-Mirror thinks that the distribution systems are still not good enough. Says he: "Everyone has a computer, but try to find a specific book on Renaissance architecture, on Fifth Avenue. The computers at the publishers are going to have to be linked to the computers at the retailers. You should be able to order books and have them the next day."

As for the books being sold, nonfiction as a whole has overshadowed fiction. The paperback best-seller list reflects specialization with a string of self-help books, including *The Woman's Dress for Success Book* and *How to Flatten Your Stomach*. Yet a single blockbuster novel can sell millions more copies than most nonfiction books (and marketing plays a large role in this game, too).

Whether people read what they buy is a different story. Some 110 million television sets murmur on across the nation. But, as many have observed, they too now serve the printed word. Nothing stimulates sales like an author's appearance on television. Galsworthy's *Forsyte Saga* sent people to the Victorian novel. Marshall McLuhan may have been right, but publishers seem to be listening to the message.

Reprinted by permission of Forbes *Magazine from the October 30, 1978 issue.*

23
(BUT WILL IT SELL BOOKS?)

by Diane M. Muller

Every business has its maxim. When we marketing people in a publishing house sit down to discuss strategy for launching a new title or boosting an old favorite, many a brilliant stunt or glamorous scheme collapses in the face of the question, "But will it sell books?"

Then, when we as publishers turn to you, the booksellers for answers, they're often met, to our consternation, with another maxim, equally entrenched: "The publishers are out to get us."

That may seem to be the case largely because there is so little homogeneity in publishers' discounts, returns policies, shipping and cooperative-advertising policies. We all have different names for the same things, different titles for the people doing them and different methods of presentation. From the vantage point of the small bookstore, we may look like profit-gobbling, corporate cookie monsters. But in fact, the publishers are the ones to put money up front for author advances, production costs, legal fees, advertising and promotion expenses, to say nothing of the cost of care and feeding of the people and machines that take those books from manuscript to marketplace. And publishers are the ones who take the risk of eating warehouses full of books if the decision to publish them was wrong. We hardly want to see that all go down anyone's drain—yours *or* ours.

That expensive overhead can work for booksellers in ways that most of them don't dream possible. Every publishing house, no matter how small, has a sales department, and the larger and more diversified the publisher's list, the larger and more diversified the staff that services it is likely to be. Some of those people are there just to help the bookseller sell their books; the only real trick the bookseller faces is figuring out who those people are and how to reach them. And since promotion is the link from the store bookshelf to the consumer's, such individuals may well offer some sound professional assistance that will result in profit for everyone.

It probably makes sense to start with your sales rep. He or she can forward requests to the proper person at the publishing house, as well as give you their names for future reference. If that proves to be an unsatisfactory channel, either the sales manager or sales-promotion manager—both of whom are likely to be listed in the *ABA Book Buyer's Handbook*—will usually have the power to make decisions for you. Sometimes they may refer you to the advertising or publicity department, or to another person in their own department, but since those people are the direct link between the publisher and the distributors, they will surely not bounce you from pillar to post.

Once you know *whom* to ask, you ought to think about *how* to ask and *when* to ask. It is best to put your requests in writing. This policy has several advantages: first, your request is on the record; second, it is represented in your words, leaving no room for misinterpretations or transcription errors; third, a written request allows the person answering it to give a thoughtful, considered response. A phone call, catching the expert unawares, may result in a distracted answer. (If writing does not draw an response within a reasonable period of time, *then* try the telephone.) Your requests concerning a specific book should arrive on the right person's desk as far in advance of publication date as possible. This gives the publisher a chance to incorporate your suggestions into the plans before budgets and time become so tight that there is little flexibility left. There will be times, of course, when a promotional inspiration occurs to you when a book is already on the shelf or (better still) flying off the shelf for no apparent reason. Do not let this timing discourage you. Sometimes the most serendipitous promotions are the most successful.

Now, you've got the name of the person in charge of the promotion of a book you are very high on. What do you ask for? Before answering that question, ask yourself the publisher's adage: will it sell books?

It's a good idea to organize your objectives before approaching the publisher. Once you know pecisely what they are, it will be easier for the publisher to offer suggestions about how to achieve them. Remember that for the publisher, it is a question of the bottom line. Sure, it would be prestigious to have that bestselling author in your shop 200 miles from the nearest airport, and it never hurts to ask, because who knows? Maybe the author has a mother or favorite fishing hole in the next town and plans to be in the neighborhood anyway. But before feeling offended because the publisher says no, think about the time and cost involved on your part, the publisher's and the author's. You may find that you would need to sell several hundred books just to break even.

Think creatively as well as realistically. Maybe there is a local author who would draw crowds, or perhaps you can stage a local event that would attract the media and offer you and the author some long-range exposure. Sometimes it makes sense to steer clear of the obvious bestsellers and look for the sleeper, the book with regional appeal or perhaps political import. If your state is dealing with the question of the Equal

Rights Amendment or legalized gambling or Proposition 13, why not organize a local symposium featuring the author of a relevant book as the expert on the subject? You will be performing a public service, getting news coverage for your store, making the author feel like a star and, we hope, selling some books. Once you offer the handle, the publisher can usually help you plan the event and will often be glad to supply promotion materials that can save you a lot of time and money and give you the ammunition you need to marshall your forces.

There are a number of small stores that have carved a niche for themselves in their own communities, and a unique place in the hearts of publishers. In every such case that comes to mind, the magic common denominator seems to be the team-like rapport between store, consumer and publisher. The store is no longer a merchant establishment but rather a participatory member of the community. After all, most of us in bookselling and publishing have an emotional commitment to what we're doing. Otherwise, we could all be leading a more financially lucrative existence selling Cadillacs or Coca-Cola. There's no denying the personal touch in this business. We are all a part of the processs of disseminating ideas.

Different stores involve their publics in different ways; again, the publisher can sometimes offer suggestions. Kramerbooks in Washington, D.C., for instance, took some available space and built a café. The bookstore, Kramerbooks & Afterwords, has become, in the most literal sense, a social center.

When ABA's associate executive director, Bob Hale, was managing Hathaway House Bookshop in Wellesley, Mass., he originated and developed what is now one of the most successful author series in the country. The series, sold on a subscription basis, is organized to the point that it is relatively painless for the author, entertaining

to its audience (700 each day) and profitable for the bookstore from a financial and public-relations point of view. The publishers know it is a sure thing, and the store has little trouble attracting big names. True, the store is located near Boston, and the reputation of the series was earned by long, arduous hours of work, but the fact remains that Hale and the series succeeded where many have failed.

Discount Books in Washington, D.C., ties promotions into city festivities and presents the publisher with a clear proposal of what they intend to do, what it will cost, and the other specifics involved; the publisher has only to say yes or no. For instance, Discount Books conceived a promotion called "Operafest," which combined their book and record departments in a month-long campaign designed to promote opera. They solicited co-op dollars from publishers and record companies to run radio and print ads, opened their doors for an opera discography, featured a contest and had autographing sessions in the store. The result was a 34 percent increase in overall classical volume in the first seven days. Similarly, they tied into the D'Oyly Carte Company performances at the Kennedy Center in D.C. by offering the company's complete Gilbert and Sullivan collection at special prices to the public. This idea can often be a handle for bookstores in communities with colleges or cultural or sports centers.

By seizing on a theme that needs no "sell" to the public, any store can merchandise that theme with windows, ads and point-of-purchase displays. Publishers often are eager to participate. A little co-op money goes a long way here. This type of promotion affords the independent bookseller a distinct advantage in that he or she has the autonomy to carry off this sort of thing, where a chain store might find it difficult. Small booksellers should be aware that publishers are bound by fair trade laws to give every advantage to the small store that it gives to the large one. Both large and small bookstores have their advantages. It makes sense to capitalize on those advantages, rather than being defeated by the *dis*advantages.

That is valuable to remember when you seem to be confronted by a frustrating bureaucracy. It also helps to remember that author appearances and co-operative advertising dollars are not the only—in fact are not always—the abracadabra that produce book sales. Often, by being resourceful and joining forces with other departments in your own store or with other merchants in your town or shopping center, or even with other bookstores, you can combine co-operative advertising dollars and put together a plan that can be merchandised to everyone's benefit.

You know your inventory and your customers and your areas of strength better than we do. If you don't have a clearcut marketing plan, most publishers will be happy to work with you and will offer sound advice. And if you already know just what you want to do, we can provide you with tools. Radio tapes, television commercials, point-of-purchase displays, photographs, give-aways, print ads, exhibits of original material from books, mounted interiors from books, contest proposals and marketing guidance are all available either free or at a reasonable cost.

It used to be that all you had to do was stick an interesting-looking person in the window, hang a sign around his neck reading "author," open the door and wait for the book to sell like hotcakes. Or so they tell me. Things are a bit more sophisticated these days, and television has made us all blasé about celebrities.

Yet, somehow, millions of books are sold in the country every year, and most of them are sold in bookstores. The successful bookseller has several tough assignments that his or her predecessor didn't face. But basically the bookseller's success depends on the ability to make the right buy from the publisher and the right sale to the customer.

It is a shared responsibility—and challenge.

Reprinted with permission from the January 1979 issue of American Bookseller. *Copyright 1979, Booksellers Publishing, Inc.*

THE BOOKSTORE

1728 Bissonnet • Houston 77005 • 713 527 8522

Mary Ross Rhyne

Dear Reader:

Have you been left out of the fun while others discuss inflation and recessions? Do the words "community property" send a shiver up your spine? Would you like to be able to read the Wall Street Journal during breakfast at the Avalon Drug?

As part of our continuing effort to cheer you as things go to pieces around us, The Bookstore is proud to announce a series of talks for women on money matters:

"¢ on Saturday"

by

Robbie Moses, Ph.D.

Paine, Webber, Jackson & Curtis, Inc.

Meetings will be at The Bookstore from 10-11:30 AM on the first Saturday of the month, beginning February 3. Programs will include book reviews, information on investments and personal financial analysis, market topics, and occasional guest lectures, including a CPA. A list of suggested reading will be available; if you can't attend but would like the list, just call or come by The Bookstore. Most of the titles are in paperback; all will be available at The Bookstore.

If you'd like to attend, will you let us know by mailing or bringing by the coupon below? An evening group can be added, and in the case of an overflow, another series covering the same material will meet on third Saturdays. Please tell us what suits your schedule.

Other questions? Call Ms. Moses at 654-0200, or The Bookstore at 527-8522.

$$$

Name_____ Phone_____

Address_____ Zip_____

___Yes, I'll be there at 10 AM on the first Saturdays starting the 3rd.
___An evening meeting suits me better; best night is_____
___I can attend third Saturdays if another group is needed. I'm bringing
_____friends (that blank is for a number, not an adjective).

Comments:_____

Advertisement reprinted with the permission of Mary Ross Rhyne and The Bookstore, Houston, Texas.

SECTION FOLLOW-UP
WHERE MARKETING HAPPENS

You can bring the people to the products or the products to the people. It sounds simple, but "place utility" is not the only issue. For the marketers of food to cook, food already cooked, or food for thought, lots of questions remain:

1. Who decides—and on what basis—on the assortment of products the customer sees? The arrangement of those products? What's promoted? What prices are charged? Is the marketer "closest to the consumer" making the decisions? Should he or she make them?

2. Do consumers want change—in the way they they buy milk or the way their purchases are added up at the supermarket? Do business buyers want change, if a scanning system or a duty-free warehouse saves somebody money? How do you market change to any group? Why would you want to?

3. How can a hamburger chain franchisee or the manager of one Sears store practice "the marketing concept," given the factors under his or her control? Does "Dear Reader . . . " offer some ideas?

4 THE PRICE OF SUCCESS

How much? Maybe that's the shopper's first question. The answer? "It depends" —on the government, on inflation, on competitors, on how competitive things really are, and on what's actually offered for that "price."

How much "should" the price be? You can find plenty of arguments on that issue too. Some of them are reprinted here, and as the saying goes, you pay your money and take your choice. How much money? Well, it depends . . .

25

THEY LET THE AIRLINES COMPETE

For her two-week vacation last summer, Martha McKee took her 70-year-old mother, Lucille, to Los Angeles to visit relatives. They flew—using a reservation made well in advance. And they saved enough money that it was almost a case of two being able to fly as cheaply as one.

Martha's mother would certainly not have made the trip at double the fare. Even Martha would have considered the bus as an alternative. They personify the kind of "new traffic" that has come to airlines since the U.S. Civil Aeronautics Board (CAB) decided in 1978 that they could abolish the "floors" on airline prices and relax somewhat the limitations on routes.

The airlines have staved off deregulation for years. They conceded that unfettered competition would lead to lower prices, but they testified that those lower prices would lead to poorer service: less frequent flights, fewer cities served, less comfort for passengers, and eventually, even slimmer margins of safety. In other words, the argument ran, a lower margin for the airline on each ticket sold would force the airline to pack more passengers into fewer flights to stay in business.

On the other side of the argument were visions of Martha and Lucille McKee, who were in effect being priced out of airline travel for the convenience of business travelers whose firms were paying their way. The business traveler traditionally has been viewed as not price-conscious but schedule-conscious. Thus, the airlines' "service" package has been heavy on convenience. Pricing has been designed to keep the carriers financially afloat while they ran convenient—but often unprofitable—schedules.

MARKETING THE SCHEDULE

One airline executive declares: "The most important thing on a passenger's mind when he chooses an airline is the schedule. There may be a little bit of loyalty to a certain line or hostility to another, but in general, if you go at five o'clock, and I want to go at five, I'm going to go with you. This means that you have to work back from the schedule, make your whole system start there."

A case in point is Braniff Airlines, which has achieved considerable success by considering passenger preferences in its routes and schedules. According to *Texas Monthly*, Braniff also exhibits considerable skill in purchasing what Russell Thayer, Braniff executive vice-president, calls "the right aircraft."

Braniff has a "radial" route structure, with its center at Dallas, which is harder to coordinate than long cross-country routes like those of TWA, United, or American. "On a system like this," Thayer says, "the purpose of each connection is to feed the overall network. You try to start flights as far back as possible, so you can build up the traffic for the longer hauls. You start by analyzing traffic out of the smaller stations. Take Austin—a state capital, a lot of good traffic coming out of there. We found that the main long-haul destination from Austin was Washington. The next most important destination was Chicago. You keep that in mind, while you do the same thing with the other cities all over the system. You try to weave them together to make the connections.

We're a high-frequency, short-haul airline, and we pay more attention than other lines do to the most convenient timing of the flights.

"Once you have the schedule, you look at the equipment and see what's going to be most effective for the specific market you're serving." The Braniff fleet is composed almost entirely of two tested if unromantic workhorses. One is the Boeing 727, used for flights inside the United States; the other, the DC-8, is for the long hauls to South America. Because it has only two basic planes, Braniff doesn't have to juggle its equipment around; repairs and scheduling also become easier.

"Once you've got the equipment and the scheduling," Thayer continues, "then you market the system; you tell people what you're offering. We have schedules at all our ticket counters; a lot of other lines think they're too expensive to print up. You don't use your advertising to talk about legroom or frills. You tell people where you go and when. It's all part of the coordination—really, coordination is the key to our success. You have to coordinate four elements. First, the kind of equipment you purchase. Second, how much of it. Third, the scheduling, and fourth, the marketing. At some lines, the equipment is chosen by the engineers, and the amount is determined by how many planes they're getting rid of. The scheduling is set up for the convenience of the maintenance men, and marketing has to push what's left. That's no way to run a railroad."

HOW BIG A PIE?

The Braniff analysis, it must be noted, applies principally to the business flier who is choosing between airlines rather than deciding whether to fly at all, and the reasoning that "schedule equals marketing success" stemmed from the idea that business fliers would forever be the airlines' bread and butter. Expanding the "pie" of fliers to be shared among carriers simply seemed unprofitable before 1978; a CAB study showed that cutting a $100 fare to $80 would attract only 14 more passengers, and would add to the airline's cost the meals and baggage handling for those 14 extra passengers.

Then Congress passed the Air Deregulation Act. Not only could fares drop, but the CAB practice of strictly limiting routes was eased. The CAB will lose its authority over routes and fares altogether by 1983. More routes were added by more carriers between more cities; consequently, the convience advantage offered by air travel grew just at the instant that the price shrank. Unsurprisingly it became clear that the CAB estimates of "price sensitive" new traffic had been dramatically low—and that the new routes themselves were one reason.

BUSINESS FLYERS REACT

The extra passengers lured by low fares and more direct routes jolted the business flyer, however. Those previously not-so-crowded planes were now filled with kids, college students—and the McKees. They were attracted by light-hearted advertising that focused on gimmick names: *Chickenfeed* fares, *Small Potatoes* fares, *Peanuts* fares, and the like. But the business flier was not entertained.

The solution? Pricing to the rescue: airlines saw the opportunity to apply what deregulation had taught them—that cutting prices did in fact increase volume, just as the economist would have predicted. This time the cut came in the first-class fare; traditionally it was 30% over the coach ticket in price, but it was lowered to be only 20% above coach. United Airlines, the nation's largest, led the way, also installing separate first-class ticket counters at 20 airports to provide an obvious benefit to those willing to "trade up." Other airlines followed suit.

Then a strike hit United. When it ended after 55 days in May 1979, that carrier knew it had lost the loyalty of some flyers. To win them back would require more than a price cut; those were no longer spectacular. The solution they hit on—and American Air Lines imitated—was to give each passenger during a three-week period a coupon. The coupon entitled its owner to fly anywhere on United at half price.

Like many price moves, this one had unintended consequences. Major airports immediately attracted hordes of brokers, who accosted each deplaning United or American passenger with the offer to buy the coupon. The price might be $20; the value to whoever bought the coupon from the broker might be more than $100, if the coupon was applied against a transcontinental round-trip, for example.

Furthermore, the traffic on short-hop United and American flights with $15 fares skyrocketed. Travelers collected a coupon with each flight, resold it for $20 or $25, then hopped a return flight—for another $10 profit.

All in all, however, the coupons accomplished what the marketers intended. People flew United in June to get the coupons. Then people flew United in the summer and fall to take advantage of the discounts provided by the coupons.

Thus, as the first year of deregulation closed, the right to compete had raised the service level and the price level for the business flier who had moved up to first class, but had lowered the price to Mrs. McKee, her mother, and thousands of other non-business fliers. Their service level, meanwhile, had been lowered only to the extent that special "deals" required them to reserve well in advance—and to elbow their way through many other passengers with special deals.

SOURCES

1. "Airlines Try to Soothe Full-Fare Passengers." *Business Week*, September 18, 1978, p. 27.
2. Cox, Clayton, "The Name is the Name of the Game." Houston *Post*, January 21, 1979, Sect. C, p. 17.
3. Fallow, James, "The Great Airline War." *Texas Monthly*, December 1975, p. 76ff.
4. Loving, Rush, Jr., 'The Pros and Cons of Airline Deregulation." *Fortune*, August 1977, pp. 209-217.
5. Robinson, Linda, "Airline Deregulation: Clearing for Takeoff . . . " *Houston Business Journal*, December 25, 1978, p. 1.
6. "United Airlines Flies the Profitable Skies." *Sales & Marketing Management*, January 1979, p. 32.

26

MARKETING IS HELPING BRITISH POSTAL SYSTEM SHOW HEALTHY PROFIT

by Robert D. Hershey, Jr.

LONDON—For years officials of the loss-ridden U.S. Postal Service have argued that toting the mail cannot be a paying proposition in the modern world. One way or another, they say, taxpayers' money must be found to fill the yawning chasm between income and expenses.

But look what has happened in Great Britain. After a long string of losses, postal operations have become profit-making centers—earning $41 million in fiscal 1977 and $77 million in the year ended March, 1978.

What's more, the service is unquestionably better here. Almost 93 percent of first-class letters are delivered the day after they are mailed. Every address in the country is covered by 9:30 a.m., and in urban areas there is a second delivery as well.

Britons have such confidence that their mail will not go astray—or that they will know quickly if it does—that few of them bother with return addresses.

The price for all this is about the same

© 1978 by The New York Times Company. Reprinted by permission.

as in America, where the standard rate recently climbed to 15 cents.

Comparisons between the two operations are not entirely fair since it is a far bigger logistical problem to serve a dynamic, continental country like the United States than a tight-knit island nation such as Britain—and one that had been experiencing a decline in mail volume as well. But the main reason for Britain's success seems to lie elsewhere.

"I think the main difference is our relationship with the government," said Denis E. Roberts, 61, the avuncular managing director of Britain's postal system. "In 1975 the government did the finest thing it could ever have done: it pulled the rug from under us. It said, 'We're not going to make up your losses any longer.' "

Roberts said the previous losses were caused mainly by an inability to raise prices.

"We found ourselves in a situation where on the one hand costs were increasing while on the other hand prices were pegged by government. The fact that you're in loss means you are demotivated. It also distorts the market and you get business you otherwise would not have got if you had been pricing properly."

The biggest problem had been Britain's parcel service, which was so inexpensive that its losses amounted to half of its revenues. After officials announced the decision to abandon it—putting 17,000 jobs in jeopardy—they won a 19 percent rate increase on parcel mail. Now this division is poised to break even, Roberts said.

There was also a dramatic increase, nearly a doubling, in ordinary letter rates during 1975. "We have a much easier ride when we go for increases than you do," Roberts said. "The American post office has got to go through a much more long-winded and slower process and the process is much more legalistic; people can file objections. Once we've started to go for a price rise, and assuming the government is not operating a policy of restraint, we can do the whole thing in about three months. There's a bit of a commotion when we do it, but I think, too, that the price lobbies here are not as strong."

Nigel N. Walmsley, an aggressive 36-year-old appointed last year to head the post office marketing unit, said he thought the difference between the British and American practices was really grounded in their "political philosophies." Americans, he suggested, will not stand for a government agency throwing its weight around in markets—air freight service, for example—where it has not been given a monopoly. And the United States insists that all customers be treated equally. No such niceties apply here.

The uninhibited British post office has launched vigorous advertising campaigns to get the business it covets even if this means capturing it from private carriers. The post office also is using its powers to negotiate individual contracts with big mailers, offering hefty rate reductions to hundreds of mail order and other companies.

"We regard marginal pricing as quite important, and we're allowed to do it," Walmsley said. About 50 percent of parcels in Britain are now sent under contract, and so far no one has taken offense at the marginal pricing, he said. "Marginal" pricing considers the distribution network as already paid for, and thus pegs the rate for extra pieces of mail to the additional cost of moving them. This, of course, yields a much lower rate than a price that requires all mail to pay its share of overhead.

Apparently, the pricing system here not only relates postal rates more accurately to costs, but also gives the customer more flexibility as well. With letters for example, the difference in postal rates for the two classes is based on speed of service rather than on what the letters contain, the criterion used in the United States.

First-class letters, delivered the first working day after collection, cost about 17 cents. Second-class letters, 95 percent of which are delivered by the third day, cost 13 cents.

Customers can tailor the service to their needs and their willingness to pay. Indeed they switch back and forth so much, Roberts noted, that the system finds it difficult to project how much revenue will be raised by specified rate increases.

British postal operations are far from ideal, however. Productivity is relatively poor, and union opposition has resisted both work-measurement programs and mechanization that are designed to improve it.

The American post office, by contrast, moves about nine times as much mail, over much longer distances, with only about 3½ times as many employees.

"There's certainly room for improvement in labor productivity," commented James Gwynn, secretary of the Post Office Users National Council, a watchdog body. "But if you look at international comparisons, the postal system in this country is as good as most and better than many."

The British post office, one of the world's earliest, has long been an innovator. In fact, it was the postal system that introduced the postage stamp, in 1840. Until then, the person who received a letter paid for its delivery. Because it was the forerunner, Britain is the only nation not required to print its name on its stamps.

Innovation has not died out. In recent years the British post office has developed the most advanced postal coding system. Much of its expertise is offered to other governments through a consulting service.

The Post Office, which is the umbrella body that through separate divisions runs the country's telephone system, its mail and competitive data processing and remittance operations, was converted from a government department to a nationalized industry in October of 1969. This gave it an early dose of the commercial freedom that has helped postal operations, surviving losses that rose above $200 million in 1975, to become profitable.

Roberts is now called on to assess the performance of his trans-Atlantic cousins:

"They've still got a loss, still got a subsidy," he says. "But their train is now going in the right direction. What I do think they need is a much greater ability to market."

27
WHAT WE SHOULD HAVE LEARNED ABOUT CONTROLS

by Walter Guzzardi, Jr.,
Research associate: Aimee Morner

While it is going too far to assert that man learns nothing from history, the question remains whether he learns enough. Late in 1974, when there was a broad consensus that the nation's No. 1 enemy was inflation, the country was swept with a yearning for wage and price controls. A Gallup survey in November showed that 62 percent of the American people favored a return to controls. The New York *Times*, Senate Majority Leader Mike Mansfield, and scores of Democratic candidates called for controls. After the election victories, the Democratic party conference, meeting in December in Kansas City, supported an "across-the-board system of economic controls," to be administered by a new agency "whose members are confirmed by the Congress."

Then the rate of inflation slowed, and the demand for controls subsided somewhat. But the collapse of the economy brought forth a new interest in controls: we could apply massive stimulus to the economy and then, it is argued, use wage and price controls to save us from another round of inflation. Obviously, advocates of controls have

From Walter Guzzardi, "What We Should Have Learned About Controls," Fortune *(March 1975). Reprinted by permission of the publishers.* © *1975 Time Inc.*

lost none of their confidence about what controls can accomplish.

KRISHNA WOULD DO BETTER

The confidence is badly misplaced. In principle, just about everything is wrong with wage and price controls. They constitute a surrender of our basic beliefs in the efficiency of free and competitive markets, and in freedom of action for business and labor. By garbling the vital signals usually conveyed by the free pricing system, controls misallocate resources, create shortages, and deter capital investment. Delicate price relationships that have gained wide social acceptance are upset by controls; impossibly difficult moral judgments by men are substituted for the neutrality and anonymity of the marketplace. Regulations become ludicrously complex, and businessmen waste energy and ingenuity devising ways to circumvent them. Sometimes for brief periods, and especially when they are riding with deep currents in the economy, controls seem to be successful in reducing the inflation rate. This illusion may be their most damaging feature; it may encourage government officials to think that they can get away with inflationary monetary and fiscal policies—ensuring a price explosion later.

In short, prayers imploring the great god Krishna to keep the dollar sound are liable to accomplish more than wage and price controls. At least the prayers, even if they are offered up in uncontrolled amounts, cannot hurt anything.

All these theoretical deficiencies of controls found practical expression during our recent, dismal experience with them. This adventure began in exhilaration: on August 16, 1971, the day after President Nixon announced the wage-price freeze, the Dow Jones industrial average shot up thirty-three points on what was then an all-time record volume of 31.7 million shares traded. But the euphoria soon drained away. The elaborate structure of controls collapsed in confusion and defeat last year, when controls were mercifully ended.

THE BIGGEST FAILURE EVER

We now behold the aftermath of the great experiment. The economy has been afflicted with the highest rate of inflation since a brief period following the end of World War II. The decline in real output of goods and services in 1974 was the sharepest since 1946. Surveying the ruins, George Shultz, former Secretary of the Treasury, whose usually influential voice was overruled when the decision for controls was made, describes the three years of controls as "the biggest failure in the history of economics."

The persistence of faith in controls, in the face of all the countervailing evidence, is in part explained by the dynamics of American politics. Henry Adams described politics as "the systematic organization of hatreds." When Americans are outraged by inflation, and when elections are just around the corner—a particular coincidence occuring both in 1971 and 1975—politicians are especially susceptible to the "do something" syndrome. So the air is blued with talk of controls.

But the demand for controls also has to be viewed as the triumph of an idea. For more than twenty-five years, that idea has been propounded by an eloquent and witty economist whose countless books and articles, promoted by a jet-set lifestyle, have made a wide public impression. John Kenneth Galbraith's arguments for controls have the attraction of simplicity. Galbraith concedes that controls would be useless or worse in a truly competitive economy. But he believes that our economy is shielded from competition by two great aggregates of power: big business and big labor, of which big business seems to be the greater sinner. These giants order prices upward, so that they can increase their profits and wages at public expense. The only preventive is to clamp controls on them.

Occasionally, parts of the Galbraithian theory (the adjective "Galbraithian" has become as much a part of the vocabulary of economics as "Keynesian") get support from other economists. Usually, however, they are only transients on Galbraith's turf, there for special reasons. Their agreement with Galbraith is partial, incidental, expedient, and ephemeral. Galbraith remains the presiding philosopher of controls.

Vital to Galbraith's thesis is the argument that wages and prices in "concentrated" industries—those in which large corporations with unionized labor have a major part of the market—set the level of prices for the economy at large. But this thesis presents several difficulties. Despite the high visibility of the auto, steel, and chemical industries (all "concentrated"), they represent only a corner of the total economy. Union labor represents only about 22 percent of the labor force. The industrialized sector, not all of which is "concentrated" anyway, comes to only about 28 percent of the economy at large. The service sector is much larger. It includes the services of lawyers and dentists and mechanics and repairmen—and, in view of the way their charges have gone up, it seems fair to conclude that their selflessness in fighting inflation has not been more notable than that of corporate or union executives.

Agriculture, so important to economic stability, is the property of neither big industrial operations nor big labor. And the biggest employer and the biggest consumer in the country is the government, whose power to print and spend money is the true engine of inflation. To control only corporations and

labor unions, in short, is to stabilize a part of an immensity.

Furthermore, Galbraith's assumption that price increases come faster in concentrated industries is being rapidly destroyed by hard analysis. Detailed studies directed by J. Fred Weston, an economist at the Graduate School of Management at the University of California at Los Angeles, reveal that the concentrated industries show a "negative relationship between the degree of concentration and the percentage of price change." Partly because of more rapid gains in productivity in concentrated industries, Weston has concluded, "The role of concentrated industries is to blunt inflation."

WHAT DID YOU SAY A TRANSACTION WAS?

The thousand practical difficulties involved in controlling an economy as vast and dynamic as ours, with its wide dispersions and complex interactions, showed up from the first day of controls in 1971. The body of supreme controllers, the Cost of Living Council, was obliged to enforce a policy handed down from Camp David that prices during the August, 1971, freeze should be fixed at the level of "the substantial volume of actual transactions" occurring over the previous thirty days.

But Arnold Weber, the first executive director of the COLC, soon made a dismaying discovery: "Transactions in the same category of goods or services often took place at different prices, and the term 'transaction' was itself imprecise." For example, should previously concluded wage contracts that provided for increases during the freeze be regarded as "transactions," and allowed to take effect? The COLC decided they should not. But in a perfect example of intrusion by politics, Congress later reversed that decision, made the payments retroactive, and added a provision for fringe benefits as well.

CURIOUS BEHAVIOR OF CARS AND CABBAGES

Another source of frustration to the controllers arose from the undeniable but inconvenient truth that many products—cars and cabbages, to mention two—sell at different prices at different times of the year. The need for an adjustment for "seasonality" was easy to perceive, but hard to fill. Could resort hotels charge more over Labor Day than they charged over the Fourth of July? Was Halloween candy a seasonal product? Once quietly cared for by the free market, these problem children were now dumped bawling and squawking into the laps of mere men, who found them impossible to pacify.

From birth to death, the age of controls floundered hopelessly in agriculture's muddy fields. So many farms grow and sell so many different products on so many markets that to control them all would be expensive, complicated by "seasonality," and, even admitting the farmer's undying dedication to the national interest, probably unworkable. So raw farm products had to be exempted for the entire time that controls were in effect.

The result was administrative chaos. Was honey a "raw" food—or processed by the busy bees? What if the honey were strained or drained? What about fish and other seafood when "shelled, shucked, skinned, or scaled"? Cucumbers went up but pickles were controlled; popped corn was controlled, raw corn was not. Since broilers were cut up and packaged before being sold, they were considered a processed food, and their price was frozen. When the price of feed went up, the farmer simply discontinued production; the nation was shocked at pictures of thousands of chicks being drowned.

In the economy outside of agriculture, controls showed numerous large defects. One great weakness of the system was that controllers never found an equitable way to deal with the time function in the pricing system. Contracts that provide for increases in wages over a number of years incorporate the inflationary expectations of both parties. Controls unfairly interrupt the agreement before it is fulfilled. William Poole, an economist at Brown University, explains that a similar process takes place with capital. When corporations borrow long-term money and agree to pay high nominal interest rates, they do so on the assumption that in later years they will be compensated by inflation —i.e., their money costs will remain fixed, while the prices they charge rise. To disallow those price rises is to take away an advantage that at that point is the borrower's due.

Controls were also unable to cope with the complexities of the international economy:

—At one juncture, the world price of zinc stood above the domestic price. To honor their commitments to their customers, domestic producers of zinc were selling at the lower price. But they had no incentive to expand the supply, and customers who didn't have commitments soon found themselves facing shortages.

—Reinforcing bars, widely used in construction, are made from another internationally traded commodity, scrap steel. Controls on the bars were imposed at a time when the price was very low. But scrap was not controlled, out of fear that too much of it might be exported. Makers of the bars soon found the cost of their raw material shooting up and had no way to pass on the increases. Production was interrupted and construction hurt.

—Baling wire is used by farmers to bundle crops. Before controls, much of the wire was imported from Japan. But prices were going up elsewhere, and the Japanese producers were withdrawing from the U.S. market when controls were put on. U.S. Steel found that the last price at which it sold baling wire, which was the controlled price, would bring a loss to the company of about $100 for every ton of baling wire it shipped. Under conditions so discouraging to production, the wire remained in short supply.

GUESSWORK BY GOVERNMENT

Phase II, which succeeded the freeze in mid-November, 1971, really amounted to an effort to substitute government judgments about prices for the sophisticated operation of the free pricing system. Phase II provided that a percentage of "allowable" cost increases could be "passed through" by corporations as price increases, but only after an application had been approved by the regulating authorities—a process that usually took several months. A ceiling was put on profit margins. Wage increases were limited to 5.5 percent, with "exceptions for gross inequities." "Tier I" companies—the 1,500 largest, ranked by sales—were the prime targets of the regulators.

Hendrik Houthakker, a former member of the Council of Economic Advisers and a top economist at Harvard, points out that the ceiling on margins did indeed keep some efficient firms from raising their prices. But this had an unintended effect: it put the squeeze on smaller and less efficient companies. Some may have been driven into bankruptcy. Thus controls on profits may have increased concentration throughout the industrial sector—hardly the outcome that

Galbraith, Houthakker's "dear friend down the hall," would desire.

Just that outcome seemed likely for a while in the paper industry. About 27 percent of the industry's output comes from small, nonintegrated mills, which rely on the big companies for their pulp. But pulp is internationally traded, the price was higher abroad, and the small mills were running short of their raw material. Some products disappeared from the market, and some small mills were hard hit. The whole industry came close to being restructured by government.

AN UNKIND CUT FOR SERVICE

One hidden cost of controls was the time that managements spent in order to find ways to defeat them. In the lumber industry, some companies cut one-eighth of an inch off plywood sheets, described the cut as "a service," and then increasd the price. Since domestic lumber was controlled but imported lumber was uncontrolled, lumber was "exported" and then "imported"—sometimes in fact, and sometimes merely on paper while the lumber sat in the yards.

Under Diocletian, the Roman emperor who was the first wage and price controller, the penalty for violation was death. Under Nixon, there were monetary fines; there was also the damage that might be done to a company's reputation. Corporations therefore generally took controls as seriously as they take income-tax laws. They did not want to be caught in violation but would use all legal means to escape unnecessary costs. The 1,500 Tier I companies filed 4,741 requests for price increases in the first nine months of Phase II. Even if there was double-dipping, the arguments they made must have been pretty good: 93 percent of the increases were granted.

Since the profit-margin ceilings were not applied product by product, but in the aggregate—total corporate profits related to total sales—multi-product corporations had lots of options besides cutting prices at the high end of the line. They could shift around their cost allocations. They could start up product lines that might be unprofitable for a year or two, and thus hold down the average margin. If all else failed, companies could beat the margin ceiling the same way they could beat an excess-profits tax: by relaxing cost controls and finding ways to spread around the money they would otherwise give away.

Corporate ingenuity also found other outlets. General Motors made some standard equipment into optional equipment on some models. Some companies introduced "superior" products at higher prices than the ones being replaced. Cheaper products were phased out, leaving only the more expensive available. Alternatively, many companies that kept their full line on the market achieved savings by allowing quality to deteriorate.

In recent weeks, Chairman Henry Reuss of the House Committee on Banking, Currency, and Housing and other influential voices in the Congress have been talking about credit controls. The Nixon Administration had at least the wit to avoid these. However, it did make some efforts at controls in the field of finance, with dubious results. At first the committee on Interest and Dividends, chaired by Arthur Burns, tried jawboning to slow down the increases in the prime rate. But the distortions in the money market were so great that, as George Shultz recalls it, the jawboning "was backed off from, and there was a lot of language that saved everybody's face."

Then, in response to the complaint that only big business could afford to borrow, the committee attempted to enforce a "two-tier" prime rate. It was designed to allow the prime to increase for small business only as fast as bank costs rose; for big business, the prime could reflect overall market forces. For a time there was a substantial differential in favor of small businesses. Eventually, rates for everybody went sky-high.

GRIEVANCES ON ALL SIDES

Looking back on their experience, large numbers of corporations say that they were hurt by price controls. Some 100 of 125 companies with annual revenues of over $50 million that responded to a questionnaire from the National Association of Manufacturers said they suffered "financial damage" because of controls. Virtually every one of them stated that it experienced "unusual difficulties" in getting important raw materials or supplies during controls.

The misadventures of RCA show the harm that controls can do to a single corporation. During the freezes, Banquet Foods, an RCA subsidiary, had to buy food-stuffs at uncontrolled prices and sell its prepared food at fixed prices; it was squeezed relentlessly. Hertz, another RCA subsidiary, similarly had to absorb great cost increases, in this case of fuel. RCA makes thousands of products and has thousands of suppliers; rather than compute, apply for, and wait for cost pass-throughs under Phase II, it negotiated a "term-limit pricing" agreement with the government. The rule about TLP was that companies opting for it could have a maximum overall annual increase; for RCA, the increase was 2 percent. But the administrative convenience of the TLP had its costly aspect. Says Chairman Robert Sarnoff: "Some suppliers raised their prices for TV components by as much as 229 percent."

Like business, labor also had means to fight controls, but also ended up claiming it was damaged. When Congress granted those retroactive wage increases and new provisions for fringe benefits in the Economic Stabilization Act Amendments of 1971, Congress was responding to labor's lobbying. In industry after industry—coal, railroads, and aerospace—settlements were made in excess of the 5.5 percent limit. The Construction Industry Stabilization Committee felt obliged to allow tremendous "catch-ups" in the construction field. When the wage for plumbers in San Francisco went up from $12.85 to $15.20 an hour, economist Otto Eckstein said the increase marked "the end of moderation." Such increases were cited by labor negotiators as justification for comparable gains in other fields—prompting a rebuttal from economist Arthur Okun to the effect that "I don't view it as equity that, when one chicken gets out of the coop, all the others have to be let out too."

Still, organized labor rapidly concluded that controls were helping business and hurting labor. Even before George Meany walked off the Pay Board in 1972, he turned on his sometime ally, President Nixon, and depicted him as "the handmaiden of big business . . . ready to let everything of a social nature go down the drain to keep big business happy." Behind those hot words there probably lay a cool assessment: that continued cooperation with controls would result in labor surrendering to government its basic purpose—gains for its membership—and perhaps even its basic right, the right to strike.

Claims of both business and labor about the unfairness of controls to each have to be appropriately discounted. The ultimate, hard question about controls is what they do to the inflation rate. And the short answer is that they make it worse.

In a free economy, the reasonable expectation of an adequate return is what attracts new capital. That capital is used for new and more efficient facilities that increase supply, meet growing demand, and provide an elemental anti-inflationary force. And to constrain prices discourages such investment.

A study by a leading New York bank shows that the gap between planned and actual capital spending was larger during the control years than at any other time since 1953. Alan Greenspan, now chairman of the Council of Economic Advisers, agrees strongly with the inference that controls were the principal deterrent to investment. Greenspan believes that after the dollar was devalued in 1971, and the American steel industry became more competitive in world markets, a burst of badly needed capital investment would have gone into the domestic steel industry—had it not been for controls. Because of them, steel supplies in later years were less abundant and steel prices higher. Concludes Greenspan: "I argue that controls are not anti- but pro-inflationary."

Controls also keep prices high in other ways. When controls are on, explains Beryl Sprinkel, chief economist at the Harris Trust & Savings Bank in Chicago, producers tend to keep their prices at the ceiling level. And when controls are anticipated, no business is likely to cut its list prices. In fact, when controls seemed imminent last fall, there was an immediate flurry of anticipatory price increases.

THE MARVEL DEMOLISHED

While the proof of what controls have done to inflation is all around us today, there were periods during the great experiment when things looked pretty good. At the end of the freeze, G.N.P. prices were increasing at only a 2.6 percent rate and the consumer price index at a rate of only 2.2 percent. But over the next three months, the post-freeze "bulge" wiped out the gains. The consumer price index's annual rate of increase doubled.

Toward the end of Phase II, controls once again seemed to be working pretty well. For all of 1972, the year of Phase II, both G.N.P. prices and the C.P.I. rose by only 3.4 percent. President Nixon's Economic Report to Congress for that year hailed the controls program as "the marvel of the rest of the world."

But the marvel was scheduled for quick demolition. Some supporters of controls still insist that all would have gone well had Phase II been left in place. However, huge inflationary forces were building up in 1972, and no controls program could have contained them. In 1972 government policies provided for individual income-tax cuts, elimination of some important excise taxes, and the effective devaluation of the dollar. Huge increases were made in the money supply; currency, demand deposits, and time deposits, which had grown at a rate of 7 percent for the second half of 1971, rose by 11 percent in 1972. The budget deficit was $23 billion for fiscal 1971 and another $23 billion for fiscal 1972. All this stimulus brought victories of a rather special sort: in the fall of 1972, Nixon won his election. The Dow broke 1,000.

In 1973, the bubble burst. The prices that deliver the message of excessive aggregate demand had been partly suppressed by controls, but now, controls or no, they made headlines. For the five months of Phase III, which first eased controls and then tried to tighten them, the C.P.I. rose at an annual rate of 8.3 percent. Food prices went up over 20 percent. Wholesale commodities went up 22.2 percent; wholesale farm produce jumped 48.9 percent. A frantically imposed freeze for sixty days beginning in mid-June, 1973, was halfhearted, ridiculed, and ineffective. Phase IV's effort to control areas in which price increases had been especially large—food, health care, insurance, petroleum—was futile. Every inflation indicator went through the roof in 1974. The great experiment was over.

THEY SHOULD HAVE TRIED HARDER

For the devout, all the aberrations born of controls, and the bad record they made, proved only the inadequacies of the controllers themselves. Galbraith has expressed the view that "any controls program run by Republicans is bound to be fouled up." Arthur Schlesinger Jr. remarked that "controls will work well only when administered by people who believe in them"—thus making it possible to explain every past failure, and every future one as well, by a shortfall of faith.

Controls never bring gains that are more than fleeting and illusory. And the price of these gains is added inflation. But that cost is not the only reason to avoid controls. The more they are used, the more they acquire undeserved legitimacy as an anti-inflationary instrument. The idea is spread that somehow government can be grossly irresponsible in managing the economy, and then, by more intervention, save the country from the consequences. In this way too, price and wage controls make worse what they set out to repair.

28

GYPSUM TRIAL SHOWS HOW PRICE-FIX PLAN SUPPOSEDLY OPERATED

by David McClintick,
The Wall Street Journal

It was a raw, bleak Monday, Feb. 15, 1965, in Portland, Ore. Two conservatively dressed businessmen arrived at the airport on separate flights, met and drove into the city to join a third man. Then, for four hours, the three conferred over dinner at Canlis, a plush restaurant atop the Portland Hilton.

The out-of-towners were Robert C. Gimlin, a vice president of U.S. Gypsum Corp., the nation's largest manufacturer of gypsum wall and ceiling board, and John W. Brown, a senior vice president of National Gypsum Corp., U.S. Gypsum's prime competitor. They dined with William H. Hunt, executive vice president of Portland-based Georgia-Pacific Corp., which was then on the verge of entering the gypsum business.

More than 10 years have passed, and Mr. Brown is dead. But the meeting in Portland still is haunting Mr. Gimlin, Mr. Hunt and a lot of other people. The Justice Depart-

ment has alleged in court that the meeting was a small but important part of a nationwide conspiracy, lasting at least 13 years through 1973, to fix prices illegally in the gypsum industry. The conspiracy allegedly involved sabotage, intricate scheming among executives and managers and an array of coverup ploys ranging from falsely documenting prices to lying under oath by executives.

SIX BIG COMPANIES CONVICTED

All in all, authorities say, the conspiracy was one of the largest and longest-lived price-fixing schemes in U.S. history. And they say it cost consumers of gypsum board, a staple in countless homes, office buildings and other structures, many millions of dollars in inflated prices.

Over the past several months, the nation's six largest gypsum makers and 10 of their highest executives or former executives have pleaded no-contest to federal criminal charges or have pleaded innocent and been found guilty by a jury in Pittsburgh of taking part in the scheme. The companies are U.S. Gypsum; National Gypsum; Georgia-Pacific; Celotex Corp., a subsidiary of Jim Walter Corp.; Flintkote Co., and Kaiser Gypsum, a subsidiary of Kaiser Cement & Gypsum Corp., 37 percent owned by Kaiser Industries Corp. Two other big companies, Johns-Manville Corp. and Fibreboard Corp., and 146 individuals were named in an indictment as unindicted co-conspirators.

During the alleged conspiracy, the companies together sold more than $4 billion worth of gypsum, over 90 percent of the industry's total volume.

The companies and individuals convicted by the jury still protest their innocence, and they are appealing their convictions. Among other things, they point

From David McClintick, "Gypsum Trial Shows How Price-Fix Plan Supposedly Operated," Wall Street Journal *(October 3, 1975). Reprinted with permission of the* Wall Street Journal. © *1975 Dow Jones & Co. All rights reserved.*

out that some gypsum prices actually were lower at the end of 1973, when the government brought its charges, than in earlier years. The government doesn't deny that, but argues that without price fixing, prices would have been even lower.

THE COMPANIES' ARGUMENT

In court, the defendants' lawyers also argued that, if the companies seemed to violate the Sherman Antitrust Act, it was only because they were trying to comply with another federal law. That law, the Robinson-Patman Act, generally permits a manufacturer to sell to one customer at a lower price than to other customers only when the lower price is necessary to meet competition for the first customer's business. So when the companies conferred with each other about prices, the argument went, they were merely trying to verify the prices being charged such customers.

This rationale, the government alleged, was cooked up after charges were brought. If the companies' contacts with each other had been legitimate, prosecutors said, the companies would have kept careful records of their discussions instead of destroying many records. The jury apparently accepted the government's view.

Despite criminal prosecution and civil law-suits, price fixing is considered widespread in some industries, partly because its rewards—higher prices and bigger profits—often may seem worth the seemingly small risk of getting caught and penalized for violating the antitrust laws. In the gypsum case, Judge Hubert I. Teitelbaum gave only suspended prison sentences and imposed fines ranging from $50,000 to as little as $1,000. Still, the companies have paid out abut $70 million in damages to gypsum dealers who filed private civil suits to recover the

money they lost in paying illegally high prices.

BACK TO 1951

How the conspiracy worked can be pieced together from court records—a 15,000-page trial transcript, 5,000 documents put in evidence, the grand-jury indictment, a 350-page government bill of particulars and other material.

Because of the statute of limitations, the prosecutors, led by Justice Department antitrust specialist John C. Fricano, had to prove that violations occurred within five years prior to the date of the indictment, Dec. 17, 1973. But they were allowed to present voluminous evidence that the alleged conspiracy began earlier. Price fixing on gypsum, the government says, began before 1951. In that year, a federal court in the District of Columbia, enjoined U.S. Gypsum, National Celotex and other companies against it.

Later in the 1950s, the government said in court, U.S. Gypsum's current chairman, Graham J. Morgan, executive vice president Andrew J. Watt and, by implication, executives in most of the rest of the gypsum industry, knew that prices still were being rigged.

So were other sales terms that affected the gypsum companies' revenues and earnings, the government said. A former credit manager for Oakland-based Kaiser Gypsum, Richard L. Downing, testified at the Pittsburgh trial that in 1957 or 1958, he and credit managers for other gypsum companies with West Coast operations met at a hotel in Long Beach, Calif., and agreed to raise the interest rate charged to customers who bought on credit to 6 percent from 5 percent. It is illegal not only for companies to band together to charge the same prices but also to fix other sales terms that deprive customers of the benefits of competition.

There was testimony that the companies knew they were risking antitrust violations. The government alleged that U.S. Gypsum, based in Chicago, declined to send a representative to the Long Beach meeting because of the "danger" that the agreement would be detected. But U.S. Gypsum's credit manager later agreed to impose the credit terms set at the meeting, the prosecutors said.

Testimony also suggested that the companies fixed uniform methods of shipping wallboard to customers. Usually the companies would deliver only by rail, so that a construction company or retail-supply customer would have to locate on a rail spur or truck its gypsum-board shipments from a rail yard. Fixing the delivery method, the government said, stifled competition.

When a producer stepped out of line, the government tried to show in court, other producers got tough. In 1960, a Texas building contractor, Claude Huckleberry, built his own gypsum plant in El Paso. Because his competitors weren't trucking material to customers, Mr. Huckleberry figured—correctly, it turned out—that he could win a lot of their business by trucking gypsum board directly to customers at no extra charge.

SABOTAGE AT A PLANT OPENING?

Though the El Paso market was relatively small, the big companies apparently considered Mr. Huckleberry's company, Texas Gypsum, a serious threat. In growing, Texas Gypsum might encourage other small companies to deliver by truck and ultimately cost the major producers a lot of business or force them to offer truck delivery themselves.

In December 1960, one month before Texas Gypsum's plant was to open, Martin Hardin showed up in El Paso to visit Mr. Huckleberry. Mr. Hardin was president of American Gypsum, a small Albuquerque producer, but the evidence showed that his visit was made on behalf of other gypsum companies, too.

Over coffee at a bowling alley, Mr. Huckleberry testified, Mr. Hardin delivered a message: "U.S. Gypsum, National, Celotex, Flintkote—he named them all—had agreed that if I didn't stop trucking they would move in and kill me"—meaning, drive him out of business.

Undeterred, Mr. Huckleberry went ahead. In January 1961, his gypsum plant was ready. He invited a New York banker, an El Paso newspaper reporter and several other guests to the plant for a demonstration. Suddenly the machinery in the plant began running in reverse, slopping "slurry," a plasterlike ingredient of gypsum board, onto the floor. "We were waist deep in slurry before I could get everything shut off," Mr. Huckleberry recalled.

THE "QUALITY" TESTS

Mr. Huckleberry fired Texas Gypsum's plant manager, William A. Kincaid. The government implied in court that it was more than coincidence that Mr. Kincaid previously had worked for U.S. Gypsum and returned to U.S. Gypsum after he lost his job at Texas Gypsum.

The Texas Gypsum plant started operating anyway, and the company won 72 percent of the gypsum-board market in the El Paso area in a few months. At the same time, the lackluster competition in the area grew fierce. U.S. Gypsum, National and Kaiser rented warehouse space in El Paso, filled it with 150 to 200 railcar loads of gypsum board, slashed prices well under Texas Gypsum's and hired trucks to deliver the board.

Nor was that all. According to a Texas Gypsum customer, salesmen from five major gypsum companies asked him for samples of Texas Gypsum's board to test for quality. "I began to get the drift of what was going on," said the customer, John D. Tinsley, a Dallas lumber dealer. He said he gave four of the five salesmen samples of their own companies' board. Some salesmen, he says, reported back that the "Texas Gypsum" board was inferior. "I doubt if anyone knew which board was which," Mr. Tinsley testified.

Texas Gypsum lost much of its new business. Because deals between companies to drive a competitor out of business are as illegal as price fixing, Mr. Huckleberry filed a private antitrust suit against his big competitors. Eventually he sold his company and got out of the gypsum business. The buyers settled the suit out of court.

FIXING KICKBACKS

Demand for gypsum was rising in the late 1950s when Mr. Huckleberry was planning to enter the business, which he did in 1961. By 1965, however, construction activity in the U.S. had become less stable, and demand for gypsum board was diminishing. But the government says the gypsum companies stepped up their efforts to keep prices high. It was at this time that Mr. Brown of National Gypsum and Mr. Gimlin of U.S. Gypsum flew to Portland and met with Mr. Hunt of Georgia-Pacific.

Mr. Gimlin testified that his encounter with Mr. Brown was a coincidence, the dinner with Mr. Hunt was impromptu, and nothing illegal was discussed. In any case, on July 1, 1965, with demand for gypsum wallboard at one of its lowest points in some time, Georgia-Pacific announced a price increase of $4 a thousand-square-feet on fire-resistant board effective Sept. 1.

In mid-July 1965, Mr. Watt, of U.S.

Gypsum, traveled to the West Coast. On July 14, he had breakfast in Portland with Mr. Hunt of Georgia-Pacific. Mr. Watt then went to Oakland to confer with Claude E. Harper, a senior executive of Kaiser Gypsum. A few days later, U.S. Gypsum announced a price increase comparable with Georgia-Pacific's. By Aug. 27, four days before these increases were to take effect, all major producers had announced similar increases. The big companies agreed to pay $2 a thousand-square-feet to wallboard installers in Oregon and Washington who purchased the companies' gypsum board through dealers. The kickbacks were paid by cashiers' checks that didn't show the original source of the funds.

A few months later, the government alleged, in September and October, the companies agreed to adjustments, to take effect in December, that would again boost prices more than 15 percent in some parts of the country.

From Oct. 12 to Oct. 15, the Gypsum Association, the industry trade organization, had a semi-annual meeting at Ponte Vedra, a Florida resort. Mr. Watt of U.S. Gypsum was named chairman of a task force to, among other things, plan the December price increase, the government said in court. A group of U.S. Gypsum executives refined the plan at several meetings between Oct. 25 and Nov. 5 in Mr. Morgan's office at U.S. Gypsum. Details of the increase were coordinated by telephone, the government alleged, between Mr. Morgan and National Gypsum's chairman, Colon Brown, in Buffalo.

To effect the increase, the government said, the companies decided to eliminate kickbacks and cancel industry-wide discounts from list prices, leaving list prices themselves unchanged. On Nov. 17, U.S. Gypsum announced its new terms. The other companies announced similar terms by Dec. 1. The companies also agreed to centralize pricing decisions in top management in order to police their agreements better, the government said.

Shortly after Dec. 15, when the changes took effect, the companies announced another change; on March 1, 1966, they would tighten and make more uniform the credit terms extended to customers.

This threatened a California wallboard dealer, Richard L. Downing, the former Kaiser Gypsum credit manager. Mr. Downing met with James D. Morgan, chairman of Flintkote, and told him tighter credit terms would force his company out of business. Flintkote agreed to impose the new terms on Mr. Downing's company over a two-year period to give the company time to adjust. On Feb. 21, Mr. Downing persuaded Kaiser to consider giving his company the same treatment.

A DEAL CALLED OFF

But when Mr. Downing met with National Gypsum officials on Feb. 23, they rejected his request that National Gypsum extend similarly easy terms. Mr. Downing hinted to National officials that the other two companies had agreed. National, according to testimony, quickly accused Flintkote of violating the industry's agreement. The government said it was a typical display of the industry's clout in policing its deals when, the next day, officials of Flintkote and Kaiser phoned Mr. Downing to back out of their deal with him. Later, Mr. Downing sought easier terms from Fibreboard, which also refused him. The government said Mr. Downing's company, and others, were forced out of business by the new and stringent credit terms.

The 1965 and 1966 price and credit agreements, the Justice Department alleged, set a pattern for illegal arrangements that were "conspiratorily achieved and maintained" into the 1970s. The gypsum

companies appeared to be aware that they were on dangerous ground. In November 1966, Georgia-Pacific's lawyer urged Mr. Hunt to insure that the company's contacts with competitors were legal. The lawyer also recommended that Georgia-Pacific change the title of its "pricing administrator" to "something less suggestive."

The government charged also that some of the companies later tried to conceal their price-fixing contacts from the court handling civil suits against them and from the federal grand jury investigating them. National Gypsum was fined $5,000 by the federal court in Washington, D.C., for criminal contempt of court. The company at first failed to produce subpoenaed desk calendars of its chairman, Colon Brown. The calendars, later produced, were used to help reconstruct Mr. Brown's movements and contacts with executives of competing firms.

PRISON TERMS SUSPENDED

Mr. Brown was convicted of conspiring to violate the Sherman Act, fined $50,000, given a six-month suspended prison term and put on probation for three years. Jay P. Nicely, a vice president of National Gypsum, was fined $1,000, given a six-month suspended prison sentence and put on probation for one year. Mr. Watt, of U.S. Gypsum, was fined $10,000, given a six-month suspended prison sentence and put on probation for one year. Convicted separately as corporate defendants were U.S. Gypsum, National Gypsum, Georgia-Pacific and Celotex. (Mr. Gimlin, of U.S. Gypsum, and the late John W. Brown, of National, who took part in the 1965 Portland dinner meeting, were named unindicted co-conspirators.)

Other defendants didn't contest the charges. They were fined, given suspended prison sentences of either 30 days or six months and put on probation. These defendants were Mr. Morgan, of U.S. Gypsum, fined $40,000; Mr. Hunt, now retired from Georgia-Pacific, $40,000; William D. Herbert, president of Celotex, $20,000; Mr. Harper, former president of Kaiser Gypsum, $40,000; Robert A. Costa, former vice president of Kaiser Gypsum, $20,000; George J. Pecaro, retired chairman of Flintkote, $20,000; and Mr. Moran, chairman of Flintkote, $20,000.

The gypsum companies have paid $70 million in damages from private civil antitrust suits. Ordinarily, such damages would be deductible from taxable income; but the criminal convictions, if upheld on appeal, would make two-thirds of the damages nondeductible. That could cost the companies about $22 million in extra taxes.

If the convictions are overturned, the big gypsum makers still face trouble. Sources say it's likely that the Justice Department soon will file a civil antitrust suit seeking to force them to divest themselves of certain manufacturing facilities and end certain joint operating agreements in order to create, one source says, a "more competitive environment" and a greater number of "aggressive single-plant producers."

29
PRICE INCREASES CAN BE HARD TO DETECT

by Milton Moskowitz
Los Angeles Times

There are many ways to increase prices.

The simplest way, of course, is to charge more for a product or service.

Another way, not easily detected, is to reduce the size or weight of a product. That's what the candy manufacturers do.

Still another way is to charge for a service that was previously offered free. The airlines are adept at this maneuver—and they have now been joined by the largest corporation in the nation, American Telephone & Telegraph.

Ma Bell has decided that you have been getting a free ride on information calls long enough—and it's time you dug into your pockets to pay for this service. "Information," or what the phone company now calls "directory assistance," is what you dial when you want to get the number of a friend or an establishment.

Since the phone company publishes directories for all localities, it says that you might just as well look up the number instead of bothering the operator.

In fact, if you did that, the phone com-

From Milton Moskowitz, *"Price Increases Can Be Hard to Detect,"* Houston Chronicle, *February 18,* © *(1975)* Los Angeles Times. *Reprinted with permission.*

pany could get rid of a lot of those operators, which is what it wants to do.

To dissuade you from calling its operators for information, Ma Bell wants to do the following: Every time you call to get a number, the operator will ask you for your number; you will be allowed three to five calls a month with no charge; after that, you will be socked with a 20-cent charge per call.

This is more than just idle dreaming on the part of the phone company. It's moving on this plan, area by area, gaining approval from the local regulatory agencies. Telephone subscribers in Cinncinnati began paying the extra levy last March. The surcharge went into effect last month in Georgia. Florida is the next target.

Wherever you live, you may expect the telephone company to seek the same penalty.

By charging for a service that it once rendered as an obligation, Ma Bell is pioneering in territory that will no doubt be watched closely by other companies. Look at it this way.

The reason most people call to retrieve a number is because they eventually want to call that number, right? They can't use the service unless they know the number—and everyone in business knows that you always try to make it easier for customers to use your services. That's why it made perfect business sense for Ma Bell to provide free information service.

But AT&T has apparently reached the stage of maturity—or is it senility?—where it does not have to make it easier for its customers. Force them to use the directory. If they don't, charge them for information they need to use the service that they pay for.

It's a beautiful example of taking advantage of your monopoly position. The airlines, which are strapped for money these days, will surely see how they can adapt this practice to their business. Why give out all that free information about flight departure and arrivals? Start charging people for this kind of information.

This is an idea that could spread like wildfire in the business community. Ma Bell, thanks!

SECTION FOLLOW-UP
THE PRICE OF SUCCESS

As the textbooks claim, the "free market" sets prices where supply and demand meet—if the government isn't setting the price somewhere else, or "competing" companies aren't setting prices in concert. Even in a free market situation, the manager is not so much setting the price as guessing where demand will be at every price and assessing trade-offs. That assessment takes the form of questions—to be asked about airlines, a postal system, a candy bar, telephone directory information, or any other product:

1. How does the price for one of an organization's products affect the rest of its marketing effort? Is a low price providing volume sales and therefore cash to promote a product of which potential buyers are unaware? Or is the low price putting a "cheap" image on other company products? Or is it bringing in store traffic to buy other products? Or is it doing two or three of these things?

2. How are prices set in a given industry—any industry described in readings in all sections of this book? Do manufacturers, growers, or publishers set a retail price? Do retailers take a standard markup? Does it have to happen "the way it's always been done?" Why or why not?

3. What happens to published prices in any industry when products get scarce, or over-abundant? What alternatives did the airlines have to the half-price-off coupons they distributed in 1979? What alternatives does a government have to price controls?

5 PROMOTION: MORE THAN A HAPPY MEDIUM

What the marketer tells prospective buyers, and how he or she tells it—both are part of promotion. Packaging, advertising, and person-to-person selling are all ways to tell the story. The story itself may differ depending on what buyers want and need to know; purchasing a computer for the state of Illinois is not like buying Girl Scout cookies.

One reason that promotion gets so much attention is its cost. Modernizing the Quaker man on an oatmeal box can cost many thousands of dollars. And even for a company that markets to poultry farmers, promotional expenses are certainly not chickenfeed.

30
THE TRAVELING SALESMAN IS NO JOKE

He will bring his company more than ten million dollars worth of business this year. But basically he spends his time offering technical advice to customers and pumping them for price information. His title is "branch manager" for an industrial marketer; informally, he is a traveling salesman.

His job has advanced far beyond the role of a wandering peddler or the city slicker who befriended the legendary farmer's daughter. He has a college degree, technical training, and served in two different jobs at company headquarters before they sent him out in the field.

Rick Wilson, a fictional composite of several such salesmen, works for a division of a leading U.S. manufacturer of aluminum products. The division markets to the transmission departments of electric utilities, and its principal product is "conductor"—the huge overhead lines that carry power. In addition, Rick's division sells utilities the fittings and accessories that go into the building of electrical substations. Everything is described in a catalog, complete with technical descriptions, list prices, and the phone number of Rick's office, to be called at no charge to the customer. His efficient secretary will take the order and send the caller a confirmation.

Then what does Rick do all day? Here is a typical week:

Monday he starts the day at his "branch office"—the total staff consisting of himself and the secretary. He wants to see the mail before he heads out of town; a shipment to the large utility he'll be visiting has been delayed, and he's hoping for some word from the plant on that problem. Also, any technical memo from headquarters is important; they average about three a month on new uses for products or results of research on product use under unusual conditions. His company maintains a large research department, but uses it as a marketing tool; Rick is welcomed by engineers in the companies he visits, largely because he knows more than they do about what his company's products can and can't accomplish.

He takes one of those engineers to lunch Monday; a man in the transmission department of the utility in the city where Rick lives. Deliberately, the branch office and his home are in the city of his largest customer, and of all their engineers, Rick tries to see 24 at least once each month. He talks about conductor problems to some; about substations to others. He sees the substation- and transmission-department purchasing agents even more often, and if possible, invites them out for a round of golf.

At lunch or on the golf course, he works prices into the conversation. This utility buys by competitive bidding, but it doesn't make the bids public. The marketer who bid low last time wants very much to know how much higher he could have bid and still have been low man. Or, if he didn't get the bid, he wants to know how much lower he would have had to go to win. And have prices changed since the bidding? That's what Rick's company pays him well to find out: as he sees it, the only way they can sell anything without that knowledge is to come in far below the market price, and that's no way to make a profit. There are ten companies in the conductor field, all making virtually the same product. His firm is the leader and would be chosen if everybody's prices were the same, but catalog prices mean almost nothing. The big question is: "What's the market price today?" Rick has expertise and friendship to offer in exchange for that information.

He goes back to the utility's office with the engineer he took to lunch, sees one or two more engineers there, but certainly doesn't expect an immediate order for his trouble. "Maybe this particular man won't need anything that we carry for two or three months," he says. "But if he's never seen me, when he *does* need something, he'll buy from the company that's been paying some attention to him."

The products Rick sells are usually specified by the engineers by brand name. Theoretically, though, the purchasing agent has final say. And he takes into account such "company policy" factors as the knowledge that Rick's company has an aluminum plant that buys its power from this utility. Not surprisingly, that utility does a lot of buying, in turn, from Rick.

Tuesday morning Rick heads out of town, and by noon reaches another city and another engineer to take to lunch. This is the man whose order is late, and Rick wants to sit down with him to find out exactly what parts of the order he needs immediately. Then Rick will call the plant and have those items shipped by air freight. The plant won't be happy; the extra transportation cost comes out of its budget. But Rick has the authority to make that decision. On the other hand, he won't make them any unhappier than necessary; he'll try to get the company's engineer to give him the shortest possible "urgent" list. Rick doesn't want the plant people as enemies; he wants them to put forth every effort to get future orders out on time.

Actually, he believes, one of his most difficult jobs is "selling" the people who keep his customers supplied. "The plant people

don't seem to understand that we're trying to sell this stuff; sometimes they act like they think it's going to be dumped in the ocean," Rick complains. If things get too rough, he can threaten to call the plant manager, and about three times a year, he does. Usually, though, he relies on pleas, with overtones of urgency.

Besides the large utilities and his own plant, Rick has a third group of people to deal with, and he'll see one of them Tuesday afternoon. This group comprises his company's distributors, who handle all the marketing to the small customers in the area and stock some items ordered by the major utility as well.

The distributor in this city deals exclusively in products made by Rick's company, and will be its distributor as long as the company is convinced he's selling as much as can be expected and it doesn't get complaints about him. So, although he's an independent businessman, he wants to make a good impression on Rick and show him that he's been diligent about having his salesmen call on the small rural co-ops in the area, who provide the bulk of his orders.

At the same time, though, Rick wants to "sell" the distributor on the value of doing even more; Rick, after all, gets credit toward his quota for everything this distributor sells. Rick has no intention of putting pressure on distributors, but he does help them out by going with them to see their more important customers who may need technical advice which Rick can provide. He's pumping the distributors about prices at the same time, since one of the jobs of the distributors' salesmen is to pump their own customers. "What do you hear they're paying for 26/7?" is the question of the day every day.

In another city in Rick's territory, Rick will help the distributor in one additional way: the utility there is municipally owned, and the local distributor is the man called on for bids when the utility is ready to make a purchase. So Rick not only tells his distributor what the material will cost him, he also helps him figure out what everybody else will tack on for profit, and to work out his actual bid. Rick, the company, and the distributor are thoroughly interdependent—and they know it.

Tuesday Rick is on his own for dinner, because he needs to get an early start Wednesday toward a smaller town 300 miles away, where there's a branch of the utility company he's just been visiting. He only gets down there once every other month, and when he does, it's the same round of lunch with one or two engineers, then back to the office to see two or three more, then dinner with the purchasing agent. Power companies have been doubling their capacity every ten years; consequently, even the smallest branch can be expected to have some expansion underway.

Thursday Rick heads back, with about 500 miles of driving ahead of him. Friday he'll see a few more engineers from that large utility in his own city. Next week he'll head out for three days to the east, instead of south. The week after that, he swings through the northern part of his territory. He can never add a customer; he's already calling on every utility in his territory that's large enough to be worth his time, and the distributors are calling on the rest. And he could probably never lose a customer entirely: some of the items in his catalog are made by, at most, one other company. But for conductor—which makes up 90 percent of his volume—a utility has plenty of alternate sources.

Rick reads one monthly trade magazine. He belongs to one club, the local Electric League. Members meet for lunch once a month; power company managers, consultants, contractors, and salesmen like Rick. They have parties, a golf tournament, and

work together to sponsor National Electric Week.

What else does Rick do with his time? Once a year he sets his sales quota for the next year, a process that involves asking each customer what he expects to buy next year. Rather than make a series of phone calls to get the estimates, he tries to bring the question up when he's with each customer, and that means he may have to start asking about next year more than a month before the quota is set. About this same time, he makes up his budget; estimating what the secretary, the office, and his travel expenses will cost the company in the coming 12 months.

Another responsibility he handles is to take surveys on possible new products. If a salesman or a customer suggests a new product to headquarters, or if headquarters develops an idea on its own, the next step is to see how many customers might want the item if it were added to the catalog. So while Rick is talking with the engineers he normally contacts, he'll ask what they think of the new idea.

For new products that the company introduces, Rick has the assignment of making sure that customers understand what the products can do. So perhaps once a year, he'll give a presentation at each power company for all the company's engineers who might need to know about the new item.

Sales meetings are another responsibility. There is a national meeting each year, plus approximately three regional meetings. A meeting can run as long as three days. These meetings are where Rick learns all the specialized product uses and problem-solving tips that he passes along to his customers.

The possibility of product shortage is also discussed at the meeting. More and more, customers are responding to rumors of shortages by stockpiling. That practice makes it difficult to schedule production, because the rumors may hit many customers at once, and make for huge upswings in demand. Then as the rumors subside, customers use up their stockpiled material, and a plant that ran on overtime for weeks finds itself producing at less than capacity. The moral, Rick and the other salespeople are told, is to have enough facts on hand to counter the rumors when necessary, in the hopes that unwarranted stockpiling can be kept to a minimum.

Rick works on straight salary, about $35,000 a year, plus expenses and a company car. He's worked for the same company nearly 20 years, and he's let them know that he has no interest in being promoted to one of the few positions where he would be in a territory so large that he would have other salesmen to supervise. He started out as a salesman in one of those large metropolitan branches, but the transfer ten years ago to his own branch gave him, as far as he's concerned, the ideal situation.

"If you want to keep moving up, you ought to find reasons to get to headquarters every once in a while, and I don't bother," Rick says. His idea of real satisfaction, he says, is to sell a utility a higher percentage of its conductor than he expected to; to take a really large order. It's a different kind of thrill than the one conventionally provided by the farmer's daughter, but for today's traveling salesman, it may be considerably more realistic.

31

TO COMPUTER SALESMEN, THE 'BIG TICKET' DEAL IS THE ONE TO LOOK FOR

by Thomas Ehrich,
The Wall Street Journal

At the age of 29, Kim Kelley is already something of a legend around Honeywell Inc. "He's the one who cried when he made his sale, isn't he?" a fellow Honeywell salesman asks him with a chuckle.

Indeed he is. Kim stood there in his customer's office last June and bawled like a baby. And for good reason. Kim had just shaken hands on a $8.1 million computer sale to the state of Illinois. He had gambled his whole career on making that sale. He had spent three years laying the groundwork for it, and for three solid months he had been working six days a week, often 14 hours a day, competing against salesmen from four other computer companies.

It was a make-or-break situation for Kim Kelley, and standing there with tears of joy and relief streaming down his cheeks, he knew he had it made. A bright future with Honeywell was assured, and he had just

From Thomas Ehrich, "To Computer Salesmen, The 'Big Ticket' Deal Is the One to Look for," Wall Street Journal (January 22, 1974). Reprinted with permission of the Wall Street Journal. © 1974 Dow Jones & Co. All rights reserved.

made an $80,000 commission—more money than he had earned in all four of his previous years with the company.

Looking back on it now, Kim says "It was pure hell." And his wife, Sandy, agrees emphatically: "I'd never want to go through it again." Such is the life of the "big-ticket" salesman who pursues multimillion-dollar contracts while others sell in bits and drabs. Lured by fat commissions (1 percent of the equipment's total value in Honeywell's case), they devote months to delicate planning and months more to the heat of battle, all to make one big sale.

GAMBLING A PIECE OF YOUR LIFE

"You're playing for big stakes, and what you ante is your life," says Dick Kuszyk, a Honeywell computer salesman in Pittsburgh. He just "gambled three years" of his life, he says, to sell a $4.5 million computer to Jones & Laughlin Steel Corp. Before he finally clinched the deal, his home life got so hectic that his wife packed up and went home to her mother for seven weeks.

A Honeywell salesman in Denver, Don Sather, was so wrapped up in trying to sell a $250,000 prototype computer system to Mountain States Telephone that he barely found time to slip away when his wife gave birth at 1:08 a.m. last August 15. "I stayed through labor and delivery, and then went back to the office," he says. He made the sale.

Kim Kelley thrives on such high-stakes action and always has, according to his mother in Davenport, Iowa, Mrs. Dorothy Rynott. He was aggressive even as a paper boy; he pulled in $150 in Christmas tips one year. After a year at the University of Iowa he spent a year in California cooking pizza, selling shoes and hustling at pool. He returned to Iowa, married his high school sweetheart in 1965 and prepared to follow

the career of his late father, who had been a tire salesman. For four years he wandered from one retail sales job to another. Finally, in 1969, he landed at a Honeywell sales office in Peoria, Ill.

VISITING THE LEGION HALL

He was sent to Springfield in 1970 and told to keep four or five big sales simmering but to put only one at a time "on the front burner." Kim wasted little time picking his target, the state government, the biggest potential customer in his region. His long-range strategy was to devote at least half his time to pursuing the state, and to use the balance to scratch out small sales elsewhere to meet his annual quota of $500,000 worth of new equipment.

For three years, he patiently made daily rounds of key state offices, pausing a few minutes in each one to drop off technical documents or just to chat. He pursed the bureaucrats further at after-hours hangouts like the American Legion hall.

"People don't buy products, they buy relationships," Kim believes. To that end, he even molded his personal life to suit his customers' preferences. He bought a big Buick and expensive suits, even though he could barely afford them. "People like to deal with a winner," Kim reasons. "They don't buy $8 million products from some guy who's worrying can he pay his rent." On the other hand, he says, it doesn't pay to appear *too* prosperous; for that reason, he quit his country club when he sensed that state employees resented his being able to afford it.

Thanks to a succession of nonstate sales, Kim's income was steadily, if unspectacularly, expanding, from $18,000 in 1970 to $22,000 in 1971 and $25,000 in 1972. The state bought hardly anything. In those three years, Kim made less than $3,000 in commissions on sales to the government.

THREE-MONTH SCRAMBLE

But when the break finally came, Kim was ready. Toward the end of 1972, the Illinois secretary of state asked for bids for a massive new computer system. Five manufacturers responded: Honeywell, Burroughs, Univac division of Sperry Rand, Control Data and International Business Machines.

In the ensuing three-month scramble, Control Data was eliminated because of "high cost," according to Noel Sexton, head of a technical committee assigned by the state to evaluate the bids. IBM was never in strong contention, says Hank Malkus, who was then division administrator in the secretary's office. "IBM doesn't tailor its equipment to a customer's need. They just say, 'Here's our equipment, you make your system fit it,' " Mr. Malkus contends. (An IBM spokesman, asked to comment, says: "IBM feels it offers an extremely broad range of products . . . We strive to combine all these products in each proposal to provide a prospect the best possible solution to his data-processing requirements.")

That made the contest a three-horse race between Honeywell, Burroughs and Univac. "The equipment was close," says Patrick Halperin, executive assistant to the secretary of state. "But the staff felt far more comfortable with Honeywell because they felt Kim had been more thorough in his marketing."

Indeed he was. Kim dealt solely with the committee. "Some of the other vendors put more emphasis on selling to the front office and tried to play on previous friendships," Mr. Sexton recalls.

Kim fed the committee information, not persuasion. "When we asked to see customers," says Mr. Malkus, "Kim just gave us

a list of Honeywell users and said, choose." Univac, on the other hand, annoyed committee members by discouraging them from interviewing users.

Kim flew in Honeywell experts and top marketing officials from Boston, Minneapolis, Phoenix and Chicago to answer technical questions on engineering, financing, installation and service. "He showed the ability of his firm to cooperate," says Mr. Halperin.

"Incredible attention to detail" helped, too, Kim thinks. The committee was asking for new bits of information daily—things like how much air conditioning his equipment would need. Kim answered every question within two days, always hand-delivering replies to each committee member. "That gave me five minutes more selling time with each one," he explains.

A SLOW PLANE RIDE

Kim hates to fly, but he flew the six committee members and their bosses to Atlanta to meet Honeywell users, to Phoenix twice to see performance tests at a Honeywell facility there, and to Houston to interview another user. When he could, he used Honeywell's "slow propeller plane," carefully chosen, Kim says, to allow more selling time in the air. Kim and his secretary arranged everything—hotel and plane reservations, rental cars, meals, meetings, even the committee's spare time.

For the Houston trip Kim even made a dry run by himself beforehand, so he'd know the best flights, how to find the Hertz counter, good restaurants and ways to avoid rush-hour traffic. The committee had picked up a rumor that Tenneco Inc., in Houston, was dissatisfied with its Honeywell computer. Kim knew the rumor to be false, but wanted to let Tenneco itself tell that to the committee. He persuaded Tenneco to give the committee a bargain rate at a hotel it owns, and while scouting Houston, he learned that two companies there were having trouble with a competitor's equipment. He dropped hints about them to Pat Halperin, who took the bait and spent his time in Houston talking with a disgruntled customer of another vendor. "I left nothing to chance," Kim says. "Detail is what sells computers."

Kim's hot pursuit of the sale meanwhile, was taking a toll on his family. Sandy Kelley says the "tension" was dreadful. Kim "snapped" at their three-year-old daughter, Brook, and had only a few hours on Sundays to spend with her. "Every morning she asked if Daddy would be home tonight," Sandy says.

"I'd keep lists of things I wanted to talk to Kim about," Sandy says. She resented having to manage the family alone, even the new house they were building. "When Kim walked into the new house for the first time, he was like a stranger." Had this happened earlier in their marriage, she says, "it might have reached the point of breaking up." As it was, what she did most was worry. "I'd wake up in the middle of the night and wonder what I'd do if Kim didn't get the order. I knew he'd be crushed, and I didn't know how it would affect our lives."

A GRIN, A HUG AND TEARS

Kim was worried sick himself. When Hank Malkus gruffly ordered him down to the state capitol last June, Kim knew it was "decision day," but he didn't know who had won. He paused only long enough to vomit into a wastebasket before hurrying to Mr. Malkus's office. Minutes later, Mr. Malkus was grinning, his secretary was hugging Kim, and Kim was crying.

By now, Kim has recovered his poise and made his peace with Sandy and Brook. He's busy supervising installation of the equipment, a chore that will take him until next September to complete. How well he handles this job and how smoothly the equipment performs later are important in keeping his new customer happy and in paving the way for future sales to the state.

And Kim is also stalking other big game. He put the finishing touches on a campaign with A. E. Staley Manufacturing Co. in December and expects to close the $1.8 million deal in February. It was a relatively easy sale to a long-time Honeywell customer that Kim had worked diligently to provide with special service. Now the Illinois Department of Revenue is "going on the front burner," Kim says. His goal: an $8 million to $10 million sale of dual computers sometime in 1974.

Meanwhile, Kim is still a bit astonished when he thinks back on what he endured to make his first big sale and when he looks at his current bank balance. He got 40 percent of his commission, or about $32,000, when he signed the contract in August. He'll get the rest when it's all installed next September.

Kim traded in his 1972 Chrysler (which he bought after driving the Buick awhile) for a new $9,250 Lincoln Continental (paying the $5,430 balance in cash), turned Sandy's old Ford in for a $2,200 used Volkswagen and paid cash for a $2,000 dining-room set. But the Kelleys have no plans to continue their spending spree.

"A year from now our lives will be the same, except that I'll have $60,000 more in cash," Kim says.

And he likes that just fine. In fact, when Honeywell recently rewarded Kim by promoting him to sales manager, he requested "demotion" in order to avoid going on straight salary. Honeywell refused but did allow Kim a special status where he runs an 18-person sales office but stays on commission. His salary is $12,600 a year; he expects more than three times that much in commissions next year. Kim says he expects to move high in management eventually, but right now, "I can't afford the pay cut."

32

HOW TO WRITE AN AD FOR THE YELLOW PAGES

1. **ILLUSTRATION**
Make sure your picture carries out or reinforces your promise. It's worth 1000 words. Note how things like the rolling pin give that "just baked" feeling.

2. **SUPPORT STATEMENT**
Authenticity is assured when you state the research source for your claims.

3. **PHONE NUMBER**
Make it stand out. That's the main reason you're here.

4. **SPECIAL SERVICES, BRANDS AVAILABLE**
If you do something other people in your line of business don't do, be sure to say it. If the brand names or lines you carry are important to the consumer, mention them.

5. **SLOGAN**

BAKERY GOODS SO FRESH THEY'LL BRING YOU BACK TO MOTHER'S.

No matter what time of day you buy bakery goods from us, they're always fresh from Your Mother's Oven.

We get up at four in the morning like other

bakers. But instead of baking all our goods at once, we bake a few at a time. All day long.

It's this attitude toward freshness that's helped us earn our four-star rating from the American Institute of Bakers.* The same attitude that keeps bringing you back to Your Mother's Oven.

*A.I.B. rates member bakers each year. Four stars is the highest rating given.

YOUR MOTHER'S OVEN
CUSTOM CAKES DELIVERED THROUGHOUT THE CITY

59 West St.   914-4952
Open 8am-6pm Except Sunday

BAKED FRESH ALL DAY LONG.

This doesn't always have to be a clever line. Better to have a message you want people to remember and to associate with your business.

(6) CREDIT CARDS ACCEPTED
Cash is a disappearing commodity. Make sure people know which credit cards you accept. A picture is the quickest way.

(7) HOURS OF BUSINESS
Shoppers are looking for this information. It may mean the difference between a sale or a customer who goes elsewhere.

(8) NAME-LOGO-ADDRESS
Tell shoppers who you are and where you are. If a diagram, picture or landmark helps locate you, use it.

(9) BODY COPY
Yes, people do read body copy. This is where you must convince the reader. If you have research facts supporting a claim, include them.

(10) HEADLINE
This is the most-read part of any ad. Make a promise you can keep. And make it an important benefit for the consumer.

The Yellow Pages is more than just a book of phone numbers.

It's an opportunity to present your strongest message at the time consumers are ready to make a purchase.

Never underestimate the pulling power of your Yellow Pages ad.

It's the most readily available and reliable source of information for newcomers moving into your town.

Overall, the Yellow Pages reaches more people than any daily paper, radio show or television program.

Three out of four people turn to the Yellow Pages for shopping information. They use it an average of 40 times per year — nearly once a week.

Eighty-nine percent of these references are followed by action. Either a visit, phone call or letter.

Most importantly, your ad runs every day of the year. That way you are certain to reach people when they are interested in and ready to purchase the type of product or service you offer.

Just try to think of another advertising medium that can work this hard for you. Even if you're already using another medium, think how valuable a good Yellow Pages ad can be in tying your other advertising together at that crucial step just before the consumer makes a purchase decision.

That's why it's so important for you to have a strong, effective ad.

Make your Yellow Pages ad big. Make it bold. Make it stand out. And consider running it under more than one business or product classification if you have more than one important product or service to sell. Or if more than one category applies to your type of business.

Do all this and you won't have to worry about going down in people's minds as just a number.

The Advertising Medium Where You Can Afford To Stand Out Every Day.

 Southwestern Bell

33
A WHIZ OF A QUIZ FOR ATLAS COPCO

by Don Korn

Most marketers who use direct mail consider a 5% return on any one mailing to be an excellent response. That's why Bernard Burke has to point out that it's not a typographical error: he really got a *50% return* on a mailing he did last year. What's more, that particular piece was not one that you could simply sign and return, but a quiz that required respondents' time and thought.

Burke is director of marketing services, Atlas Copco, Wayne, N.J., the U.S. arm of Sweden's Atlas Copco AB, a leading manufacturer of construction and industrial machinery. "We're still fairly new in this country," says Burke. "As recently as two years ago, our market share in air compressors was minute. We compete with such companies as Ingersoll-Rand, Joy Manufacturing, and Gardner-Denver, and we are struggling to gain visibility. At the end of 1976, we were preparing to introduce a lightweight, quiet compressor that has genuine product advantages, so we decided to use sales promotion to increase recognition."

Burke, who is responsible for both advertising and sales promotion, did market research on the construction industry, concentrating on Atlas Copco's West Coast and Midwest regions. He came up with some 2,000 contractors who were prime prospects

Reprinted by permission from Sales & Marketing Management magazine. Copyright 1978.

for the new compressor. "We found out that these contractors tended to be golfers," Burke said, "so we asked our ad agency, Poppe Tyson, New York City, to prepare a quiz, which it did with the help of several local club pros."

The result was a four-page direct mail piece in full color. Two pages showed a golfer teeing off next to an XAS-160 compressor, with the headline "Think like a pro," and some copy describing the machine. The other two pages showed layouts of nine golf holes, with situations. For example:

> *Hole 7.2 Down.* Pro sliced his iron shot on a par 3. His ball is resting on a hard surface level with the green about 10 yd. off the green. The green is soft and wet. Did he (A) putt, (B) chip on with a 4-iron, (C) play a sand wedge?

The mailer included a scorecard on which respondents could circle A, B, or C for each hole. The scorecard was perforated, converting to a postage-paid reply card. "We sent it out to those 2,000 target contractors and received more than 1,000 answers," says Burke.

The mailing piece was also run as an insert in regional construction magazines, pulling another several hundred entries. Everyone who entered received a cardboard tube that contained three golf balls stamped "Atlas Copco"; an answer sheet with a reply card attached, to be used for requesting more product information; and a reprint of a four-color, "Think like a pro" ad that appeared concurrently in national construction magazines. Atlas Copco salespeople gave winners of the contest graphite drivers and other golf equipment. (The answer to Hole 7, incidentally, is [B]).

Besides the industrial advertising, the golf theme was augmented by two one-day golf outings, held at country clubs near Los Angeles and Chicago. District managers and regional managers selected contractors to be invited; the company's local distributors were also there. "We provided lunch, golf, cocktails, dinner, and prizes for all," says Burke. "It was a great way to build distributor and customer relations." Reinforcing the "Think like a pro" theme were notepads, bumper stickers, and do-not-disturb signs, all intended to remind recipients of Copco.

Burke notes that although the sales force helped to make up the invitation list and then followed through with its customers, the entire program, including the golf outings, came from the advertising and sales promotion budget. About 15%-20% of his entire 1977 budget went toward this campaign, and he says that it was well worth it: "Our market penetration has increased sharply, with the West Coast and Midwest leading the way. And we've added many top-quality distributors, which was another of our goals."

To follow up, Atlas Copco is using a sports quiz direct mail piece, which touts the entire line of XAS compressors as having "Pro-power." Questions on this mailer, sent to 10,000 contractors nationwide, range from the college team that gained the most yards in a Rose Bowl to the longest odds ever quoted on a legitimate horse race. Once again, there is a perforated answer sheet that converts into a reply card.

This year's industrial Pro-power ads are two-page spreads, and Burke has added a co-op program, with ad slicks supplied to distributors for their own use. Only one golf outing is scheduled this year, but he hopes eventually to expand to four or five per year. Golf, he has found, is a sales promotion vehicle that suits Atlas Copco to a tee.

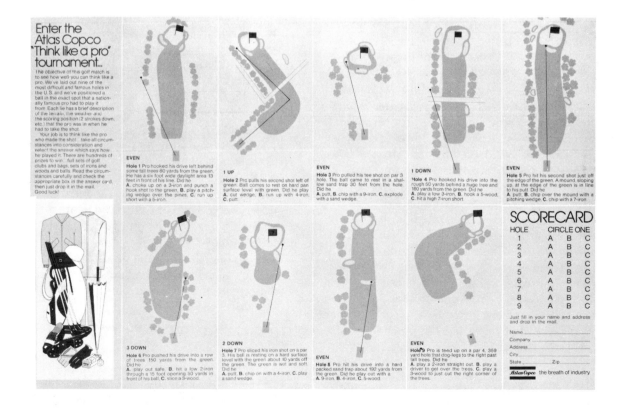

34

UNSUNG HEROES: DIRECT RESPONSE WRITERS PERFORM MINOR MIRACLES

by Bob Stone,
Advertising Age

"Marketing know-how is the key." Sixty percent of total response is due to media selection." "The proposition is what counts."

Statements like these could give direct response writers inferiority complexes. The fact of the matter is, the direct response writer is the unsung hero of direct marketing.

For the most part, media selection and marketing are mechanical; writing is *creative*. Every direct marketing program which succeeds is evidence that direct response writers have performed minor miracles. Day after day they literally breathe life into raw substance.

Every assignment handed to a direct response writer is presented with the dictum: *Perform a miracle*. Here's the product, the proposition, the market. Prepare a mailing package, an ad, a commercial which will command readership, be absorbed and produce positive action. And don't forget—we're going to count the responses to see whether you succeeded or failed. And when you're

From Bob Stone, "Unsung Heroes: Direct Response Writers Perform Minor Miracles," Advertising Age, September 1, 1975.

finished with this assignment we've got another and another and another. Talk about pressure—direct response writers have got to have ice in their veins!

DIRECT RESPONSE WRITERS UNITED

Truly professional direct response writers are members of an elite group, a group which could rightfully claim the status of America's most select club—the U.S. Senate. No one—not even the government—could compute the hundreds of millions of dollars of goods and services moved through the miraculous creativity of this elite group.

Direct response writers in New York have formed their own club—The Direct Marketing Writers Guild Inc. Let me quote from the thinking of one of the professional members of the guild, Gene Schwartz. In an article titled "I Listen With My Ears," he states, "The first step: The essential step in turning an item into an ad, is turning yourself into a listener. You listen two ways: First with your ears, and then with your eyes. You hear everything you can about the product, and then you read everything you can about the product.

"The thing that astounds me when I read most ads, or work with most writers, is that they really haven't bothered to listen deeply enough. This is most obvious in book copy, where you can check the ad against the text. But it also stands out quite clearly in product advertising, where you can check the ad against the way the product works for you. Lazy ears produce bad ads. Here's what I've discovered about sharpening mine:

HOW A PRO WRITES TOP COPY

"1. Sit down with the owner of the product— the man who's hiring you—and pump hell out of him. Put on a tape recorder and have him talk for three or four hours.

"Ask him where the product comes from, what it does, what are its problems and how he's tried to cure them, why it's better than its competitors, who likes it, who doesn't like it, what proof he's got that it works, what strange uses people have got out of it, what funny stories he has accumulated in regard to its manufacture or use, what problems he was trying to solve when he created it, how he would improve it if he had unlimited money, what causes most of his refunds, who works for him to help him make it, how it is made, how he keeps up the quality, who writes him what about it, etc.

"2. Talk to his customers. Do it in person, or on paper. See if they agree with him. If they don't, find out why.

"3. Listen to his competitors. They often tell you more about the opportunities they're missing in their ads than the opportunities they're seeing and therefore seizing. Let them write a possible head or two for you —out of the body copy of their ads.

"4. Then put all the material down, in one big pile, and underline it. Start blending it together, like you'd made a cake. Give first priority to your head and subheads, then the body claims. And then type it up, preferably adding little of yourself except as selector and condenser."

As evidence of the power of his listening technique, Gene Schwartz cites two tremendously successful headlines. He heard Joe Cossman speak his most successful fishing lure head: "Swims Under its Own Power," and he was smart enough to use it. A gentleman by the name of Harry Lorayne blurted out to Schwartz his longest-lived book head: "Give Me 15 Minutes and I'll Give You a Push-Button Memory."

Is it any wonder that Mr. Schwartz consistently produces minor miracles? He listens intently, he digs, he probes, he

assimilates. Then, and only then, does he unleash his creative writing talent.

Direct response writing pros use a variety of techniques for approaching the moment of truth. But they all have one thing in common: They dig, dig, dig. The hack, on the other hand, just sits down to write. Miracle performances don't happen by accident—they're created.

GREAT WRITERS ARE SELF-EFFACING

Perhaps one reason why great writers seldom receive the recognition they should is that most are self-effacing. Two great direct response writers of this ilk who immediately come to mind are John Daples and Tom Collins. Such writers see themselves as catalysts between product and prospect.

The attitude of the successful writer is one of self-effacement. John D. Yeck of Yeck Bros. Group, Dayton, O.—a distinguished direct response writer—has this to say to young writers: "The most important thing to learn in communications is *I don't matter.* You must say to yourself, 'What I think I'm writing or saying doesn't matter. Only the other person counts; what he understands my words to mean is what matters. I don't.' Only the real pros can assume an attitude like that.

There is no substitute for a professional direct response writer. The immortal Maxwell Sackheim, whose mail order ads have helped fulfill the dreams, hopes, wants and desires of millions of people, makes this plea for professionalism in his book, "My First Sixty Years in Advertising" (Prentice-Hall, Englewood Cliffs, N.J.).

"To stoop to the use of second-rate copy and to buy cheap design to fill expensively paid for space will ultimately show in de-

"Will you help me
find 975 Gentlemen
who are seeking
a Custom Cigar Maker?"

Dear Sir:

My name is Tom Timmins. I'm a custom-cigar maker, have been for 51 years and I'm looking for 975 gentlemen who will settle for nothing less than fine, custom-made cigars.

For each of these 975 men I have a thrill in store, a thrill that will take them back to happier smoking days, days when the fantastically mild and flavorable Cuban leaf could be savored, enjoyed, and lingered over.

You may be one of the men I am seeking. Or you may be able to lead me to a friend of yours who is seeking a custom-made cigar. When you bring the two together--custom-cigar maker and custom-cigar smoker--you bring about as happy a friendship as one can possibly imagine.

If you do like fine cigars and if you recall with mouth-watering nostalgia the pre-Castro tobacco, then you'll be interested in a true story that has all the elements of a cloak-and-dagger novel ... and beats James Bond 007 right off the map!

The incredible story begins in 1963 when the Castro embargo hit the cigar industry like an atomic bomb, wiping out our supply of this choice tobacco. Not a pound of Cuban tobacco has arrived in this country since.

The embargo meant little to the giant producers of cigarettes and cigars. They merely switched their source of supply. But the story was different for custom-cigar makers. Lesser quality would mean ruin. And here is where the cloak-and-dagger thriller comes in.

A daring group of expatriate Cubans, unsympathetic to Castro and the Communists, banded together and made a pact that would cost them their lives if discovered.

One dark night, under the cover of a storm, they put to sea in a small boat and ran the bristling gauntlet of Castro's gunboats. Their small craft, tossed and driven by giant waves, carried a precious cargo--tobacco seeds bound for Tegucigalpa, Honduras.

In Tegucigalpa, an area with soil, water, temperature, humidity and other climate conditions similar to those of their homeland, these modern-day pilgrims planted those seeds. They taught the Honduran farm owners and farm hands how to till the soil properly, how to irrigate, fertilize and cultivate the crop. They showed them how to hang acres of cheesecloth canopy over "shade" tobacco, and built huge barnlike curing sheds.

Their first harvest was mostly seed crop; but they did cure a limited amount of leaf (it takes up to two full years!). Thus, after three years, they were able to test it. The results: Caramba -- Magnifico!

The supply is still very small--but it has increased enough to put some on the market. It is our good fortune, because our clientele is select, to be able to satisfy the wishes of our good customers and gradually increase our list.

That's why we are coming to you at this time to see if you would like to sample the pleasure of this fine tobacco. Or, if you are not interested at this time-- perhaps you can recommend a friend. Either way, we would appreciate hearing from you.

Will you do us this favor, please?

A special card is enclosed. Please punch out the perforated "cigar box." If you would like to try the Thompson Variety Cabinet of 60 cigars--made from fine mild tobaccos--put the "cigar box" in the YES slot. This will be your request for us to mail the Variety Cabinet to you POSTPAID AND AT ABSOLUTELY NO OBLIGATION TO BUY.

On the other hand--if you wish to pass up this offer at this time, we will appreciate it if you will put the "cigar box" in the NO slot and return, thus releasing the Variety Cabinet to someone else.

On the chance that you will put the "cigar box" in the YES slot, I would like to further explain our NO RISK OFFER. It means just that. We'll ship the Thompson Variety Cabinet of 60 fine, fresh cigars to you POSTPAID. Smoke one, or a half dozen, or a dozen with my compliments. If these cigars aren't all you expect and a great deal more--return the remainder by parcel post--I'll pay the postage and you'll owe nothing. And if you are delighted--the complete cost is only $8.90.

So, I will certainly appreciate it if you will return the YES or NO card in the postage-free envelope today. It has been nice chatting with you--if only by mail.

Sincerely,

Tom Timmins

Tom Timmins

P.S. If you will return the YES or NO card in the postage-free envelope today, I'll sure appreciate it.

Thompson & Company, 200 NORTH EDISON, TAMPA, FLORIDA

(Prime example of creative direct response copy above proves Max Sackheim's assertion that "Good copy is the poetry of advertising.")

creased profits, leaving in the minds of the readers a question as to the quality of your goods."

Max Sackheim gives direct response writers their proper due when he says, "Good copy is the poetry of advertising. It is taking a plain fact and making it plainer and more impressive by the art of language. It is a song which lures and educates and prompts to action."

35
MAKING THE MOST OF MARKET RESEARCH

Agri Marketing

There they were. A feed company going into the 1974 marketing program and caught with their recognition down. Down bad— 14.2 percent below average recognition score among feeders.

Now here they are. Going into the second half of 1975 full force after coming out of last year with about 15 percent increase in sales tonnage . . . and coming out of the first quarter of this year with an even better record.

All this taking place while cattle on feed in their area were down somewhere around 33 percent and hogs on feed at the minus-30 percent level.

And while the nation as an average was reporting overall feed tonnage down 1 percent during 1974 and complete feeds down 4 percent and supplements down 20 percent during this year's first three months.

As their radio spots so aptly put it, "Golden Sun is rising."

Through careful marketing research and a philosophy of "advertising must be dictated by the marketplace," Golden Sun Feeds, Inc., of Estherville, IA is shedding light on a lot of things these days.

They've just acquired the inventory

From "Making the Most of Market Research," Agri Marketing, *September, 1975.*

and property related to Rath Packing Company's animal and poultry feed business and with that expect to add about 100 dealers to their already growing force of some 365-plus dealers in Minnesota, South Dakota, Iowa, Nebraska, Wisconsin and Illinois. Golden Sun Feeds is a subsidiary of John Morrell and Company.

They've just moved into a $1.8 million corporate headquarters and feed manufacturing facility in Estherville that looks more like a missle launching site than a feed mill. And is certainly a far cry from conducting business in offices above a warehouse like they've done for 50 years.

They've equipped themselves with four modern manufacturing plants (prior to a fifth in Maquoketa, IA, with the Rath acquisition) in the Midwest—none over 10 years of age: Estherville; Sioux Falls, SD; Grinnell, IA; Fremont, NE.

They've taken home a first place trophy for farm publication campaigns at the National Addy Awards presentation during their first year in print advertising.

And they've obviously gotten rid of that minus customer awareness nemesis. How all this came about and continues to come about is the Golden Sun soap opera you're going to read here. How a little company with a lot of guts huffed and puffed and is now giving some bigger companies sleepless nights.

Except this soap opera is virtually suds-less. Golden Sun has known where they were going and how they were going to get there all along. Mainly through good solid market research.

"Share of market only comes after share of mind," according to Harry Hauber, the company's vice president-sales. So, back in July of 1973 Golden Sun decided to go outside for some assistance in their marketing programs. It was all a part of a master plan to increase sales volume, enlarge the market thru both added dealers and areas, and to do something about

that minus customer and dealer recognition factor.

That's where the outside agency comes in. The Jaqua Company of Grand Rapids, Michigan, came aboard during July of 1973. Golden Sun's first agency ever. Their job: spread the word and increase awareness.

Up to that time, Jaqua research was soon to find out, dealers felt advertising could be more effective in different areas of media. Dealers were concerned that Golden Sun products were not known well to new customer prospects.

And more in-depth research showed that feeders in the market area were buying for three reasons.

1. Because they trust the dealer.
2. Because the dealer offers services they need.
3. Because the dealer has a good product.

Farmers interviewed by Jaqua rated most competition as good quality and indicated little brand loyalty for a particular manufacturer. In a majority of cases so much so that the feeder indicated he'd not change dealers if the dealer changed brands.

Farmers were eager for some helpful selling, not just order-taking.

The people from Jaqua talked to dealers and sales people, too. All with the clients' permission and all as a part of research that John McGavin, Jaqua account executive for Golden Sun, likes to call a "situation audit." Put another way, a realistic appraisal of a marketplace. And hopefully from an objective source, devoid of internal company politics.

Questionnaires, telephone calls, personal visits. To feeders, GS dealers, competitive dealers and Golden Sun salesmen and regional managers.

But the survey didn't even get past the

threshold until Jaqua people had actually visited the field, ridden with GS salesmen before putting together the questions that would later make up the market survey. Questions that only come from someone who knows what he's asking about.

Golden Sun ranked better with dealers than with feeders in name recognition. But still behind five or six other feed companies in the market area.

Research done and bound into volumes, Golden Sun marketing personnel in consultation with the agency people now had to put together a creative platform that would work.

They call it a creative platform because:

—It's carefully constructed to gain the most mileage from the inroads previous Golden Sun advertising had accomplished.

—It's built on research, not ivory-towered by some agency account man or dictated from the company president.

—It's a foundation on which to build new strengths in order to improve communications at all levels. And to build on in the future when more time and money is available.

—It identifies Golden Sun in a memorable and meaningful way in the minds of the feeder.

—Most importantly, it's a creative platform designed to talk "with"—not "at"—the feeder.

—It employs the association of "sunshine" with Golden Sun Feeds, Inc., as an intended design element. The logo had come off well in research and a good dealer sign program was consistent and being used already.

—It offers maximum return on an advertising/promotion dollar investment and holds itself accountable for future measurement.

John McGavin is a strong proponent of actually measuring advertising effectiveness. He says with the initial benchmark set by early market research a follow-up survey, which is now in progress, can measure gains (or losses) in realistic terms.

Other criteria, too, were set for the campaign: memorability, flexibility, credibility and longevity.

GS wanted to build a name that matched what was being accomplished. Because Golden Sun was already doing a lot of things right.

Good dealer training and recruitment. A premium program that employs short-term (60-day) promotions. A feed facts booklet that has questionnaires over each section that new dealers complete and submit.

Territory manager organizational concept that keeps the central office out of the picture. That keeps the regional man on the scene after the fact (the meeting, feeder seminar, open house) to answer questions. Not a here today, gone tomorrow sort of centrally developed plan.

Territory men are brought into the five Golden Sun plants frequently for briefings and nutritional workshops,

A dealer advisory board that actually does something is operating with a dealer from each territory who visits other dealers in his area after each meeting.

Fall promotion events and ham days give still more life to marketing programs.

And a new computerized Feedlot Management Simulation program that's probably the most sophisticated and has the greatest potential yet of any in the industry.

So Golden Sun wasn't a company just struggling along a ton of feed at a time. "We were doing a good job of serving our customers," says Bob

Hammond, GS president. "It's just that we felt we could do a better job telling people what we were doing. New customers and customer growth are the lifeblood of the company."

That brings us back to the creative platform.

"If a campaign is good enough, it can work in all directions," says Jaqua's McGavin.

And Golden Sun's Harlan Kolsrud, company merchandising manager, amplifies. "We developed a campaign that tells farmers we know they have some problems we can't do anything about. But others we can . . . like feed."

And from all that comes, "Put some sunshine in your life." Theme for Golden Sun's promotions.

In essence what their print ads and radio spots say are: "We at Golden Sun are cognizant of you, Mr. Feeder. Golden Sun and its entire dealer organization are going to do our best to help you with your problems. We can't do anything about the weather or the hours you put in. Farming is hard work.

"We can help you by providing you with the feeding program that's right for you. We aren't going to preach to you or tell you why our company is the greatest in the world. We want you to succeed and profit. We want to 'put some sunshine in your life.' It's our sincere effort to help."

Print ads are dark and dreary with four-color rainy day illustrations and only a few words of copy. Photographs were ruled out because of expense and problems in shooting in the rain. Jaqua research shows testimonials don't work—farmers are too proud; they already know what works. So these ads don't sell feed. They say "our dealers have the knowledge to help you . . . go see them." The one bright element in each ad is the sunshine tag line.

Radio spots, thru a cost-share dealer program that tallied up a better than 85 percent dealer response, use a catchy country rock music approach that any one can hum along with after a couple of listenings. And one that fared well in national competition against such competition as Volkswagen.

The program is working. Increases in brand name recognition and awareness are coming in unsolicited. The dealer's role is being enhanced and identified and current customers are being resold while new customer prospects are being attracted.

Now a new campaign is underway just this month with still more emphasis on dealers. Not product-sell advertising, though. Instead, prods to go to a dealer for answers to questions and some directions.

Research conducted after last year's campaign indicates a desire on both dealer and feeder levels to brighten up the promotion, put more life into the message. New radio spots are quick tempo and full of life.

New versions, new treatments. The sun is up all over Golden Sun land.

58 percent of dealers questioned say this year's ads directly helped boost feed sales. Territory men agree. And competitive dealers rate the campaign still higher. But Jaqua and Golden Sun both say that good readership reports on ads isn't enough. Now they have to go back to the same survey audience originally used and see what happens.

They're doing that right now. Golden Sun and The Jaqua Company aren't afraid of the results. If necessary, they'll just start all over again. Because they believe in their market research philosophy.

36

CORPORATE LOGOS ARE HIS GAME, BASS IS HIS NAME

by John Revett

LOS ANGELES—"What I'd like to do next is a country," said Saul Bass. "Just a small country would be fine, you know, and you could do it about the same way as a corporate ID program. Not with some wild-eyed guy rushing up and shouting, *'I love that blue'!*"

The man who has produced some of the world's most recognizable corporate, product and services symbols was in a jovial mood. He had just finished giving Girl Scouts of America a new look and had gotten a standing ovation from franchisees of Der Wienerschnitzel after presenting a new logo for the fast-food chain at a meeting in Las Vegas.

All around him in his office on Sunset Blvd. were the symbols and designs of a career that begain with the "arm," the unusual, sharply angled "Man with the Golden Arm" film logo of the early 1950s, and expanded from there to major company IDs and product packaging. On the floor, a small fleet of model planes bearing Saul Bass designs, including the familiar U-shaped flare of United Airlines and Continental Air-

Reprinted with permission from the January 8, 1979 issue of Advertising Age. *Copyright © 1979 by Crane Communications, Inc. Logos designed by Saul Bass.*

lines' gathering stream of white lines inside a red circle. On the walls were dozens of other Bass designs ranging from AT&T's Bell Telephone bell to Quaker Oats' modernized Quaker man.

Gesturing around the room at the collection, Mr. Bass commented on how some of his designs got where they are ("We told AT&T they had a powerful medium in their thousands of trucks, but that they weren't using it and the trucks looked like Army surplus") and also discussed some of the problems he sees in corporate designs today.

"What's happening is an institutionalization of corporate ID. There's been a tendency to sterilize the whole thing," he said, "with symbols becoming cold, monolithic and symbolically abstract. I find it a tendency that is not sensing corporate requirements very well. Why? Well, I can't think of any corporation that can't use some expression of responsiveness to human needs, and to the society in which it exists."

John Hancock Mutual Life Insurance Co. dropping the famous John Hancock signature (which it later returned to) "was a huge communications error," Mr. Bass said. "Can you imagine? Somebody 'modernized' it. I can't think of anything more upsetting."

He declined to name specific logos or designs in use today that reflect his feelings about "sterile" symbols, but hinted that Quaker may have considered eliminating the Quaker man when the company decided a new logo was needed. Keeping the Quaker man in a new form was "a must," said Mr. Bass.

Saul Bass & Associates is now Saul Bass/Herb Yager & Associates. A former Ogilvy & Mather vp, Mr. Yager has been with Mr. Bass for about four years and is now a partner as well as the "business" end of the company. But at first it was Saul Bass alone, creating logos for movies.

His design for "The Moon is Blue" attracted attention, and then came the "Man

with the Golden Arm" logo. The "arm"

represented "total commitment to the film," Mr. Bass said. "The arm symbol became the ad because it telegraphed the essence of the movie. It was an Otto Preminger movie and it might not have happened if it hadn't been him. He's strong and independent.

"At that time, the idea of a company or a movie consistently identifying itself hadn't really been accepted. Film titles had been inventive earlier, when there were movies that opened with titles written in the sand that would be washed away by waves and flower petal titles that would be blown away. But then things dried up for awhile, and you had eight different campaigns for a movie. I call them 'See, see, see' campaigns. 'See the gorilla break out of his cage.' 'See the barbarian horders.' The idea was that if one campaign didn't work, maybe another would. The 'arm' symbol changed that for films and it carried over into corporate programs."

Alcoa and Celanese were among the first Bass corporate ID programs to focus on one unifying symbol. Later came Bell Telephone and Rockwell International. "When we first talked to AT&T about the Bell program (about 10 years ago), their research showed the old Bell symbol had a 73% recall. That seemed great, but when we thought about it, that should have been 90%. We got it up to about 91% (with the new Bell logo)," Mr. Bass said.

Regarding airline designs, "we've got a handy dandy Bass and Yager theory," said Saul Bass. "It goes this way: One of the major

issues in air travel is the question of fear of flying. It's always there implicitly and a lot of people think about it whether you're the kind of person who 'flies' the plane or the other kind who goes into a kind of cocoon condition.

"One way of dealing with this problem is the look of the plane. The plane is the package and you want the outside to be pizazzy, but you can also use it as a kind of reassurance service. So you come to the question of the stripes. We see them as being reassuring, so you have to refresh that cliche of the stripes and deliver the central message of an airline—that it's high technology. At the same time it has to be simple because you don't want people to think you're fooling around with the outside of the plane and they're thinking, 'why don't you pay attention to the engine?'"

As a result, Bass-designed airlines retain the "cliche" stripes and depend on color

schemes and some stripe variation, as in the Frontier Airline stripes which curve up over the fuselage, for style distinction.

"You won't see us doing planes without stripes," said Mr. Bass, who feels airlines like Braniff that have left them off make the mistake of giving passengers the impression they're "in a floating jelly bean, which is not the kind of plane you would want to get into."

Neither Mr. Bass nor Mr. Yager would comment for the record on whether they will be involved in development of a new logo and airline design for Western and Continental airlines if the Civil Aeronautics Board approves the merger of the two Los Angeles-based carriers. But they made it clear that they view the corporate ID problems involved as difficult ones, beginning with the question of a name. Western Continental is the name submitted to CAB with the merger application.

Mr. Bass did say his work in progress includes logos for two new movies, a Stanley Kubrick film called "The Shining" which is in the works at Warner Bros., and an independent Otto Preminger movie based on Graham Green's novel, "The Human Factor."

According to Mr. Yager, beginning next spring Bass-designed "message" packages will be used for all Girl Scout cookies instead of different designs from different cookie makers. The idea came from Bass de-

GIRL SCOUTS

signs used on packages of cookies made for the Girl Scouts by Burry, Quaker unit, aimed at selling the idea of contemporary Girl Scouting "like a spread in a magazine," said Mr. Yager.

Der Wienerschnitzel's problem seemed a bit simpler. The fast-food chain had a "D/W" logo followed by Der Wienerschnitzel spelled out across the roof. "Relying on words instead of a symbol is a communications error," Mr. Bass said. "The key is the sign, because these people are nose to nose with McDonald's, Burger Chef, Wendy's, and the sign has to kick off an impulse, usually within four seconds, or you're dead." So, in his first venture into fast-food design, Mr. Bass created a bright orange, sausage-like "W" symbol with a shortened "Wienersch-

nitzel," roughly in the shape of a hot dog, underneath.

How's it going to work out? "McDonald's has a nonverbal symbol—the big 'M,' the arches. Well, this is better than McDonald's," Mr. Bass heartily declared.

37
MARKETING TO THE PUBLIC INTEREST

Frank C. Nicholas,
Beech-Nut Foods Corporation

This is the story of a lawyer who became an infant formula marketer, then a baby-food marketer, then an innovator in the public interest as well as the interest of his company. This is the story of why baby food has changed, and how the public found out about it.

INTRODUCTION

In 1972, I was an attorney in tranquil Bucks County, Pennsylvania, involved in the corporate aspects of acquisitions, mergers, and venture capital.

I was looking for investment opportunities for some of my clients and for myself, and I heard that the Baker Laboratories division of Pfizer might be available for purchase.

Baker Laboratories was a producer of high-quality infant formula. Infant formula is a modified milk that is used by mothers in feeding their newly arrived babies when they are unable to or elect not to nurture their babies with breast milk. However, when I communicated with Pfizer, they initially advised me that Baker Laboratories was not for sale. I pursued Pfizer, who finally agreed that Baker Laboratories was for sale.

And somewhat later, Pfizer agreed to sell me Baker Labs at 27% of their initial asking price. We paid $700,000 for Baker. I borrowed $300,000 and Pfizer took back $400,000 in notes. It was slightly leveraged!

POWER OF THE MEDIA

During the period of negotiating with Pfizer for the acquisition of Baker, I became impressed with the viability of the communications media and their incredible ability to instantaneously disseminate information. The information disseminated seems to be absorbed as if by osmosis into the minds of those who see, hear, and read what which is disseminated.

During 1973, for example, I became acutely aware of that which was being published about problems with "added" salt and "added" sugar. The research scientists, the medical doctors, and the nutritionists were publishing information that was instantaneously communicated through all forms of communication media—the fact that "added" salt was bad because it caused problems later on with high blood pressure. If you have high blood pressure, the doctor will tell you to absolutely go on a salt-free diet.

The same research scientists, nutritionists, and medical doctors were telling us that "added" sugar was bad because it caused a life-long fight with obesity and dental problems. You would never believe the number of allergies that are attributed to "added" sugar. Children with circles under their eyes, itchy noses, short attention span, irritability, inability to sleep—watch out! The medical profession tells us that sugar is the culprit. And, of course, sugar has been known to cause heart problems.

And the more vocal consumer groups were asking why? why? why? Why was it necessary to add sugar and salt to foods?

I am not referring to the consumer activists that eat buffalo meat and head cheese and drink goat's milk. I am talking about the well-informed, well-trained consumer activists. And I began to ask myself: If the medical profession tells us that sugar and salt are bad, and the consumer activists want to know why sugar and salt are contained in the foods, then why are the processors of food putting sugar and salt into the food? I couldn't find the answer!

Market research report after market research report confirmed the fact that consumers did not want sugar and salt in their food and particularly not in baby food. The same research reports told us that the consumers did not want artificial colors, artificial flavors, flavor enhancers, or preservatives in their food. Consumer affairs people echoed that which the market research told us. Consumers overwhelmingly wanted to get back to the basics in their foods.

THE NEXT ACQUISITION

During the process of acquiring Baker, I became impressed with the level of confidence that a mother placed in a producer of infant formula. Envision, if you will, the nuance surrounding the decision-making process of a mother when she selects a particular brand of infant formula to feed to her child. Nothing, as you all well know, is quite as precious or is more dependent upon its parents than a baby that is taken from the hospital to its home. A mother places an incredible level of confidence with an infant formula company when she selects a particular brand of infant formula. I became immediately impressed with the fact that it required a substantial amount of effort to create this level of confidence and yet, the mother used formula for such a short period of time. Mothers begin to feed formula at birth and continue for a maximum of approximately eight months. Our surveys show that 79% of mothers will introduce solid foods to their babies by the end of the second month and yet, there is no infant formula company in the baby food business and no baby food company is in the infant formula business. Why not?

The leading producers of infant formula are pharmaceutical companies who have surrounded their products with esoteric names like "Enfamil," "Similac," and "S.M.A." and yet, infant formula is a food that is designed to sustain life and is not designed to correct or impede existing or anticipated medical difficulties. Pharmaceutical companies seem reluctant to distort their medical image by producing and marketing food.

Now, it seemed to me that if you can convince a consumer to use one of your products at one period of time, why not develop or acquire products that the consumer can use in a successive period of time—"link" one phase with the next? Therefore, about one month after my partners and I acquired Baker, I decided that I would look into the matter of acquiring a baby food company.

I communicated with Squibb, who owned Beech-Nut Baby Food. My first communication was in the middle of October. Squibb advised me that Beech-Nut Baby Food was, in fact, for sale and that it was, in fact, being sold to Cavenham of England. I suggested to them that the negotiations might blow up. It was suggested that my statement was improper. I pursued Squibb two weeks each during November and December. The deal with Cavenham was to have been consummated on January 15. On January 17, I read in the *Wall Street Journal* that the deal had blown up. I communicated with Squibb. They didn't even remember my prior eight or ten conversations. But 42 days later, Baker Laboratories acquired Beech-Nut Baby Food, that had a net worth of $28.5 million, for $16 million—with $16 million in borrowed funds. Squibb lost $5 million in

1972 in the baby food business. Few, if any, companies want to absorb a $5 million loss.

LEARNING TO INNOVATE

One thing that impressed me as I was studying the baby food business was that all three companies were manufacturing essentially the same product, with the exception of one whose quality is somewhat less than the other two. All three companies put their product in the identical-shaped jar and used the identical-shaped cap. The difference was in the label.

Oh yes, there were line extensions such as "blueberry buckle" and "pumpkin pie pudding," but nothing had really been done in the way of innovation.

The food industry had become the target of critics who believed that the industry had not been responsive to the medical profession and to mothers and consumers and their changing nutritional and dietary needs. Baby food manufacturers in particular have borne the brunt of this criticism.

I made it a specific act to consistently leave my office and travel about the U.S. talking with the various individuals and consumer groups that were leveling criticism at the food industry and particularly those screeching at the baby food industry. I read medical literature. I talked with mothers-to-be and to mothers who had just given birth to their babies and was astounded at the level of knowledge that these various individuals, groups, and mothers had of nutrition. Mothers, as an example, were talking about their babies' inability to metabolize salt.

I talked with outside research people. I talked with Beech-Nut's internal research and development department.

I remember, very clearly, about four days after Baker acquired Beech-Nut, when I went up to our plant in Canojaharie, New York, and went to the research and development department where there were three men in white coats who faced ten persons, principally women, who were sitting in cubicles tasting baby food. I asked one of the men what was going on. He told me that they were considering the introduction of a new item in the baby food line and that they were securing the reaction of the panel to the baby food. One individual in the cubicle would say "There's something wrong with this; add a little sugar," or "Maybe you should add some salt." Another one would say "This is pretty flat; can't you add something to it?" I asked the R&D department for whom Beech-Nut made baby food? They suggested, by indirection, I was a wise-guy.

It's a reasonable assumption that for over 40 years, the producers of baby food have been making baby food to suit the mother's taste. A mother, as you know, will taste the baby food prior to the time that she gives it to her baby. And, if the baby food tastes great to her she usually is of the impression that it's great for the baby. Wrong! The mother's taste, like yours and mine, has been distorted over the years with sugar and salt and seasoning and spices so that when we taste something we don't really taste the food that we are eating; we taste the things that have been added to mask or change the basic nature of the food. Babies, on the other hand, when they are born, do not have a sense of taste. Babies, when they are born, have that which is called "mouth-feel." They will take food into their mouths, suck on it, and check on the viscosity, the texture, the lumpiness, and the thickness. Babies will accept or reject food on that basis. The babies' taste buds do not begin to develop until they reach five or six months of age.

So, in substance, for over 40 years, I believe that baby food companies have been making baby food to please a mother's distorted taste. The food is consumed by the babies who do not have a sense of taste. Something of an inconsistency.

M.S.G.

Do you know why you and I like Chinese food so much? M.S.G.—Monosodium glutamate! Walk into the kitchen of a Chinese restaurant and you would find that the main ingredient in any "wok" is M.S.G. When M.S.G. hits your taste buds it's like kissing a spark plug with the engine running.

Why haven't any of the producers of baby food removed the sugar and salt from the baby food? Real simple: when the mother tastes the baby food and it is not up to her taste standards, the mother will not, logically, buy that brand of baby food again, but will buy baby food that is consistent with the way she believes baby food should taste.

When I suggested to our research and development department that we should consider the removal of sugar and salt from our baby food, the director of our R&D department, in a fit of pique, advised me that the statement that I had just made was consistent with the belief that he privately held for some time: that I didn't have the slightest idea of the real world of making baby food! And, he was correct. Because when we made apple juice for babies we would take a wide variety of apples from a wide variety of sources with a wide degree of maturation, squeeze these apples, and measure the acidity of the juice. Then someone would shout, "Put eleven bags of sugar in batch 09432."

The truth of the matter was that the producer who took the sugar and salt out of his baby food had taken the first step to put himself out of business. And yet, the research scientist, the nutritionist, and the medical profession, and the consumer activists were shouting, "Stop adding sugar and salt to foods."

INNOVATION IN THE PUBLIC INTEREST

Beech-Nut made the decision that we were going to make baby food for the babies. We removed all the added salt from all our products and all the added sugar from 94 of our products. The only place we add sugar is where the product would be so tart or bitter it would not be possible to eat it, such as in an apricot or a plum.

It was a massive job to change the formulation in 132 of our products. It was just not that easy a task simply to remove sugar and salt. We learned, for example, after six months' inquiry, that the "golden delicious" apple has a relatively consistent level of acidity once the apple has reached its full maturity and size. So at that point in time, the apple juice tastes great without the addition of sugar.

Fruit juice for babies, in addition to having added sugar, was always packed in a tin can. Did you ever drink a can of beer that had made its way to the back end of the refrigerator, and no one knew about it? It doesn't make much difference if it's the sixth beer, but when it's the first, there is a noticeable "tinny" taste.

We decided that we would put the fruit juice in a glass jar and thread the glass jar so that it would accomodate a nipple assembly. All the mother need do is twist off the top and twist on the nipple assembly. Previously, the mother would have to wash the can opener, wash the top of the can, puncture the can, pour the contents into a previously washed bottle, twist on the nipple, throw the can away, and clean up. Now all the mother needs to do is to twist off the top and twist on the nipple assembly. In 1975, we sold 1¼ million cases of fruit juice for babies with added sugar in tin cans. In 1977, we sold 4 million cases of fruit juice for babies with no added sugar in glass.

In February 1975, Beech-Nut began

producing baby food with no added salt and no added sugar. We began changing labels as inconspicuously as possible. Beech-Nut produces peas for babies in June and July; when we make peas, we make enough peas to last us until the next June or July and probably into November or December because we don't know precisely how much we will sell. As a consequence, Beech-Nut, as well as all the producers of baby food, have approximately 18 months of inventory ahead of them in their warehouses, in the warehouses of the stores, and on the shelves of the stores.

In 1973, 1974, 1975, and 1976 Beech-Nut made virtually no expenditures in advertising or promotion. Our leading competitor, I am told, spent less than a million dollars on advertising or promotion. That's not much advertising for a 400 million dollar market. Why? Because the number of babies being born had dropped precipitously—there was an excess of capacity—and because the baby food industry had been in a violent price war.

However, when an industry is at "parade rest"—when an industry has not been innovative—a well-placed bomb will make an amount of noise in geometric proportions. And there is an incredible tendency to use negative industry conditions as an excuse for not innovating. So we probably chose an ideal time for our innovation.

Now—can you imagine how the taste buds of the mother who believes that carrots should be seasoned with a tablespoon of butter, salt and pepper, and possibly M.S.G. react when she tastes Beech-Nut carrots? You are right! The first reaction is WOW—Beech-Nut carrots are really flat!"

Flat it is and flat is the way the International Academy of Preventive Medicine says baby food should taste to the mothers, because in a jar of Beech-Nut carrots there is nothing but carrots with water necessary for preparation. There are no artificial flavors, no artificial colors, no flavor enhancers, no preservatives, no sugar, no salt.

Baby food with no added salt and with no added sugar in most. Marketing to the public interest? Yep! Marketing to the interest of Beech-Nut? You bet! Sales are up 26%.

TELLING THE PUBLIC

I am sure it's patently obvious that to make an appearance on the "Today" show with Tom Brokaw and Betty Furness, one must have something that is of substantial interest to the many millions of viewers. Our public relations agency was able to place me on the "Today" show on January 5, 1977, for a total elapsed time of 13 minutes.

Beech-Nut held a press conference on January 5, 1977, which was attended by over 90 representatives of the media. There were television cameras stretched for about 40 feet. That night Beech-Nut was on all four of the major television networks. John Chancellor featured Beech-Nut on NBC. Beech-Nut's move to take the sugar and salt out and why we took it out was on virtually every local television and radio station in the United States. Beech-Nut's action was on all of the wire services, was in every major newspaper. It had been said that never in the history of the introduction of a new product or an innovation of any product had so much publicity been had.

Beech-Nut implemented a massive public relations program of consumer education, all of which was to the effect that added sugar and salt was bad, and that babies should not be fed foods that tasted great to the mothers.

Our public relations people convinced me that the communications media would, indeed, be interested in talking to and meeting with the chief executive officer of a major company. I went on the road in January and spent three or four days out of every week visiting every major city in the United States. A typical week would find me in Cleveland, where I would be on an average of three television shows and four radio shows and visit the major newspapers. The next day I would be in Columbus and then on to Cincinnati and into Louisville where I went through the same routine. I continued that schedule through December 15 last year. All of which points out that, through the communications media, the public did and does have an intense interest in nutrition.

I was on The Phil Donahue Show and the Gloria Swanson Show. As president of Beech-Nut, I was featured in *Newsweek, People,* the New York *Times, Anny,* and *Broadcasting.* We were in every major and minor newspaper with as much as a full page. The free publicity we received in augmenting our position was just absolutely unbelievable.

And our public relations continue. One of the things that struck me with substantial intensity during 1977 was the coordination it took to appear on a given radio or television show at a specific period of time during the day or evening. The availability for a slot for me on a particular show at a particular time required split-second coordination. I suggested to our public relations people that in the case of radio it might be advisable for us to write to the radio stations, giving them copies of *Newsweek,* the New York *Times, People,* and the various publications so they would have some idea of what we are attempting to do, and tell them that I would be available to talk either by tape or live on their radio show. On the days that I am in the office and in the early morning or late in evening I will appear on eight to ten radio shows a day. It's an incredibly effective method and again points out the fact that there is a substantial interest in nutrition.

I have had a long-standing policy of making myself available to people that write or call to us about a wide variety of subjects. There seems to be a very substantial belief in the minds of people in the United States that the chairman/president/chief executive officer of a company moves about only after dark and never speaks to anyone except in the presence of a lawyer and then only when everyone takes an oath of secrecy. It seems that people just love to have an opportunity to talk to the president of the company. When I call someone who has written a letter to me, I announce myself and usually note there is a long silence and often the retort, "You're kidding," or "I can't believe you're really the president of Beech-Nut."

Beech-Nut is regarded as the innovator —the leader in introducing new concepts in the baby food industry. Once one takes that position, one must constantly keep ahead of the game. And we are continually taking the necessary steps to effect that objective.

Beech-Nut's activities have been recognized by prominent associations. The International Academy of Preventative Medicine, which consists of medical doctors and dentists, gave Beech-Nut their annual award for nutrition; they believe that we are changing the feeding habits of babies in the United States by introducing them to natural foods, so that when they are exposed to food with sugar and salt they will not like it. Beech-Nut won the coveted "Silver Anvil Award" for the nation's number-one most effective public relations campaign in 1977. The Juvenile Diabetes Foundation will recognize Beech-Nut this month for our contribution to the health of diabetic children. And we continue to listen to the medical profession, to mothers, and to consumer activists.

COMPETITIVE REACTION

Our major competitor's first comment on that which we had done was that it was a marketing "ploy." Two months later they said that salt was an essential ingredient. Two months after that they said "that continued research will guide the use of this essential mineral." Two months after that they said that they would produce "one line with salt and one line without salt." Finally, in October 1977, 32 months after we had begun making baby food without sugar and salt, they announced that Beech-Nut has caused so much confusion that they were going to take the salt out of their baby food. Beech-Nut has been credited with upsetting the status quo in the baby food industry.

Beech-Nut has introduced the "hot line," which is our way of making information about infant nutrition and child development available to the mother when she needs it the most. All the mother need do is pick up the telephone and call toll-free to get an immediate answer to the question that concerns her. We have assembled a notable group of authorities in the pediatric, nutrition, and child development field who recorded their answers to over 50 questions parents ask most frequently about infant nutrition. Beech-Nut's hot line is in operation Monday through Friday from 9 a.m. until 4 p.m. eastern time. A member of our consumer affairs staff will match the mother's question with the answer. If none of our recorded messages is suitable, we make arrangements to get the answers to the caller.

In June 1974, I learned that a producer of infant foods in Germany had captured 90% of the German baby food business with a highly unique, nutritious baby food product. I went to Germany to get more details on the product. There was nothing even remotely close to this product on the U.S. market. Milupa, of Germany, took infant formula, wheat or rice cereal, and fruit that had been reduced by a special process in Switzerland to powder, blended these three ingredients together, cooked them, and then instantized them much like instant coffee. Beech-Nut executed a joint venture with this German company and began to produce this innovative, highly nutritious product, which

we call Beech-Nut Cera-Meal. You have heard people say that fat babies make fat adults and that fat babies are not healthy babies—I believe it is absolutely true. All the mother need do with Beech-Nut's Cera-Meal is add water so she can control the calories.

CONCLUSION

In summary—Beech-Nut sells more units and makes more profit when we market to the public interest. And that's what *all* of us should be doing.

Reprinted with the permission of Frank C. Nicholas from his talk at the American Marketing Association 61st International Conference, Philadelphia, PA, June 1978.

SECTION FOLLOW-UP
PROMOTION . . .

3. Which communicators have positioning statements--comparing "our" brand at least implicitly to others in the industry? What are those statements?

Marketers spend promotional budgets in hopes of gaining greater awareness, interest, desire, and action, we're told. So it seems reasonable to examine in that light each promotion in this set of articles:

1. What is the apparent objective of: Visits by an aluminum salesman? Direct mail from Atlas Copco? The Yellow Pages bakery ad? The Beech-Nut Foods public relations campaign? Will these marketers and the other marketers described here be able to measure whether or not their objectives were achieved? Which objectives offer the easiest measurement chore?

2. What markets are the target of each promotional plan? To whom do the organizational marketers—of aluminum, computers, air compressors and animal feed—aim their messages? What can you tell about these target segments, and the target consumer segments from the other articles, by reading the messages directed to them? What do the communicators think they already know or believe about each product category?

6 GOVERNMENT FINGERS IN THE MARKETING PIE

The brand manager for a nationally marketed fruit-flavored drink tells it this way:

"Suppose I want to change ingredients, or change the label, or change the price, or start advertising on TV, or start shipping by train instead of truck. Suppose I want to do anything—well, before I think about it much, and before I ask my boss, I talk to the company lawyer."

The lawyer and the brand manager both know the extent to which marketing is very much the business of government. If you market lipstick or aspirin, an agency of your government checks on possible health hazards. Do you market cereal? No problem—unless you're so good at it that the competition is bowled over. Do you market to children? The FTC hopes they'll be old enough to take your message with a grain of salt—not sugar.

From every direction, there are government fingers in the marketing pie, counting the cherries and making sure the number is as advertised. And if you market a lemon to an unsuspecting buyer, we have laws covering that problem, too.

38

THE SOGGY CASE AGAINST THE CEREAL INDUSTRY

by Walter Kiechel III

On April 26, 1972, the nation's four largest manufacturers of ready-to-eat cereal found themselves confronted with a novel, even mysterious FTC antitrust suit. Now, after six years, 200 trial days, and 29,000 pages of transcript, the novelty has begun to wear a bit thin, but the mystery lingers on. The government has completed the presentation of its case, and cereal-company lawyers see in it only a muddle of untested economic theory, garbled fact, and contradictory testimony.

Last month, one of the four companies, Quaker Oats, got off through a combination of smart lawyering and government confusion. That leaves the three other giants of the industry—Kellogg, General Mills, and General Foods, each with a market share considerably larger than Quaker's 9 percent —in a proceeding that probably will drag on into 1979.

THE ATTACK ON OLIGOPOLY

What's been on trial in Room 7313 of the FTC's Washington offices is the structure of

an industry. Government lawyers now concede that few, if any, of the manufacturers' actions are per se illegal. No, says the FTC, it's the oligopolistic structure of the cereal industry, the concentration of around 90 percent of the business in the hands of four companies, that ensures "supracompetive" profits, cheats consumers, and renders illegal otherwise innocuous practices.

The government's star witnesses have testified not about collusive deals struck in smoke-filled motel rooms, but rather about industrial-organization theory and whether that theory corresponds to the reality of the cereal industry. At least, that was the original intention. In the course of the trial, it has become apparent that many of the theoretical components of the FTC's case were jerry-built, some of them just for this proceeding. Submitted to cross-examination, witnesses and theories have been demolished and, in some instances, even withdrawn by FTC counsel.

The evidence presented so far on the behavior of the cereal companies shows an industry that is bitterly competitive in every respect but price. Hundreds of thousands of dollars are invested to develop a product that will have unique "mouth feel." New brand after new brand is thrown into the fray, each supported by heavy marketing outlays. Fickle consumers go from Alpha-Bits to Wheaties looking for a taste or texture or color that captures their fancy. Procter & Gamble couldn't come up with such a product—as revealed in the FTC testimony—so it scratched its plans to enter the competition. When we're beating each other's brains out every other way, the cereal companies have said in effect, why compete on price, which consumers say isn't that important?

At the heart of the FTC suit is what some lawyers call the "puzzle." Picture a manufacturing industry dominated by a few large firms. Each of the firms is profitable—

From the April 10, 1978 issue of Fortune. *Reprinted with the permission of* Fortune *magazine.*

in fact, more profitable than the norm in most other industries. One would expect "entry," some new company trying to shoulder its way into the market for those high profits. But no one enters. Are there natural barriers to entry, such as the economies of scale that obtain in steel making? No. Hence the puzzle.

Well, says the FTC in its theory that purports to explain the "puzzle," then there must be artificial barriers erected by the oligopolists to preserve their "supracompetitive" profitability. Protected by these barriers, the companies can settle in for some cozy "noncompetitive" behavior: avoiding price competition and acquiescing to the status quo of existing market shares. They don't need to resort to the "anticompetitive" behavior of a rapacious monolopy seeker— fixing prices, secret rebates—and so they avoid the proscriptions of antitrust law as traditionally construed. But in the end, ac-

cording to the government, the consumer has to pay more for the products of a noncompetitive industry than he or she would under conditions of "perfect" competition.

The legal hook on the end of the theory is Section 5 of the FTC Act, a notoriously open-ended prohibition of "unfair methods of competition." Referring to the suit against the cereal makers, one company staffer involved in the proceeding says, "It is an economic case with a taint of law rather than a legal case going to economics for justification."

To prove its case, the FTC has to establish that the structure of the cereal industry corresponds to what is pictured in the agency's untested theory. Confronted with a recalcitrant fact or two, the government's witness must fit fact to theory, theory to fact, or admit that the two bear no relation. In the presentation of the government's "case-in-chief"—the main body of its argument—FTC

witnesses did all three, blurring whatever theoretical and factual clarity the case may ever have had.

NICHE FOR A NEW MONSTER

The basic problem facing the government was put simply by a cereal-company lawyer: "We had some beautiful facts." All too often, the beautiful facts tended to undercut the government's theory.

On the question of profitability, the FTC decided that accounting rates of return, the stuff annual reports are made of, would not provide a sufficiently accurate yardstick. As a result, the government had a witness develop a sophisticated model to calculate economic rates of return. In fact, it turned

out to be two models, or one model with two differing sets of assumptions.

While both showed Kellogg and General Mills to be quite profitable, the first model had the effrontery to show that General Foods had no excess profits. A change of assumptions brought a change in results. Significantly, both models showed that Quaker had almost never exceeded the multi-industry benchmark of profitability. Under one set of assumptions, the company actually had a negative return on its cereal operations.

A keystone in the government's case was the theory of brand proliferation as a barrier to entry. Assume, as seems reasonable, that the average consumer has only a limited amount of "perceptual space" (a term frequently used in the trial) to devote to the consideration of cereal products. By flooding this space with different brands of cereal, the big companies were supposedly able to take up all available room. With Franken Berry and Count Chocula out there, where's the niche for a new monster at breakfast? Once again, the presence of Quaker in the case proved embarrassing to the theory. In twelve years of rapid introduction of its own new brands, the company had gone from a 2 percent market share to 9 percent, precisely what a potential entrant was not supposed to be able to do. Obligingly, a loophole was discovered: Quaker was already in the industry, so its rise was a special case.

SKIRMISHES OVER SHELF SPACE

A related problem was product differentiation. Why should the addition of a marbit (a bit of marshmallow) justify a new cereal and an ad campaign? The FTC wasn't opposed to "cakes and ale"—the consumer's simple pleasures—but frowned upon ten kinds of cake, some with marbits, some without. The respondents' debunking process here consisted of little more than providing the commission with rudimentary knowledge of cereal marketing. Government witnesses from the cereal industry, many of them not that happy about the cause they had been subpoenaed to serve, were sounded out on the importance to a cereal's success of unique "mouth feel." Where the consumer found this quality lacking, testimony showed, the product tended to live a nasty, brutish, and short life.

In another area—the grocery store— the critical variable for a cereal company is "facings," the number of full-front presentations of its different products that it can get a store to carry. The grocer, on the other hand, thinks in terms of turnover, keeping popular products in stock while minimizing dogs.

From these potentially convergent interests, and Kellogg's belief that it seldom received the space justified by its sales, came the Kellogg shelf-space allocation plan—one that other cereal companies have emulated. With the grocer's cooperation, Kellogg would monitor the traffic in all brands of cereal then propose to the grocer how he might allot his cereal shelf space to maximize turnover.

In shelf-space allocation plans the commission found a sinister mechanism for dictating what the grocer would stock. The assumption was that the big companies would carve up the existing space among themselves, thereby preventing a new entrant from joining their ranks. The only problem was proving it.

At the beginning of trial, government counsel scheduled some thirty-three retailer witnesses to testify to the cereal companies' coercive tactics. By the time the FTC's case was in, only five such witnesses had been presented. Even these did not testify as originally anticipated by the commission. We control the shelf space, said the retailers; while we're happy to accept recommendations, the final decision is ours. One witness told of fistfights between rival salesmen competing for facings.

Quaker Oats had an especially sophisticated shelf-space allocation plan. This, together with other evidence of its singular competitive feistiness, impressed economist Michael Glassman, one of the government's chief witnesses. He was also troubled by the prospective cost to taxpayers of continuing the case against Quaker, particularly since the cost would be way out of line with the insignificant punishment to be meted out. Quaker, after all, was not to be broken up or forced into royalty-free licensing of its trademarked brands, as the others were. In open court Glassman suggested that Quaker should be dismissed from the case. Such cost-benefit analysis persuaded FTC lawyers to concur in the Quaker motion for dismissal that quickly followed.

DISSOLVING THE ENCHANTED CASTLE

Moreover, Quaker had also impressed the judge, and therein may lie the larger significance of the dismissal (which it is unlikely the FTC Commissioners will overturn). If Administrative Law Judge Hinkes is willing to look at the conduct of an individual company apart from the overall industry structure, then perhaps the spell that the FTC is trying to cast—look at the *gestalt* or total picture, not at the participants—may be broken, and the FTC's enchanted castle in the air dissolved.

It's a forbidding edifice, and one that casts a long shadow. If the government ultimately prevails, the consequences will not stop with the dismembering of the big cereal companies. If it becomes the law that an industry dominated by three or four companies must be broken up simply because of its structure, then the door will be open to a radical restructuring of the industrial sector. Not only will Froot Loops and Cheerios be affected, but also, potentially, typewriters and oil, chocolate and chewing gum, automobiles and soap.

39
THE NEW MONOPOLIES

Consumer Reports

Tough times make for tough talk about enforcement of antitrust laws. It's happened in past economic downturns, and it's happening now—for good reason. Economic concentration costs consumers dearly.

According to a complaint by the Federal Trade Commission, for example, consumers pay 15 to 20 percent too much for breakfast cereals because three companies (Kellogg, General Mills, and General Foods) control 82 percent of the market. Other potential cereal producers, it is alleged, are effectively kept out of the cereal market because they can't compete against the enormous advertising campaigns of the big three, which spend 20 percent of gross sales promoting their products.

The direct benefit for consumers in successful antitrust action was illustrated dramatically in a landmark case charging pharmaceutical manufacturers with fixing the price of certain antibiotics, including tetracycline and its derivatives. The wholesale price of these drugs had remained unchanged for 10 years at approximately 32¢ for a 250-mg tablet. That price, it turned out, had been set by an illegal conspiracy among drug companies. After indictments were

From "The New Monopolies," Consumer Reports *(June 1975). Copyright 1975 by Consumers Union of United States, Inc., Mount Vernon, N.Y., 10550. Reprinted by permission of* Consumer Reports, *June 1975.*

handed down by the Federal Trade Commission and the Justice Department, the wholesale price of a tetracycline tablet dropped to about 11¢, a decrease of approximately 66 percent, and millions of dollars in damages have been awarded to those who bought the drug during the period the price was fixed. The Justice Department has promised to prosecute antitrust violators just as vigorously as its prosecutes fraud or civil-rights violations. And Congress late last year voted the first improvement in the antitrust laws since 1955. Criminal antitrust violations are now felonies rather than misdemeanors; violators risk three years in prison and a fine of $100,000 for individuals and up to $1-million for corporations; and procedures for settling civil antitrust cases are open to closer public scrutiny than before.

The Government's prime targets are what's called *behavioral* antitrust infractions. Familiar examples are bid-rigging, overt price-fixing conspiracies, market division by agreement, and profit-pooling. Such schemes tend to recur even in traditionally competitive markets, but they also tend to be short-lived—either because the violations of law are easy to spot and stop, or because they result in artifically high returns that tempt new entrants into the business and thus revive competition.

There's another kind of antitrust problem that's more difficult to get at. It's called *structural*. A structural problem is the anticompetitive effect that comes about natually when a small number of companies account for a substantial portion of an industry's sales—a situation economists call economic concentration.

Structural issues underlie the Justice Department's recent suit against the nation's largest privately held corporation, American Telephone and Telegraph. The charge is monopolization of telecommunications equipment and service. Structural issues are also involved in the Federal Trade

Commission's case against ITT Continental Baking Co., makers of *Wonder Bread,* for alleged attempts to monopolize the wholesale bread industry.

Some economists are saying it might be wise to break up giant corporations that cotrol a disproportionate share of an industry. The Justice Department, for example, wants Western Electric split off from its parent, A.T.&T. General Motors is another frequently mentioned candidate for dismemberment.

This report will examine why economists are concerned about economic concentration, how economic concentration affects consumers, and what might be done about it.

THE EXTENT OF CONCENTRATION

According to Professor Willard Mueller of the University of Wisconsin, the 200 largest manufacturing corporations now control two-thirds of all manufacturing assets. That's a greater share of assets than the thousand largest manufacturing corporations controlled in 1941. Mueller's statistics dramatize the trend toward industrial bigness, but they say nothing about competition within individual markets.

William G. Shepherd of the University of Michigan did examine individual industries. He reported that industries in which four firms or fewer control 50 percent or more of sales account for 64 percent of all manufacturing sales. Shepherd's finding is significant because many economists consider an industry to be a shared monopoly, or oligopoly, when the percentage of sales accounted for by the top four companies exceeds 50 percent. A shared monopoly exists when the dominant companies in a particular industry are so few that they collectively behave as a monopolist would—that is, restrict output in order to charge higher prices than would be possible in a competitive marketplace.

Shepherd concludes, however, that really tight shared monopoly is still confined to a "relatively few major industries." However few, these industries do occupy critical sectors of the economy. The list of consumer-product industries where four firms or fewer control 50 percent or more of sales includes: telephone equipment (Western Electric); cars and trucks (GM, Ford, Chrysler); soaps and detergents (Procter & Gamble, Colgate, Lever); glass (P.P.G. Industries, Libbey-Owens-Ford); and tires (Goodyear, Firestone, Uniroyal). Many other concentrated industries, including computers (IBM), heavy electrical equipment (General Electric, Westinghouse), industrial chemicals (Du-Pont, Union Carbide, Dow, Monsanto), copper (Anaconda, Kennecott, Phelps-Dodge), and others, contribute to high consumer costs indirectly, through high manufacturing costs of consumer products.

OLIGOPOLY VS. COMPETITION

Oligopolies are often the offspring of industrial mergers. The three great merger waves occurred at the turn of the 20th century, from 1925 to 1929, and during the 1960s. Between 1962 and 1968 alone, 110 of the 500 largest industrial firms disappeared in mergers. Between 1948 and 1968, some 1200 manufacturing companies, each with assets of $10-million or more, were merged with other firms.

Once an industry is concentrated, it often stays that way, because potential competitors can't get started. They run up against market factors that economists call entry barriers.

Entry barriers include: large capital outlays that may be required at the outset for operating facilities; and absolute cost advantage that established firms hold because of superior production techniques, managerial talent, or control over special resources or special patents; distribution channels that are tied up because existing companies established exclusive dealerships; and product differentiation—large-scale advertising that already established firms have employed to replace price and quality competition with promotional competition aimed at loyalty to a brand name.

In an ideal competitive market, many seller vie for the consumer's dollar. Consumers, presumed to be knowledgeable about their purchases, choose products that offer the highest quality, the lowest price, or the best combination of quality and price. By thus "voting" with their dollars, consumers determine what is to be produced and at what price. Sellers must constantly compete for the consumer's favor through innovations that raise quality and efficiencies that lower cost and permit price reductions.

But what happens when the "many sellers" of the classical, competitive model in the economy give way to a few larger sellers—that imperfect form of competition called shared monopoly or oligopoly? A study conducted by the Center for Study of Reponsive Law noted: "Because there are few firms [in an oligopolistic industry], the actions of one are noticed by the rest; each realizes that any move on its part—a price increase, for example—will generate a reaction by the other firms. Since the best way to maximize profits is to act as a monopolist would, the oligopolistic firms begin to march to the same corporate drummer. Such joint behavior has been described as 'parallel pricing,' 'conscious parallelism,' and 'price leadership'—or what one former antitrust official has called 'conspiracy through newspaper pronouncements.' The technique is simple: U.S. Steel announces a price increase of 6 percent on many major products; within two days all other firms increase their prices by an identical amount. No formal price-fixing conspiracy has occurred—yet the effect is the same."

Prices in oligopolistic industries, according to various estimates, are 10 to 30 percent higher than they would be if those industries were less concentrated—that is, if sales were divided among more firms. If the oligopolist's prices are high, they are also relatively impervious to the workings of supply and demand. Economist John Blair studied 16 pairs of products, one from a concentrated industry, the other a related product from an industry considered to be more competitive. Blair found that during the two recessions of the 1950s, the wholesale price index of every product produced in a competitive industry fell, responding to slack demand. But the price indices of 13 of the 16 products produced in concentrated industries actually rose, defying the law of supply and demand.

Demand—the consumer voting with his dollars—is supposed to be the invisible hand of the marketplace, determining supply and price. But the oligopolist's ability to control, or administer, price upsets the market mechanism.

Economist Frederic M. Scherer, now head of the Federal Trade Commission's Bureau of Economics, has estimated the loss to the economy because the oligopolist can charge higher than competitive prices. Among the factors included in Scherer's calculations: diversion of resources from more competitive to less competitive sectors of the economy caused by the oligopolist's high prices; inefficiencies due to organizational slack in less competitive industries; wasteful advertising that serves no informational purpose but instills brand-name loyalty to the oligopolist's product; and idle production facilities in uncompetitive industries. Scherer concludes that such economic losses from oligopoly and other breakdowns of competition amount to 6.2 percent of the Gross National Product. Based on the 1974 GNP of $1396.7-billion, that's an oligopoly cost of $87-billion a year.

INFLATION AND INEQUALITY

Senator Philip A. Hart, chairman of the Senate Antitrust and Monopoly Subcommittee, has conducted a 10-year investigation of economic concentration. He contends that because oligopolists can often establish price independent of the forces of supply and demand, they fuel a chronic inflation. Tight money, a traditional remedy for inflation, has little effect on uncompetitive industries because, says Hart, they "simply pass high interest rates on to their customers through price increases. The burden of tight money falls on the shoulders of competitive small business firms and consumers, without the monetary policy accomplishing its goal of checking inflation."

A second traditional remedy for inflation, lowering aggregate demand through higher taxes or reduced Government spending, may, in fact, spur oligopolists to raise their prices, according to Hart. They would do this, says the Senator, "to maintain their revenues—and profit rates—in the face of declining physical output." And they could do this because price competition had been eliminated.

An analysis by economist Gardiner C. Means supports Hart's contention. Means examined economic changes between September 1973 and September 1974, a period of falling demand (a 23 percent increase in unemployment and a 25 percent increase in idle manufacturing capacity) and rising prices (a 20 percent increase in the wholesale price index). Means found that wholesale prices increased less than 5 percent in "competition-dominated industries," including farm, leather, lumber, and textiles. But the rise in "concentration-dominated industries" was 27 percent. Included in that definition were metals, machinery, nonmetallic minerals, rubber, paper, and transportation equipment.

Economic inequality is another cost laid to oligopoly. "Market power [oligopoly] is ordinarily attained and exploited by relatively few members of society (as managers and/or owners), and their enrichment ordinarily involves a relative, and not always small, decrease in purchasing power on the part of those who face higher prices as consumers, possibly lower prices as suppliers, and lower returns as competitors," economist Shepherd wrote.

FLAWED DEFENSE OF OLIGOPOLY

A defense often made for oligopoly is that large corporations insulated from competition can introduce the kind of technological innovations that benefit society. Put another way, the oligopolist can afford to spend heavily on research and development because his profits are secure.

That's a nice theory, but there's no evidence to support it and some to dispute it. One economist, for example, examined research expenditures and concluded that "size adds little to research intensity and may actually detract from it in some industries." Another economist, using patents to estimate inventive output, found that the lower half of the nation's 500 largest corporations was more innovative than the upper half.

Two cases in point:

—The auto industry agreed in the 1950s that no company would develop and introduce an antipollution device until all could. Antipollution devices didn't find their way into cars until the

mid-1960s, long after the necessary technology was available.
—Of the 13 major production inventions in the steel industry between 1940 and 1955, not one was made by the concentrated American steel industry.

A second defense of oligopoly is that large companies can produce goods at lower cost because of "economies of scale"—efficiencies resulting from large production-plant size, multiplant operations, procurement of materials in vast quantity, preferential access to capital, transportation discounts, and other factors related to firm size.

But according to several recent studies, scale economies are exhausted at relatively modest levels of concentration in many industries. F.M. Scherer, for example, in a review of 12 industries, wrote that "in most instances, realizing the principal advantages of multiplant size did not necessitate high concentration at the nationwide level . . . national market seller concentration in most industries appears to be much higher than it needs to be for leading firms to take advantage of all but slight residual scale economies."

Summing up, oligopoly is real, costly, and usually unnecessary for economic efficiency. The country has had antitrust laws since 1890, but they've failed to ensure competition in every corner of the marketplace. Why?

For one thing, the antitrust divisions of the Justice Department and the Federal Trade Commission are underfunded. The money spent by a single corporation, Control Data, to prosecute its *private* antitrust suit against IBM exceeded the Justice Department's entire antitrust budget of $13-million in 1974. Congress increased appropriations for antitrust enforcement slightly this year. A doubling or tripling would be more like what's needed.

A more important reason for the weakness of antitrust enforcement is the weakness of the antitrust laws themselves. Those laws, principally the Sherman Act, have been interpreted by the courts to mean that mere possession of monopoly power is not illegal; there must be a proven *intent* to "monopolize." To show such intent, prosecutors must prove that industrial conspirators took concrete steps to control prices or exclude competitors.

The antitrust laws were aimed against the turn-of-the-century buccaneer who gained monopoly control of an entire industry, often with brazen tactics that were easy to prove in court. The situation is quite different when several firms, not one, collectively hold the power to act as a monopolist would. Oligopolists needn't formally conspire to control prices; they just follow the price leader. And price leadership—the "conspiracy through newspaper pronouncements"—isn't illegal under the antitrust laws. As one antitrust attorney puts it: "Much of what the law forbids today, the modern would-be monopolist doesn't *need* to practice anyway. And what he *does* need in order to ply his trade, the law often allows."

The law, therefore, should be changed. CU urges that Congress amend the Sherman Act so it reaches oligopoly, as well as monopoly, when oligopoly impairs price competition without offering consumer benefits for the resulting higher prices. And the government should no longer have to prove that an oligopolist's intent is evil; the possession of monopoly power, either collectively among oligopolists, or individually as a monoplist, should be an offense when it is detrimental to the nation's economic wellbeing. Senator Hart has reintroduced legislation, called the Industrial Reorganization Act, incorporating this change.

In addition to being outdated, sections of the antitrust law hinder effective enforcement. Senator Hart, along with Senate Republican Leader Hugh Scott, has intro-

duced another bill (S. 1284) to remedy certain of these procedural roadblocks. It would allow the Justice Department to obtain, in advance of a merger, the information necessary to determine whether the merger should be challenged. The bill would also increase the penalty for not obeying special orders or subpoenas of the Federal Trade Commission from $100 a day to a minimum of $1000 a day and a maximum of $5000 a day. And it would permit State Attorneys General to file antitrust actions and collect treble damages on behalf of state citizens. Finally, under the bill, a *nolo contendere* (no contest) plea to an antitrust charge could be used in private, treble-damage suits as evidence that a crime had been committed.

40
A LID ON KID VID?

On one side—the advocates of freedom from regulation, Constitutional protection of commercial speech (advertising), and the educational experience that comes when a child finds out that TV commercials give a less-than-perfect indication of what a product will really be like. On the other side—the advocates of healthy teeth and "good quality programming." The battlefield? Saturday morning television programs and commercials aimed at children.

In their most controversial moments, children's TV commercials have showed gleaming red fire trucks, sirens blaring, chasing off to quench dramatic blazes. "You can be the man in the driver's seat when this truck battles the big fires," enthused an announcer. "Just tell Mom . . . "

Reality, unfortunately, was a 12-inch plastic truck with no siren, that could be pushed along the floor toward imaginary blazes until it was time for the "fireman" to watch another TV program. There he would hear the virtues of another delightful toy, and in the process would be the center of a controversy that has involved the federal government in the issue of commercials directed at children.

Commenting on the issue, Nicholas Johnson, Federal Communications Commission member, stated, "Television is the candy the child molester gives your kids."

On the other hand, Seymour Banks, a vice president of Leo Burnett, Inc., one of the nation's largest advertising agencies, defends advertising to children. He says,

We suggest that the social justification for advertising to children arises from the process of consumer socialization—experience as a purchaser—both in its own right and as a training ground for other types of decision making. A significant test of maturity is the ability to make reasonably good choices and decisions in a wide variety of circumstances. . . . Involved in this long and painful process (but no more so than other maturation processes) is the learning of the proper criteria to use in evaluating products, the value of money spent now for several items versus the purchase of a larger item later, the determination of the standards appropriate to a particular age, class and way of life, and finally the development of character.

The issue of what children see on TV hit the marketing world dramatically when the Federal Trade Commission took off after advertisers in the late seventies. The agency held hearings on its suggestions ranging from health warnings on sweet cereals to an outright ban on all commercials directed at children under eight.

To put it mildly, the hearings brought out differences of opinion.

Said Harry M. Snyder, West Coast director of Consumer's Union: "Where is it written that the new family structure is child, parent, and General Foods?"

Countered radio and TV executives: "The FTC staff is behaving like a national nanny trampling the right to free speech."

Studies presented to the FTC show that the average American child was exposed to more than 20,000 commercials in 1977 as a result of watching an average of 2 or 3 hours of TV a day. That fact had caused broadcasters to cut back the permitted commercial time on shows aimed at children from 16 to 9.5 minutes per hour, but even with that reduction, advertisers were spending $500 million yearly on children's commercials.

A MIDDLE GROUND

Into the controversy, principally involving toys and cereals, came a few new ideas and considerable sentiment for compromise. Some members of Congress threatened to reduce the FTC budget if its stand was not modified. Meanwhile, however, two toy companies agreed to small fines and to the signing of consent orders barring them from misrepresentation of the performance of any toy.

The American Broadcasting Company decided to cut down further the proportion of commercial minutes in an hour of programming and to fill some of the time with messages on health and nutrition. But a more comprehensive proposal came from Kenneth Mason, president of Quaker Oats Company. He advocated government recognition that Saturday morning is a "special public interest time period" on TV, then the granting of special federal permission to major TV networks to work together to produce ten three-hour quality Saturday programs each, to be broadcast simultaneously on the three major networks. Advertisers would "circulate their commercials through the Saturday morning hours on all three networks"—saving money, because they would be seen by every child watching. The savings, by elimination of duplication (or of network competition, depending on how one viewed the matter), could be invested in higher quality programming, Mason suggested. But absolutely nobody took him up on the idea.

The National Association of Broadcasters, for instance, took the stance that nothing special was really needed in material directed to kids, since, they argued:

—Parents exert a stronger influence than television over children.
—Supporters of the restrictions have failed to prove that commercials for sugared foods increase the prevalence of tooth decay in children.
—A ban or limit on children's advertising would "impinge on the First Amendment rights of others" and would set up unconstitutional "prior restraints of commercial speech."
—Reducing or eliminating such ads would lessen the quantity and quality of children's programming.

POWER OF TV

The "kid vid" controversy has reached its present level largely because of the demonstrated effectiveness of television as a persuasive medium to the young. An early success story, for example, was Mattel Toys.

According to Mattel's founders, Elliot and Ruth Handler, TV "made" the company in 1955. After introducing the Burp Gun at the 1955 toy show, they were asked if Mattel would like to sponsor a 15-minute segment of a new TV show produced by Walt Disney. They recalled the decision this way in a news interview:

> There was only one segment left on the show, the Mickey Mouse Club, and Mattel would have to sign for 52 weeks. The cost was $500,000, not a tremendous sum, but it was just about equal to the company's net worth. So Handler signed.
>
> Mattel had been shipping great quantities of Burp Guns to its customers all summer, only to discover they were not selling at the rate the firm was shipping. Cancellations started pouring in.
>
> When the plant closed for the Thanksgiving holidays, the commercials had been on TV for about four weeks. About the only thing Mattel had heard was a deafening silence and Burp Guns were stacked in the warehouse by the thousands.
>
> When the plant opened the follow-

ing Monday, the mailbags were full of orders and the phones were ringing off the wall as retailers canceled the cancellations.

Are food commercials comparably effective? Results of a national poll back up the idea that parents buy what their children ask for, even against their better judgement. But no one can say with certainty whether TV ads or natural preferences—or both—prompt children to ask for sweetened cereals and cakes.

According to the Community Nutrition Institute, which submitted survey results to the FTC, toaster sweets and presweetened cold cereals were correctly identified by most parents as the "worst breakfast foods for a child"—but were most requested by children and frequently purchased. The survey reported that three-fourths of the parents said they bought snack-type and sugared food because their children asked for it. But nobody was saying that without the influence of TV they would have asked for broccoli.

SOURCES

1. "Broadcasters Claim Kids Sharp Advertising Judges." United Press International, carried in the Houston *Chronicle,* November 25, 1978, Sect. 1, p. 14.
2. Coates, Colby, "ABC Reform Is Not Enough, Critics of Children's TV Claim." *Advertising Age,* February 5, 1979, p. 8.
3. "General Mills Offers FTC a Deal on Toy Ads." *Advertising Age,* August 28, 1978, p. 3.
4. Joseph, Nadine, "Protection for Children Urged at Hearings on Television Ads." Associated Press, carried in the Houston *Post,* January 16, 1979, Sect. B, p. 7.
5. "Pool Kids' TV to Boost Quality: Mason." *Marketing News,* December 1, 1978, pp. 1, 8.
6. "Sweets Eat Up Budget, Poll Finds." United Press International, carried in the Houston *Chronicle,* March 6, 1979, Sec. 1, p. 6.
7. Thompson, Tommy, "The Mattel Story Romantic, as American as Apple Pie." Houston *Chronicle,* July 9, 1972, Business section, pp. 13–14.

41

SEES RED OVER FDA BAN

*by Curt Matthews,
St. Louis Post-Dispatch*

The most widely used food coloring in the United States, Red Dye No. 2, was banned by the Food and Drug Administration last week after a five-year struggle by a Ralph Nader research group to eliminate the coloring from food products.

Dr. Alexander M. Schmidt, head of the Food and Drug Administration, announced the ban on "Red No. 2" on Jan. 19 and said, "We have recently learned that our latest study cannot establish the safety of the Red No. 2."

The statement by Schmidt suggested that recent studies conducted at the FDA's National Center for Toxicological Research in Jeffersonville, Ark., raised the possibility that Red Dye No. 2 had potential as a cancer-inducing agent.

Earlier this month the FDA received a study by Dr. David W. Gaylor at the Center for Toxicological Research, which stated that rats fed high dosages of Red Dye No. 2 developed malignant growths.

The findings by Dr. Gaylor paralleled those reported by Russian scientists in 1971. It was the Russian report that originally prompted Nader's Public Citizen's Health

From Curt Matthews, "Sees Red Over FDA Ban on Food Dye," St. Louis Post-Dispatch *(January 27, 1976). Reprinted by permission of the* St. Louis Post-Dispatch.

Research Group to petition the FDA for a ban on the dye four years ago.

However, FDA Commissioner Schmidt suggested in his statement on Jan. 19 that it was only within recent months that his agency became fully aware of the cancer-inducing potential of the dye.

"Events leading to today's announcement began on Nov. 21, 1975," Schmidt said, "when the FDA asked its Toxicology Advisory Committee to undertake a review of all available animal studies."

Anita Johnson, an attorney for the Public Citizen's Health Research Group, said that Schmidt was "at the top of the heap" of persons and special interests groups resisting the ban.

As recently as Dec. 28, Schmidt said that he could not ban the controversial food additive unless he found it to be an imminent threat to public health. Johnson said that Schmidt's position was legally wrong since the dye had been "provisionally" approved in 1960 and never given permanent approval by the FDA as a safe food additive.

Under the Food and Drug Act, any food additive placed on the "provisional" list may be banned by the FDA unless the companies producing and using it can prove that it is harmless to the public.

The FDA reports that 1,377,944 pounds of the additive were used in commercial food products last year. It is by far the most widely used artificial coloring in the food, drug and beverage industries.

It is estimated by the Nader research group that the value of products sold each year containing the dye amounts to more than 15 billion dollars.

Although a number of major food and cosmetic firms have been cutting back the use of Red Dye No. 2 in recent years due to the questionable safety of the product, the total comsumption of the dye has increased dramatically since 1971. Five years ago annual consumption of the dye was about

600,000 pounds, less than half of 1975 consumption.

A major factor in the increased use of the dye has been wide market acceptance of what are commonly known as "convenience foods"—that is foods requiring little or no preparation before being served. Such foods usually require more chemical coloring and preservatives because they are often prepared under more severe conditions of temperature, pressure or agitation.

Six firms produce most of the dye used by the food, cosmetic and beverage industries. One of the largest is Warner-Jenkinson Manufacturing Co. in St. Louis, a subsidiary of the Seven-Up Co. in Clayton.

Jerome Kinnison, color product manager at Warner-Jenkinson, quoted recently regarding the impact of the FDA's ban said that "chaos impossible to describe" would result for some small food companies.

Kinnison reportedly called the FDA action "absurd" and suggested that the agency was ignoring two FDA-sponsored tests showing the dye was safe. He termed "questionable" the test results showing it as a possible cause of cancer.

Although the FDA has banned all future use of the dye in products destined for public consumption, products containing it and still in the marketplace will not be recalled.

A spokesman for FDA said that the decision not to recall products already in the market rested on an assessment of the potential danger of such products. He characterized the FDA ban as "precautionary" saying that it has not as yet been proven carcinogenic—that is, cancer causing.

"Products with the dye are not being recalled because they don't present that much of a danger," the spokesman said.

However, Anita Johnson at the public citizens' research group disagreed: "It will take a year before the market is cleared of all the products containing the dye. If it is dangerous to consume such products a year from now, it is just as dangerous to do it today."

Products generally listed as most heavily dependent on it for coloring are gelatin mixes, soft drinks and ice cream. It is also widely used in cosmetics, particularly lipsticks and face colorings.

The *Wall Street Journal* recently reported that three major diversified food product companies—Nestle Co., Nabisco Inc. and Borden Inc.—were phasing out the dye as a result of the controversy over its possible harm to consumers.

However, another major user of the dye, General Foods Corp., reportedly was continuing its use in a variety of products "with full confidence" about its safety. Among the General Foods products reportedly containing the dye are Jell-O gelatin and pudding, some flavors of Kool-Aid drink and most varieties of Gaines pet food.

Some years ago it was reported that the dye was being used in dog foods to enhance color even though dogs see only in shades of gray.

Substitutes for the dye are available according to industry spokesmen, although for various reasons are not as desirable as the product banned by the FDA.

The substitutes include Red No. 40, which does not give as deep a hue as Red No. 2, and Red No. 3, which isn't soluble in water. Another possible substitute is Red No. 4, which presently is authorized only for maraschino cherries.

According to some reports, a number of major comestic makers—including Revlon, Estee Lauder and Elizabeth Arden, no longer use the dye in the products they manufacture. A spokesman for the Cosmetic, Toiletry and Fragrance Association told the *Washington Post* that the dye is used in only 26 of the more than 17,000 products marketed by members of the association.

Research analysis conducted by Dr. Sidney M. Wolfe for the public citizen's research group shows a series of tests dating back to 1951 which link the coloring to an increase in the incidence of cancer and cancer symptoms in animals. Rats given measured dosages over a two-year period in the early 1950s by two FDA reseachers developed twice as many breast tumors as normal.

Similar tests were conducted in 1955 by the FDA. Of 100 female rats on a normal diet, only five developed breast tumors. However, in a group of 100 female rats fed measured amounts of the dye, 12 developed breast tumors.

Following similar tests on mice in 1957 by the FDA, the researchers—both doctors—concluded, "statistically , the (Red No. 2-fed) mice had significantly more total tumors than did the control (mice)."

Commenting in 1974 on the FDA's delay in banning the additive, Dr. Wolfe and Anita Johnson said, "If 10 billion dollars worth of junk food sales didn't greatly depend on this dye, the FDA might find it easier to perform its public health function."

42
HEADACHES

Wall Street Journal

Among the many blessings you enjoy without even being conscious of them one you might rise up and give thanks for is the fact that Hermann Dreser did his great work before Ralph Nader was born.

Hermann Dreser, in case the name jogs no memory cells, was the man who in the last century discovered the medicinal properties of acetylsalicylic acid. The good fortune in that is both medical and legal.

Medical, because acetysalicylic acid is one of the great wonder drugs in the pharmacopoeia; among other things it will relieve that headache, reduce that fever and diminish those arthritic aches and pains. Legal, because it is still possible to walk into your corner drug store and buy an aspirin tablet without so much as a by-your-leave from the Food and Drug Administration.

The second part of this good fortune is certainly as remarkable as the first. If we had had to wait a century before some scientist stumbled over the aspirin tablet, you can be sure you wouldn't be able to pop one into your mouth without an expensive prescription.

For it is certainly a mysterious drug. Nobody knows how it works or why. In some of its clinical applications no one can even prove by objective laboratory tests that it

works at all. If you take it for a headache and your headache goes away, the researcher has to take your word for it, and even then he doesn't know for sure why it did.

It's also not a drug for everybody. In some people it produces gastric irritation; that is, it gives a tummy ache to replace the headache. In others it produces violent skin rashes, or what the FDA might call anaphylactic phenomena. In other words, its side-effects can be counterproductive.

Too much aspirin, curiously enough, can give you a headache instead of relieving one. Even moderate overdoses can produce dizziness, nausea and vomiting, loss of vision and mental confusion. If you are foolish enough to take a hundred times the normal couple of tablets you could be dead.

From this you could make quite an indictment: Efficacy for some advertised uses not proven. Chemotherapy not understood. Variable effects on individuals with severe side-reactions in some. Overdose possibly fatal.

Grateful we should be, then, that aspirin was discovered generations ago and is protected—for the nonce, anyway—by a sort of grandfather clause. Otherwise the FDA would banish it in a moment.

If you think that an exaggeration, consider the case of hexachlorophene, a chemical antibacterial cleansing agent much used for bathing hospital patients.

It seems that somebody in a laboratory fed some rats with this hexachlorophene and totally immersed some monkeys in it full-strength for a long period of time, and upon later examination traces of it were found in the blood stream. This gives some cause for a warning against drinking it or getting in a tub full of it, but the FDA didn't stop there. On this evidence the FDA, spurred on by Mr. Nader, told hospitals to stop using it even in solution for washing patients, and proposed that the use of it in personal cleansing products be permitted by prescription only.

From Vermont Royster, "Headaches," Wall Street Journal, February 16, 1972. Reprinted with permission of The Wall Street Journal. © 1972 Dow Jones & Company, Inc. All Rights Reserved.

The results of this were quite interesting. Prior to the chemical's introduction as a cleansing agent shortly after World War II staphylcoccal outbreaks were a hospital scourge, especially in maternity wards. With the use of hexachlorophene such outbreaks became rare. When hospitals stopped using it at the urging of the FDA, guess what? Once more the staph scourge.

Fortunately doctors are reasonably intelligent people, so most hospitals have gone back to using the cleansing agent, FDA or no. So much for that.

Unfortunately the mental process here reflected is endemic in the consumer vigilante mind. Witness the flaps, past and present, over DDT, cyclamates, saccharine and something called diethyl pyrocarbonate sometimes used as a preservative in beer, wines and noncarbonated soft drinks.

DDT, you'll remember, incurred a worldwide ban as a pesticide for its alleged dangerous effects. The consequence was a baby-boom among pests, particularly the malarial mosquito, so that in many areas of the world the ban had to be banished. And now comes a report from a federally funded project by the Medical University of South Carolina, which was "unable to find any harmful effects" to humans from DDT. So much for that.

Turn now to cyclamates, a sugar substitute sweetening agent once used in diet soft-drinks, coffee, tea and such. Despite testimony from a deputy assistant secretary of HUD that there was no evidence whatever that it caused cancer in humans, it was banned because intravenous feeding of it to rats in a dosage roughly 400 times any normal dose was followed by some rat tumors.

Then there's saccharin. Unless I missed the latest bulletin, it's not yet on the ban list, but the FDA is investigating it even though it has been around about as long as aspirin with no horror stories among the clinical reports. Were I a suspicious fellow I might suspect some sweetening of the evidence by the sugar industry, especially since the research is being done by the Wisconsin Alumni Research Foundation, which *Barron's* magazine tells me is supported by those sugar people. So much for that.

And now comes word that the FDA is going to crack down on that diethyl pyrocarbonate. It has given the vintners and beverage firms 60 days to present suitable data "to show that the ingredient can continue to be used safely." This, although the FDA announcement says *"there is no evidence that DEPC has caused any harm to humans."* (Italic supplied.)

That last sentence is what gives pause. Everyone would welcome legal bans on food, chemicals or drugs where it's known that they are harmful to the human species in ordinary uses. But something's topsy-turvy when the bans are read on muddled evidence or, in some cases, on no evidence at all, or maybe just because some stupid people might take too much of a good thing.

Anyway, everything is bad for you in excess. Refined sugar used to be classed as a medicine, it's still bad medicine for diabetics, and too much of it isn't good for anybody. Too much water, unmixed with whisky will destroy your sodium balance and lead to edema.

And too much thinking about officious nonsense can produce a headache. Pardon me while I swallow a couple of nonprescription tablets of that mysterious, tricky and possibly fatal acetylsalicyclic acid.

43

SKI RESORTS REVERSE ADVERTISING POLICY, WARN OF DANGERS

by Andrew Schneider,
Associated Press

CONCORD, N.H.—In a dramatic reversal of its advertising, the ski industry is now saying that gliding down the slopes can be hazardous to your health.

The intent of the 180-degree shift in marketing, designed to stress the inherent risks of skiing, is to lessen ski area's responsibility for some accidents. The sweeping change can be seen in almost everything from reports of ski conditions to signs on the slopes.

"We're going to take the fluff out of our marketing and put it on the slopes where it belongs," says David Cleary, special counsel to the 450-member National Ski Area Association. "It may cost millions to change our image but we're going to tell it like it is."

For decades the industry has heralded skiing as a glittering, romantic, safe way to spend a day outdoors.

But as the sport grew so did the number of skiers who wound up under an X-ray machine. "A lot of them started asking the courts 'If this sport is so safe why is my leg broken?' " Cleary says.

As might be expected, the number of law suits generated by skiers increased along with their numbers.

"We had a small but increasing number of suits resulting from accidents at the areas," Cleary says. "But everything changed this year when ski operations from Maine to California had the hell shocked out of them when the Vermont Supreme Court ruled on the Sunday case."

James Sunday, 21, snagged some brush, fell and hit his head on a rock while skiing at Stratton Mountain, Vt., in February 1974. It was his first time on skis. He was paralyzed below the neck.

In June, the Vermont Supreme Court upheld a jury award of $1.5 million to Sunday. That high court judgment was interpreted by the industry to mean that responsibility for injury was shifted from the skier to the ski area.

The Sunday case overturned a 30-year-old court ruling, also from Vermont, which said skiers must accept the responsibility for the dangers that are inherent in the sport.

Officers of many ski areas admit they're apprehensive about the new marketing methods, but no one argued the need for them.

"We've got not choice but to try it," says Tom Richardson, vice president of Colorado's Aspen Ski Corp. "There are ambulance chasers all over the place and if by taking the fluff out of our ads we can protect ourselves from phony suits, then it's worth the effort."

Aspen has spent more than $100,000 for cautionary signs on its slopes. But Richardson questions how much good the signs will do.

"Skiers don't read," he says. "They're so excited and enamored by what they're doing they ignore everything else. But if it

From the Houston Chronicle, *January 17, 1979. Reprinted with the permission of the Associated Press.*

comes to court at least the lawyers will be able to say they were warned."

The Burma Shave syndrome of covering the slopes with signs can also be found in other areas. "We've got more signs than people," says Tim Cyr, manager of Maine's Pleasant Mountain ski area. "We warn them about the potential dangers of everything but breathing."

The suit-motivated changes go far beyond the signs and one of the most obvious is the modification of how ski conditions are reported.

"The days of saying conditions are good or excellent or whatever are gone forever," says Richardson. "We have killed all the adjectives and now are just reporting the facts."

The majority of broadcast ski reports now present only what trails are open, amount of new snow and surface conditions.

And some advisories are followed by some sort of disclaimer. "This report was based on conditions observed at 8:30 a.m. Skier traffic and changing weather conditions throughout the day can alter snow conditions significantly," say reports from Maine's Sugerloaf area.

Another change can be seen in promotional literature. "Last year our brochure said our ski school can teach you how to ski quickly and safely," says Cyr. "Now we just say you can learn quickly."

The danger associated with skiing was a topic rarely mentioned by ski areas. That too has changed. A brochure from the Killington area in Vermont lists and explains dozens of possible dangers.

"Alpine skiing is a sport of concentration, rhythm, motion and control," the Killington report says, warning of possible "severe climates, high winds, poor visibility, rocks, bare spots, ice, crusts, trees, towers, stumps, rain, snow, sleet and strenuous descents and bumps."

Not every ski area has made the switch.

A recent newsletter from the Gunstock area in New Hampshire says skiing "carries about the same risk that confronts a bowler."

Cleary notes that the ski area association can only suggest changes, adding: "Those who want to continue the old methods will have to suffer the consequences."

It's difficult to say how much the changes in advertising will cost but, with the new signs on slopes and reworded brochures, it probably will run into millions.

The ski areas, incidentally, do not think all this will result in fewer people taking to the slopes.

SECTION FOLLOW-UP
GOVERNMENT FINGERS . . .

What inspires each government restriction on marketing? Has some abuse by a well-known firm brought public protest? Does the general philosophy of promoting competition demand some particular law or regulation? Has some firm soughht protection from unrestricted competition and asked some legislative body for help? Or is there another explanation?

For each of the articles in this section, it seems legitimate to ask:

1. Who benefits from the restriction described?
2. Who is hurt?
3. Who promoted the limitation? What circumstances favored, or favor, its passage?
4. What marketing practices in what industries are affected?
5. What other industries might be affected next? Why those specific ones?

7 WHAT ELSE AFFECTS MARKETING?

As big a dent as government makes in the average set of marketing plans, it's by no means the only force to do so. The product changes as it crosses the ocean to a foreign market. The advertising changes as consumer crusaders toss verbal rotten tomatoes at what they consider to be exaggerated claims. The price changes, or stays the same, in response to pressure from the industry as a whole, and it rises emphatically when suppliers say "we've run out."

Meanwhile, clothing styles and lifestyles influence what consumers want to buy. So do the economics of cattle feeding—and the economics of defective products. Furthermore, as zero population growth takes hold, expected customers literally fail to materialize.

Even the organization which pays their salaries shapes the plans of the marketers—or tears them up. Does the organization have the funds to implement a marketing plan? And does that plan call for surpassing last year? If it seems by now that *everything* influences marketing—then we've put our message across.

44

LESSONS FROM THE FIRESTONE FRACAS

by Arthur M. Louis

The success of a corporation nowadays depends not only on how it makes and markets its products, but also on how it is perceived by the public. Members of Congress, government agencies, consumer groups, and the press are all scrutinizing business with an intensity and zeal rarely displayed in the past. Some of the scrutineers are bound to be hostile toward corporations—which makes it all the more important that businessmen exert every effort to demonstrate that their motives and actions meet the highest standards. In that regard, the response of Firestone Tire & Rubber Co. to its current, widely publicized radial-tire crisis may well become a classic, to be pored over by business-school students for many years to come.

Firestone stands accused of selling defective tires—the 500 series of steel-belted radials. According to the federal authorities, these tires are prone to blowouts, tread separations, and other dangerous deformities, and have been the target of thousands of consumer complaints. Records supplied to congressional investigators by Firestone and other sources indicate that there have been hundreds of accidents involving 500-series radials, and that these accidents have caused

From the August 28, 1978 issue of Fortune. *Reprinted with the permission of* Fortune *magazine.*

at least thirty-four deaths. No other radial-tire line has been associated with nearly that number. . . .

The Traffic Safety Administration, an arm of the Department of Transportation, investigated the tire for seven months before announcing that it had made an "initial determination" of a safety-related defect. . . . The agency studied 6,000 consumer reports dealing with more than 14,000 separate tire failures. It felt that the 500 radial was effectively damned both by the volume and by the nature of the complaints—which had been sent to its own offices, to Congress, to consumer organizations, and to Firestone. The agency based its decision as well on the so-called adjustment rate of the 500 radial. The adjustment rate is calculated by dividing the number of tires sold into the number that are returned—for full or partial refunds—by dissatisfied customers. Adjustments might be made for anything from a wobbly ride to a high-speed blowout. Firestone has testified that the 500 had an adjustment rate of 7.4 percent, more than twice the estimated average for other radial tires. . . .

Firestone's management has contended all along that the company has been unjustly accused. It did recall 400,000 of its 500-series radials last year—the largest tire recall in history—at the Traffic Safety Administration's suggestion. But that was because of what Firestone describes as a temporary production problem at a single plant in Illinois. Other production problems caused the company to recall a total of 10,425 more 500 radials on three earlier occasions. Nonetheless, Firestone contends that there is nothing fundamentally wrong with the tire, and it has strenuously opposed a complete recall. According to Firestone, practically all the tire failures can be blamed on consumer neglect and abuse. It claims that consumers damage their tires by overloading them, banging them against the curb, failing to keep them adequately inflated, and driving at excessive speeds.

Controversy over the 500 radial has been raging in the public forums for months, and the Firestone name has been besmirched in courtrooms and a congressional hearing, as well as in the press and on the air. As one might expect, the unfavorable publicity has caused defections from the ranks of Firestone customers. The company is having trouble selling its seven current radial lines, although none of them has been found defective. Despite extra-heavy advertising and promotion, and the creation of a special warranty, Firestone's share of the multibillion-dollar radial-tire market has slipped by about a half percent. A company officer says the drain on sales already has amounted to scores of millions of dollars. . . .

Firestone also is coping with a spate of lawsuits, charging everything from bent fenders to loss of life and limb. Since production began, the company has been hit with some 250 suits seeking millions of dollars in damages because of alleged failures of the 500 radials. Nine of the cases resulted in courtroom verdicts against Firestone, while the company has won twenty-two and settled sixty-four out of court for less than the plaintiffs demanded. The largest settlement by far —approximately $1.4 million—was made in the case of a Nevada family. Both parents were killed, and a child was left a paraplegic as the result of an auto accident in which the right rear tire—a 500 radial—blew out. Firestone felt it had a strong case, but decided not to take its chances with a jury.

The purpose of this article is not to judge whether the 500 radial is in fact defective. What does seem clear, however, is that Firestone, in its attempts to ward off disagreeable consequences and defend its honor, has often been its own worst enemy. At times, it has almost gone out of its way to provoke suspicion and doubt. One would ex-

pect a company convinced of its rectitude to cooperate fully with the government. But Firestone has repeatedly tried to thwart investigation of its tire, and has publicly impugned the motives of the investigators as well. In the process, it has simply prolonged and intensified its ordeal.

Firestone has demonstrated a penchant for blunders, some of them susceptible to the worst interpretation. Early last spring, at a time when the investigation hadn't yet become common knowledge, Firestone held a major clearance sale of 500's in the Southeast. New tires were sold in Miami and Birmingham at half the list price. Firestone explains that it was phasing the tire out, that clearance sales are a routine procedure when stocks get down to certain levels, and that it had planned for months to clear out this line. But the company should have anticipated that the government's investigation would eventually get lots of publicity, and that the sale would then appear— whether justly or not—as a desperate effort to unload damaged goods.

The Firestone 500 radial began attracting baleful attention from consumer advocates back in 1976, when the Center for Auto Safety, a Washington-based organization formerly associated with Ralph Nader, received a large number of complaints— mainly about tread separations and blowouts. During 1977, the center studied the tire complaints in its files, and found that half of them were leveled against Firestone, with the great bulk of these involving the 500 radial. Last November, Clarence M. Ditlow III, director of the center, wrote a letter about the findings to Mario A. Di Federico, the president of Firestone, and suggested— impudently, no doubt—that the company should shift half of its advertising budget into quality control.

Ditlow also turned his data over to the Traffic Safety Administration, which began its own investigation. Firestone contends that the agency bears a grudge against the company. In 1975, the agency ordered a recall of one million Firestone tires—bias-plies rather than radials—which it felt did not meet safety and durability standards. But it had to back down in the face of a company lawsuit, after the Justice Department advised that the case against Firestone was too weak.

Firestone also suggests that the Traffic Safety Administration is part of a Naderite conspiracy. Joan Claybrook, who heads the agency, is a former associate of Ralph Nader. So is Lowell Dodge, special counsel of a House subcommittee—headed by Representative John E. Moss, a California Democrat—which joined the investigation of Firestone last spring. Firestone finds something sinister in the common backgrounds of Claybrook, Dodge, and the other Nader alumnus in the case, Clarence Ditlow. As John F. Floberg, Firestone's vice president and general counsel, recently put it: "They scratch each other's backs. They get together and decide to play Ping-Pong or badminton with somebody." Firestone, he suggests, is the ball—or the shuttlecock—in the present game.

It is Floberg who has taken the most aggressive role in Firestone's response to the radial-tire crisis. He represented the company almost single-handedly at the House subcommittee hearings, while Richard A. Riley, the chairman and chief executive, has limited his participation in the public debate to a few reluctant interviews. . . . The general outlines of the strategy had to be approved by Riley, but a source elsewhere in the industry says that Firestone's tactics bear the stamp of Floberg, a combative World War II veteran who spent seven years as assistant secretary of the Navy and an AEC commissioner before joining Firestone in 1960.

One of Firestone's legal tactics was an attempt to suppress the results of a survey of tire owners conducted by the Traffic Safety

Administration. The agency says it was alarmed by the reports about Firestone's radials, and initiated the survey to determine whether Firestone was the only make that was proving particularly troublesome. It mailed 87,000 survey cards to people who had bought new cars equipped with radial tires. The respondents were asked to indicate the brands of their tires, and to tell whether they had experienced blowouts or other problems.

Only 5,400 people—6.2 percent of those surveyed—bothered to respond, but within this group, Firestone seemed to make the worst showing by far. The company got wind of the results, and learned that the agency was preparing to release them. It went into the U.S. District Court in Cleveland and asked for a restraining order, preventing the Traffic Safety administration from making the results public. Firestone argued that the survey was statistically unsound, because of the small response and for other reasons as well, and claimed that the publicity would damage the company's business. The order was granted last March.

Firestone's effort at censorship backfired. People who had been unaware of the radial-tire crisis read about the court's action, and began asking what the company had to hide. In particular, the episode aroused the suspicions of Congressman Moss, an ardent consumerist and chairman of the subcommittee on oversight and investigations of the House Committee on Interstate and Foreign Commerce. After hearing of the judge's decision, he summoned his legal aides, and announced grimly, "We'll have to hold hearings." The hearings, which stretched over four days during the spring and summer, received heavy coverage in the press and on TV, and produced still more bad publicity.

Ironically, the results of the survey reached the public anyhow. The Center for Auto Safety requested them, along with other data, under the Freedom of Information Act. Despite the restraining order, the results were sent to the consumer group, which passed them along to the press. The incident seemed to support Firestone's charges that the Traffic Safety Administration was out to nail the company. It was explained, however, that a staff lawyer had released the material "inadvertently." At the very least, the incident demonstrated that Firestone has no monopoly on blunders.

It seems clear that Firestone should never have hauled the Traffic Safety Administration into court. The company should have waited until the agency released the survey, then countered with a public statement of its own, attacking the statistical methods. Firestone might have scored some debating points this way. Or then again, the public might have dismissed the explanation as self-serving, since most people are hopelessly befuddled by disputes among statisticians. But in either case Firestone would have suffered less damage.

Firestone has tried to thwart the Traffic Safety Administration's investigation in other ways as well. Last December, the agency sent the company a long list of questions concerning steel-belted radial tires. It asked for copies of any and all complaints about failures of Firestone radials, for a list of all lawsuits against Firestone arising from these failures, and for a detailed account of any changes in the methods used to manufacture radials. The agency asked for prompt responses, but in an increasingly bitter exchange of letters and telegrams, Firestone kept insisting that it could not supply all the information requested without spending many months researching and compiling.

The agency ran out of patience, and last April it sent Firestone a "special order" —a list of the questions that had not been answered, together with additional questions that had been raised during the investi-

gation and questions about production prior to 1975. There were twenty-seven items in all, and the agency demanded a full and prompt response, under penalty of prosecution.

In a long and defiant reply, drafted by a Cleveland law firm, Firestone objected to practically all the questions. It continued to insist that they would require too much time and effort, and it questioned whether the Traffic Safety Administration had the authority to demand the information. The company argued that the agency could require answers only to "specific questions," and that some of the questions weren't specific. It also argued that Firestone was being asked to analyze documents and compile new ones, when the agency had the authority only to ask the company to make existing documents available for inspection. Firestone upbraided the agency for asking it to send copies of certain documents when the company, under the law, only had to make the documents available at headquarters. And it objected to a request for information about tires produced more than three years ago, on the ground that such tires are exempt from agency control.

The agency received the reply with something less than joy. It took Firestone to court in Washington in an effort to force compliance with its "special order." The matter is now before U.S. District Judge Thomas A. Flannery. But whatever the judgment may be, the company inevitably has raised public doubts about its good faith by refusing to cooperate fully with the Traffic Safety Administration, and by choosing instead to split legal hairs. Firestone, of course, doesn't see it that way. "I think we've been completely aboveboard," says Chairman Riley.

When John Floberg appeared before the House subcommittee, he found himself in hostile surroundings. Chairman Moss and most of the other subcommittee members were antagonistic toward the company. What's more, Floberg had been preceded to the stand by seven witnesses—two police officers, two consumers, a Firestone dealer, a writer, and Clarence Ditlow—all of whom had testified against the 500 radial. Still, the hearings offered Firestone a broad forum, and a chance to redeem itself in the public eye.

The company muffed the chance. Floberg's prepared statement was eloquent at times. But his adversaries on the subcommittee had done their homework, and they managed to trip him up. He lapsed into obfuscations and tortured explanations. The situation called for a heavy dose of candor, but Floberg came across strictly as a lawyer fighting a tough case.

At one point, Floberg stated that the 500 was one of two steel-belted radials that had been rated above all others in a Consumer Reports survey. But Lowell Dodge, the subcommittee counsel, pointed out that the ratings, which appeared in the October, 1973, issue, had been made according to tread wear, not safety.

A while later, Floberg tried to make the point that the industry encouraged consumers to take proper care of their radial tires. He cited a television ad that Firestone had run on the subject. But, as he conceded, this was not a very potent example, since the advertisement had been forced on Firestone by the Federal Trade Commission, in partial settlement of a lawsuit. The FTC had been upset because earlier ads had stressed the safety of the company's tires *without* mentioning the need for proper maintenance. The FTC also fined the company $50,000.

An adversary, Representative Albert Gore Jr., Democrat of Tennessee, wondered about the seemingly high adjustment rate on 500-brand radials. Floberg tried to show that the rate—7.4 percent—might not be out of line. He mentioned that the tire had been Firestone's most expensive, and that buyers might therefore be "more likely to seek adjustment when they are unhappy with it." He added that the industry guards its adjustment rates "very jealously" and suggested that the 500 might compare favorably with other top-priced tires. But the subcommittee had demanded adjustment data from the other major tire makers, and none of them indicated a rate even half that of the 500's on competitive steel-belted lines for the years 1975-77. At Goodyear, Firestone's chief competitor, the highest adjustment rate was 2.9 percent.

Last month, the Traffic Safety Administration made its "initial determination" that the 500 radial had a safety-related defect. It recommended that Firestone recall the tires immediately, although it refrained from issuing an order until after a public hearing earlier this month. But whatever happens from here on, Firestone has long since lost the radial-tire war. It has vividly demonstrated the wrong way of dealing with the government and the public.

45

EVERY MAN A WALTER MITTY

by Norman Goluskin,
President, Smith/Greenland
Sales Management

There's a fellow on my block—let's call him Joe—who drives a Mercedes when he has house guests but tools around in a Pinto when he's taking the wife and kids out. I've been fed a front-row brand of Scotch by him, but his garbage cans are usually topped off with empty bottles of something approaching rot-gut gin. I know something else about him: although he has a business school M.S., his favorite reading is pulp detective magazines.

As a marketing man, I get the jitters every time I see Joe.

Marketers throughout the country are pondering how to sell their products to a public that is being besieged by great political and economic stress, coupled with revolutionary new lifestyles. It's no wonder that yesterday's tools can't answer today's marketing problems.

The marketer or advertiser who isn't looking for new ways of approaching the marketplace is looking for trouble. As our culture continues to be fractioned into overlapping subgroups, and our lifestyles become more complex, our notion of how to sell products and services must continue to be current.

From Norman Goluskin, "Every Man a Walter Mitty," Sales Management, *July 7, 1975.*

Enter consumer segmentation *1975 style.*

The marketing traditionalists know the term consumer segmentation. It's been accepted by the marketing community for some time. Put simply, it means identifying a group of consumers who have a homogeneous set of needs and then offering them a product that will satisfy those particular needs. It works: the annals of marketing overflow with successful case histories.

However, the traditional use of consumer segmentation has been severely limited and has not kept up with the times. Traditional consumer segmentation never delved into the area of the many separate wants and needs within the same consumer. It never probed the many "split personalities" that make up each and every one of us at different times under different circumstances.

Originally, products were left to seek out their own segments. The common practice was to identify a point of product differentiation, then promote it. A mouthwash that promises good taste will clearly differentiate itself from one that says it tastes bad. A consumer segment then develops around the attraction of the product difference. Rossor Reeves, in his exposition of the Unique Selling Proposition, was an early and strong proponent of that type of segmentation.

Little attention was given to the significance of the product difference. The assumption was that the difference would attract a specific user group from the general population. Sure enough, it became apparent that users of one product had certain similarities that set them apart from users of competitive products.

At first, such consumer groups were defined demographically because demographic characteristics were tangible and therefore easier to measure. Segmentation was based on sex, age, education, income, geographic location, and so on. Many marketers still adhere to that single-minded system of defining segments.

Then, some marketers began to realize that demography alone does not provide a precise basis for describing consumer wants and needs. It might be found, for example, that teachers with relatively low incomes expressed interests that were more like those of the upper middle class than of many of their economic peers.

Then, consumer groupings began to be isolated in terms of their motivations. It was learned that Honda motorcycles could be sold to little old ladies in sneakers and to conservative businessmen, as well as to leather-jacketed youths. The common denominator among those disparate groups was their psychological makeup, not their demographic characteristics. Spurred on by multivariate computer statistics and increasing psychological sophistication, psychographic segmentation emerged.

Despite the many refinements of both demographic and psychographic segmentation, there is a subtle problem: the tendency to assume that the individual consumer is a constant, that once pigeonholed into a given segment, he will oblige by staying there. In fact, the human personality is a variable quantity: its wants and needs will vary depending on mood, situation, and, perhaps, the phase of the moon. Thus the principle of consumer segmentation runs the risk of oversimplification when it focuses only on those aspects of similarity within a specific group. We can no longer ignore that, at different times, any given individual may belong to any number of segments, all of which relate to a common product category.

Thus stratifications that aim at the heavy beer-drinker, the luxury-car owner, the airline traveller, or the sexually liberated are finding their audiences more difficult to define properly. Consequently their advertising messages have become less effec-

tive. The so-called psychographic profile of a consumer "segment" can be very misleading because each consumer is made up of many different layers of experience, motivation, desires, and attitudes. One person may fit comfortably into totally diverse segments during the course of a single week or even a day.

Let's examine a few ordinary life situations in which one individual may use different products at different times. Take the case of the $50,000-a-year professional man who invites a group of business colleagues to his suburban home for a cocktail party. At dinner he will use his best china, sterling silverware, and his finest linen napkins. He will end the meal with vintage brandy. Everyone is impressed and goes away thinking that his business chum has real style.

The following day—with no party on his family's agenda—he will assume a totally different lifestyle. The napkins will be paper, the sterling will be replaced by stainless, the drink will be beer, and so on. What does all this mean to the marketer and advertiser? It means that we are different people at different times and use different products that more aptly fit the segments we occupy at that time.

We will often use higher-priced brands for one purpose and lower-priced brands for other purposes, convenience foods for one occasion, elaborately prepared meals at another. Nowhere is that variation more apparent than in our dress. There is no consistency in the makeup of a consumer's psyche that suggests that he will use one and only one product at all times. When is the last time you felt extravagant and splurged on some indulgence? Contrast that with the time you didn't like springing for a reasonably priced necessity.

The combinations and permutations of products and services that are used at varying times differ markedly and cause advertisers to pull their hair out. It simply means that an advertiser must understand the varying situations when an individual might consider using one product or service over another. He must also realize that loyalties to one product or brand are diminishing and so, too, is the old idea of consumer segmentation.

THE PEN THAT TELLS

The solution may be to carry segmentation one step further, from *consumer* to *situational* segments. Identify the psychological variables that operate in different usage situations, and offer a product through advertising that satisfies the wants and needs implicit in them.

The opportunity posed by situational segmentation was clearly demonstrated in a recent Smith/Greenland study of writing instruments. The study was part of a continual probing into evolving consumer behavior and perceptions to update market patterns in different product categories.

The project involved three basic types of writing instruments: ball point pens, fine-tip porous markers, and broad-tip porous markers. Using a ball point, respondents drew a picture of someone using a ball point and described the situation. That procedure was repeated with each of the two types of porous pens. There were substantial qualitative differences in the situational and psychological meanings associated with each of the three instruments, and remarkable agreement among the panelists as to the nature of those differences.

For example, the *ball point* tends to be identified with occupational situations in which the user is constrained by a structure over which he has little control but within which he must perform in a largely routine manner. There is little opportunity for self-expression, and there is little association with one's personal lifestyle or needs. The

instrument is utilitarian and it is solely task related. Examples include a secretary taking a telephone message, an accountant working late on the books, and a student taking lecture notes.

The *broad-tip porous marker* also tends to be placed in a structured, occupational situation, but one within which the user is in control and is performing in a largely self-assertive manner. Although the structural constraint is still evident, there is considerable opportunity for self-expression, which in fact may be demanded by the situation. Here the respondents found an art director developing a layout, a shipping clerk indicating delivery instructions, and a landlord posting a notice to his tenants.

Perceptions of the *fine-tip porous marker* lie beyond structure and constraint. The situations tend not to be occupational. There is a feeling of nonconformity and self-expression, even to the point of mischievousness. There is little, if any, implication of structure. Examples here include an adolescent writing a love note, a fine artist doing a sketch, and a young boy writing graffiti on a wall.

The implications for marketing are clear. Situational segmentation should be considered for products that coexist within the same general category and where usage might overlap. In the case of writing instruments, it seems logical to assume that most consumers, at various times, find themselves in situations involving confinement, control, and freedom. Analogous situational segmentation exists for other product categories. The problem is to define them, and then present the products to suit the wants and needs involved.

ANOTHER APPROACH

These findings suggest another approach to market segmentation, that is, positioning closely allied products against segments defined in terms of use *situations* rather than use *groups*. In the example referred to above, any single person, at one time or another, might easily fit into two or more of the situational segments defined.

If consumer segmentation is properly applied, then as consumers move from use segment to use segment, they will opt for the product that most closely suits their personal needs at the time.

We all move much more quickly nowadays from one situation to the next—home, office, weekends, father, manager, provider, etc. We are constantly changing our psychological makeup as we move from one experience to the next in our increasingly complicated lives. The marketer of today must recognize something that the purveyors of comic books learned very quickly—that Clark Kent can be Superman also.

46
HOW BEEF BECAME KING

by Marvin Harris and Eric B. Ross

Although vegetarians are becoming either more numerous or more vocal, there's no sign that the nation as a whole is eating less beef these days. Americans consume more than 100 pounds per person per year much of it in the form of oddly misnamed hamburgers. That's twice as much as pork, the second most popular meat. Moreover, beef in the form of steak is our favorite prestige food. Coast to coast, rare, medium, or well done, it honors those who serve it and those who eat it far more than pork or lamb. To special guests at home or in a restaurant, we offer steak or perhaps prime ribs, seldom ham steaks, less often pork chops or mutton, and never, never horse or dog meat. In America, steak is to meat what Cadillac is to cars.

Like most cultural practices, American beef-eating seems natural until we lift our gaze beyond the smoke of our own barbecues. Throughout the Far East, hundreds of millions of people have never tasted beef and have not the slightest desire to try it. In Hindu India, steak is as unthinkable as dog chops in the United States. Less well known is the fact that the Chinese, who are not averse to eating dogs now and then, find the idea of slaughtering cattle to eat steak rather appalling. As anthropologist Martin Yang reports, "It would be insulting, or at least improper, to offer beef to a guest at an honorable dinner." The honorable host offers pork instead.

"There is no disputing taste" is an old but misleading maxim. Everybody's food preferences ought to be respected, but there is much to dispute when it comes to explaining why we have them. It's easy to dismiss food preferences as quirky, inscrutable traditions that science can never understand: Americans like hamburgers and steak because they like hamburgers and steak, and that's that. But with the price of meat setting records at the supermarket, some of us prefer to shop around for a slightly more edifying theory.

The whole question of American meat preferences has recently been raised by anthropologist Marshall Sahlins at the University of Chicago. Sahlins sides with those who feel that the search for the practical, mundane causes of cultural lifestyles is futile. Our liking for beef and our abhorrence of dog meat, he argues, "is in no way justifiable by biological, ecological, or economic advantage." It is really a cultural convention that originated thousands of years ago when Indo-European ancestors identified cattle with virility because cattle represented "increasable wealth." This traditional "sexual code of food," Sahlins contends, is not determined by any practical benefits associated with eating beef rather than other meats. Further, our beef preference arbitrarily shapes the conduct of American agribusiness and distorts the exploitation of American resources along fundamentally irrational lines. Its consequences "extend from agricultural 'adaptation' to international trade and world political relations."

We don't eat dogs, Sahlins explains, becaue they remind us of people. Cows seem human to Hindus; dogs seem human to Americans. So the people of India bestow all sorts of privileges on their cows, while Americans treat canines as if they were members of the family. If India is the land of the sacred cow, concludes Sahlins, the U.S. is the land of the sacred dog.

Our research leads us to very different conclusions. The preeminence of beef in the United States is a recent, temporary development that has little to do with ancient Indo-European cattle cults. It grew out of specific economic and technological changes brought on by the attempt to maximize the benefits and minimize the costs of meat production in the face of shifting ecological and demographic considerations. These costs and benefits also lie behind the American abhorrence of dog meat as well as other apparently inscrutable food preferences.

The U.S. has not always been the land of big steaks. Before 1875, pork was the preferred daily meat, and ham was the choice for honored guests. Even as late as 1950 pork was a bit more popular than beef. It is true that cattle were reared and consumed in substantial numbers from Colonial times onward, and in regions such as New England and the Louisiana prairies, cattle hides and salted, barreled beef formed the basis of important local industries. But nowhere did cattle rival hogs as a source of meat. Whites in the antebellum South consumed three times as much pork as beef. In his book *Hog Meat and Hoecake*, historian S.B. Hilliard writes that "this preference for pork came to be a distinctive element of Southern culture and as a food item pork completely eclipsed all others."

New Englanders were only slightly less pork-conscious. As historian H.S. Russell put it, "From the viewpoint of the family larder, the most necessary farm animal was the hog; few meals of this period anywhere were complete without some pork product." The importance of pork during the antebellum period—when the good life was "living high on the hog"—has left its mark on American speech habits. Americans still talk about "bringing home the bacon," not "bringing home the steak," and accuse politicians of "pork barrel" rather than "beef barrel" legislation.

One reason for the early preeminence of pork is strictly biological. Under favorable conditions, the pig converts plants into flesh far more efficiently than any other domesticated animal. Pigs transform about 35 percent of what they eat into live weight, compared with only 11 percent for cattle; they also have larger litters. Moreover, the hog is a creature that likes to root about for nuts and other tidbits buried in the forest floor. As long as there were extensive forests, American settlers could let their pigs feed themselves during most of the year. But what really made the hog king was the fact that American homesteaders produced more corn than the sparse human population could eat. At first, this surplus was most profitably converted into whiskey (hence the origin of bourbon as the distinctive American contribution to the world of hard liquor).

When the federal government decided to make whiskey one of its principal sources of tax revenue, frontier farmers found it more profitable to turn surplus corn into meat rather than alcohol. From then on, as the corn belt moved steadily westward across the Appalachians and beyond, so did the hog belt. By 1830, the corn-hog complex had reached the Ohio Valley, and Cincinnati, known as Porkopolis, was the major source of pork for the Eastern Seaboard as well as for the overseas trade via New Orleans. It was in Cincinnati that the technical pattern for the American meat-packing industry was first established. Workers stood in place, mechanically performing specialized operations as the pig carcasses moved past them suspended from overhead monorails. Henry Ford is usually credited with creating the assembly line in Detroit in 1913, but the prototype of Henry Ford's assembly line was Cincinnati's pig disassembly line, operating well before the Civil War.

When the corn belt moved still farther west, accompanied and spurred on by furious railroad building, Chicago replaced Cincinnati as the nation's principal meat-packing and transshipment center. But, despite Carl Sandburg's characterization of Chicago as "Hog Butcher to the World," beef, not pork, was destined to be the city's real glory.

Up to this point, about 1860, cattle suffered from two disadvantages as a source of mass-produced meat. Because the pig was a more efficient converter of corn into flesh, pork was cheaper to produce. There was also the problem of preservation. Early meat-packers had to rely on salting as the princi-

BEEF VS. PORK: RECENT TRENDS

U.S. Per-Capita Consumption, in Pounds*

Year	Beef	Pork
1977	125.9	61.5
1976	129.4	58.2
1975	120.1	54.8
1974	116.8	66.6
1973	109.6	61.6
1972	116.1	67.4
1971	113.0	73.0
1970	113.7	66.4
1965	99.5	58.7
1960	85.1	64.9
1950	63.4	69.2
1920	59.1	63.5

*Figures, from the U.S. Department of Agriculture, represent carcass weight—how much the meat weighed at the packinghouse. The National Livestock and Meat Board estimates that, allowing for bone, fat, and cooking losses, we actually ate about 44 pounds of beef and 22 pounds of pork per person last year.

pal way of getting the meat to market 'in edible condition. And pork took to salting far better than beef, which was stringier to begin with. These advantages kept pork the favorite American meat until physiology, geography, and technology combined forces to move beef ahead.

Cattle have one distinct physiological advantage over swine: as ruminants, they are outfitted with a series of stomachs adaped to eating grass; pigs, for all their omnivorous tastes, cannot digest grass. Beyond the Mississippi lay great expanses of semiarid grasslands only marginally suited for corn production, where cattle rather than pigs could more efficiently convert plants into meat. Cattle could also be driven over long distances and made to swim broad rivers to get to market; pigs are poor swimmers and notoriously hard to drive.

The cattle had another advantage, as well as some drawbacks. Herds of longhorned breeds descended from stock released by some Spanish settlers roamed southern Texas in a semiwild condition before the Civil War. But because the Eastern market was inaccessible, the animals were valued chiefly for their hides rather than their flesh. The railroads, spreading out from Chicago, soon changed all this. Where the cattle trails crossed the tracks, Chicago-based entrepreneurs built stockyards and towns virtually overnight.

As soon as Illinois livestock-shipper J.G. McCoy learned that the trail from Texas would cross the tracks being laid through Kansas at Abilene, he ordered holding facilities for 3,000 head built within 60 days. By the end of the year 1867, starting from scratch, McCoy shipped 35,000 head from Abilene to Chicago. By 1871, over 700,000 head of range cattle were being shipped by rail to the packing houses in Chicago and elsewhere, and cattle-ranching was spreading across the plains from Texas. But the stupendous potential of the Western rangelands as yet remained untapped. Most of the cattle raised on the Great Plains still reached the Eastern consumer in the form of barreled, salted beef. The more desirable

fresh beef was available only at exorbitant prices by shipping live animals all the way from Chicago, and slaughtering them at the neighborhood butcher shop.

In the late 1860s, George Hammond delivered the first fresh Chicago beef stored on ice to the Boston market. Since Hammond's beef touched the ice, it was discolored and met with consumer resistance. A few years later, Philip Armour and Gustavus Swift, founders of the huge meat-packing companies that still bear their names, introduced refrigerator cars that chilled the meat by circulating air over ice. In October of 1882, *Harper's Weekly* reported that Swift's "Chicago dressed beef" arrived in New York in cars whose doors opened directly in front of a refrigerated wholesale storage building. The overhead trolley in the car linked up with the trolley in the building (kept at the same temperature as the car) and the carcass was transferred from one to the other "without being removed from the hook on which it was hung when killed."

Thus, by taking advantage of the unexploited rangelands, recently cleared of buffalo and Indians, and by using assembly-line processing, efficient rail transport, and intensive capitalization, the giant packers undersold the local butchers and captured the Eastern markets. Swift's first shipment depressed the price of beef $4 per hundredweight, leading *Harper's* to declare, "The era of cheap beef has begun for New York."

Beef's reputation in the U.S., it seems, did not arise from some ancient, arbitrary code in which beef stood for virility, but from practical production and marketing breakthroughs that made fresh beef affordable by the urban consumer. Beef won out over pork principally because the available grasslands made it cheaper to mass-produce fresh beef than fresh pork. If pigs could still have been raised by the old system of semiwild foraging, fresh pork might have competed with fresh beef for the urban market. But by the

1870's, the corn belt had moved out of the forested regions—in fact, much former wilderness had been cleared for farmland—and the mass production of pigs had come to depend almost entirely on feeding them corn and other farm products. While cattle were fattened on corn just before slaughter, the rangelands provided virtually free food during the animals' years of maximum growth.

Based on the same analysis, we can resolve the matter of American's sacred dogs rather briefly. Dogs are carnivores and hence thrive best on meat, not grass, nuts, or grain. So why should packers produce meat by fattening dogs on meat that humans can eat? Actually, the only place where dogs have been mass-produced for human consumption was in pre-Columbian Mexico, by the Aztecs. But the Aztecs, who bred a special hairless variety of dogs for this purpose, did not have pigs, cattle, sheep, or any other efficient sources of animal flesh. Making the best of matters, the Aztecs not only ate specially bred hairless dogs, but human babies and captured enemy soldiers as well.

American dogs are not only hairy; they are also expensive animals, carefully bred for specialized functions that other animals cannot perform as well. Right now, their main job is to scare off intruders and provide company in an increasingly urban, crime-ridden, and lonely society. Our taboo on dog flesh, therefore, merely expresses in symbolic form the high value we place on these functions, as well as the more traditional ones dogs exercised when they helped men hunt or herd other animals.

Just as geographical, physiological, and technological factors explain the development of America's current preference for beef, so contemporary economic and ecological considerations will change our tastes in the future. Actually, the original economic bonanza of open-range cattle-ranching was a short-lived phenomenon. Rising land prices caused by the continuous advance of farms

into the marginal areas of the Great Plains, and overgrazing during the boom years of ranching in the early 1880s, soon obliged ranchers to use more intensive methods of stock-raising. Competition for the Eastern market also led to the replacement of the hardy but stringy longhorns with less hardy but tender Herefords. With the cutback in rangeland and increasing use of more expensive breeds, more and more of the weight gain of beef cattle came to depend on alfalfa, corn, soybeans, and other planted crops. Current feedlot operations, in which calves are force-fed a rich diet of energy-expensive grains, vitamins, and hormones, and brought to maturity within eight months, constitute an ever-more wasteful form of production.

Thus, just as much of America's housing and travel preferences depend on no-longer-cheap supplies of petrochemicals, our beef-eating ways now stand at odds with sound ecological and economic principles. Cattle have lost much of their cost advantage over swine and other more efficient sources of animal protein (such as poultry-farming and dairying) and America's taste for meat must sooner or later swing back to pork and dairy products, and include vegetable sources of protein as well.

We can speculate about the fate of beef-eaters like ourselves on the basis of what happened in older civilizations. High per-capita beef consumption has always been associated with low-density populations, pioneering in natural or artificially created grasslands. The Indo-European Vedic-speaking people of ancient northern India, and the ancestral Chinese of the Yellow River basin, were both at first cattle-raisers and avid beef-eaters. As their populations grew and farming was intensified, cattle became too expensive to be raised for meat. They were needed as plow animals, to help the crop-lands feed people rather than animals.

In China, pork gradually became the

preferred meat, because pigs could be raised more efficiently than cattle on household wastes and agricultural by-products. In northern India, the fierce summer heat, the monsoons, and periodic droughts made the pig a poor choice. So, as population density increased in the Gangetic plain, India turned to dairying as the major source of animal protein. It soon became a cardinal religious principle of Buddhism and Hinduism to protect the supply of draft animals by prohibiting the slaughter of cattle and the consumption of beef. Thus, out of the same Indo-European tradition to which Sahlins erroneously attributes the American taste for beef, a civilization arose in which beef-eating is the greatest sin. Nothing so drastic is likely to happen to us. But we are bound to lose our taste for big fat steaks just as surely as we are bound to lose our affinity for big fat cars.

From the October 1978 issue of Psychology Today. *Copyright © 1978 by Ziff-Davis Publishing Company. Reprinted with permission.*

HOW THE CHANGING AGE MIX CHANGES MARKETS

Business Week

More babies, fewer teen-agers, far more young adults, fewer middle-aged citizens, and many more oldsters than there are today. That is the new age mix of the U.S. population that will confront business a decade hence. These changes mean that business will face a different market to sell to and a different labor force to draw on in the 1980s. Companies as diverse as General Electric, Merrill Lynch, AT&T, RCA, Coca-Cola, Gillette, Federated Department Stores, and even *Playboy* magazine are already thinking hard about what they should be doing to get ready for the 234 million Americans who will be around in 1985.

The key change in the age mix of the population is the shift of post-World War II babies toward middle age. Ten years from now Americans between the age of 35 and 39 will number 17.2 million, a jump of 48 percent. They will account for 7.3 percent of the population instead of today's 5.4 percent.

"That moving bulge," says Dwain L. Jeter, development vice-president at International Multifoods, "really means that this

From "How the Changing Age Mix Changes Markets." Reprinted from the January 12, 1976 issue of Business Week *by special permission.* © *1976 by McGraw-Hill, Inc.*

company must seriously assess whether its basic outlook on the world must be adapted to a changing environment." The year 1985 will also see some population valleys of significance equal to the peak of the 35-to-39 age group. There will be fewer Americans in their late 40s and early 50s, the age range that traditionally supplies the bulk of top management talent as well as the personal investment dollars that fuel the stock market. Also reduced will be the horde of teenagers who set so much of the style in consumer markets.

On the other hand, there will be more older Americans as a result of improved health care. And, with many more people of an age when couples normally have children, a new baby boom is in the making, even assuming zero population growth.

The growth of population from 213.5 million now to the anticipated 234 million in 1985—an increase of 9.3 percent—will be well below the 25 percent rate of the past decade. This means that "there will be a slowdown in the rate of economic growth after 1980" explains Conference Board economist Fabian Linden.

Given the trends, "In order to succeed in the marketplace, you must reposition yourself," insists *Playboy's* director of marketing information, Herbert Maneloveg. With the numbers declining among the post-adolescent group that is now that magazine's prime target, the editors will emphasize more sophisticated copy with less fantasy and more useful advice on vacations, investment, and clothes.

"Age represents many other things," says Eva E. Jacobs, consumer expenditure expert at the Bureau of Labor Statistics. "It represents income, size of family, and whether they are homeowners." New BLS reports show a family headed by someone between 35 and 44 has an income close to one headed by someone 45 to 54. However, the younger family spends 16 percent less on

personal care services, 21 percent less on over-the-counter drugs, but 10 percent more on meat.

PREDICTING THE 'COHORT FACTORS'

Going hand-in-hand with the basic age distribution changes are changes in what demographers call "cohort factors." These are values and attitudes that a generation carries with it throughout its life. The 30-year-olds of 1985 will have a different outlook from the 30-year-olds of today. For instance, when General Mills recently asked adults and teenagers in the same families what expenditures they thought of as luxuries, the children were far less likely than their parents to cite a new car each year or hired household help. They were far more inclined to classify having meat at most meals as a luxury.

It is harder to predict cohort factors than to size up the age distribution of tomorrow's population. But some predictions seem certain to stick.

With so many adult women already working—close to 45 percent—the percentage is expected to go up only a point or two by 1985. But that will represent a meaningful change because the growth will come even though many of the new working women will already have small children. Since 1960 the percentage of working mothers with children under three has doubled. That trend will continue. It "will mean more company-sponsored day care, more paid maternity leave," says an executive of one large industrial company.

Moreover, working wives will increasingly fill significant jobs that add substantially to family income. Business is already planning how to woo this busier, more monied woman. "There is a pressing need that, in order to have more time for each other, the working couple has to spend less time on the rote chores of the household," insists Joseph Naines, Whirlpool Corp. economist. "Our goal is to put the burden of operation into the design of the machines." Paul N. Fruitt, corporate planning vice-president at Gillette Co., sees greater use of time-saving, convenience-shopping outlets, a trend that prompts Donald Ratajczak, director of Georgia State University's forecasting projects, to say, "I've even seen some estimates of virtually no growth in the supermarket area."

The food service industry is gleeful. "More and more women are going to insist on, and achieve, the reality of a dual career —one foot in the kitchen and one foot in the boardroom," predicts G. Michael Hostage, president of Marriott Corp.'s restaurant group.

The likelihood that parents of the mid 1980s will have only enough children to keep the population stable stems from later marriages and a more positive preference for small families. But given the huge number of women in prime child-bearing years, total births will soar. Disproportionately, the births will be of first children—which is good news for marketers. "Probably somewhere in the neighborhood of an additional $700 is expended in 'tooling up' for the initial child," says Census Bureau Director Vincent P. Barabba. He forsees first children, who accounted for little more than 25 percent of all births in 1960, representing 40 percent of births by 1985.

RCA Vice-President Robert J. Eggert sees the combination of two working parents and fewer children as creating a large potential for selling goods that today may be rated as luxuries. Other experts agree. "Being lower on the population curve, a family would live higher on the hog," sums up Rand Corp.'s Peter S. Morrison.

Companies such as General Motors and AT&T say the prime indicator they watch is not the raw population total but the number of separate households, and that is soaring. AT&T is working on new projections for the years beyond 1983 to replace those it sent to its operating telephone companies only last August.

The rapid changes in households come partly from the increased number of divorces. But to a greater extent, the changes derive from the increasing tendency of young singles to live apart from their parents and for oldsters to live apart from their grown children. The biggest growth is in single-adult households. "That's what's pushing this up, and that's at both ends of the age scale," says Malcolm Burnside, manager of economic studies for AT&T. New U.S. Agriculture Dept. projections show that while only about 15 percent of those between 20 and 24 headed a family in the years just after World War II, the figure today is around 25 percent. By the end of the century it will be almost 30 percent. Some 55 percent of those over 65 were heads of households in the late 1940s; today that is around 63 percent.

Census Bureau Director Barabba zeroes in on the way smaller families will affect the housing market. The result, he says, will be "smaller units, more multiple housing units, closer-in locations to centers of population." GE is banking on that trend. It is putting its new-product emphasis on compact appliances for smaller living quarters.

SIZING UP THE CUSTOMERS

"The 1985 customer will be much more self-confident, discriminating, less likely to follow the masses and accept something," predicts Phyllis Sewell, vice-president of Federated Department Stores. Federated stores, she says, "will be going into greater

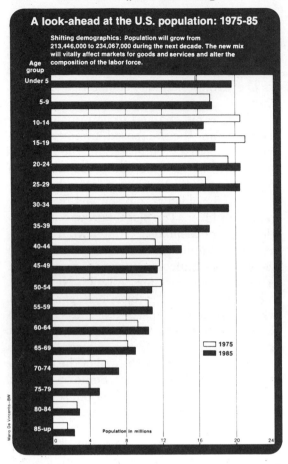

A look-ahead at the U.S. population: 1975-85

Shifting demographics: Population will grow from 213,446,000 to 234,067,000 during the next decade. The new mix will vitally affect markets for goods and services and alter the composition of the labor force.

Age group: Under 5, 5-9, 10-14, 15-19, 20-24, 25-29, 30-34, 35-39, 40-44, 45-49, 50-54, 55-59, 60-64, 65-69, 70-74, 75-79, 80-84, 85-up

☐ 1975   ■ 1985

Population in millions

Mario De Vincentis—BW

specialization within the store, with more different departments. We will be concentrating more on the fashion business and on utilitarian goods, and deemphasizing hardware and major appliances. Now," she says, "we stress the teen-ager and the young 20s. In 1985 it will be people in their 30s, with different needs."

Market planners from coast to coast repeat the Sewell analysis. "Without question, the level of family income will increase dramatically," says Howard Haworth, president of Drexel Heritage Furnishings. A maker of higher-priced furniture, Drexel has been trying to find ways to market lower-priced merchandise, but this will end. "This market," Haworth asserts, "will be moving up to meet us."

International Multifoods is also setting a new course. Vice-President Jeter says that, contrary to "all of the conventional wisdom in the fast-food industry, which says that you do not open these stores in cities of less than 100,000 people," the company now is opening its Mr. Donut shops in small towns.

Working wives, as far as auto makers are concerned, mean "a postive factor for automobile demand," says Ford Marketing Research Director Norman Krandall. For the Institute of Life Insurance, working wives mean a better chance for two-policy families. At Penn Mutual Insurance Co. the percentage of total coverage represented by "wife insurance" has risen in the past decade by 55 percent.

The median age of Americans will cross the line from the 20s to the 30s in 1981. To the U.S. Forest Service, this older population means less emphasis on skiing and hunting. Half of all waterfowl hunters are under 25, two-thirds are under 35.

For others, an older population means creation of whole new product lines. A 10-year projection of soft drink trends worked out by PepsiCo. Inc. shows a flattening of demand as the teen-age population subsides, but an increase in demand for diet and citrus-flavored drinks used as mixers. Upjohn is "flat-out" on research into degenerative diseases.

Marketers are worrying, however, over the fine points of reaching tomorrow's customer. At Gillette, vice-president Fruitt is wondering how the company will reach the customers now being sold grooming and cleaning products through daytime television if more women are spending the days at the office or factory.

A NEW TYPE OF EMPLOYEE

That same older, better-educated, less family-burdened person who will be the customer ly-burdened person who will be the customer for business a decade hence will also be the worker in the factory and the manager in the office.

"There are going to be a lot of people available," the chief demographic analyst at one major oil company says, so turnover may be low as those who have a good spot eschew job-hopping. "At the same time, they are going to have lots of education, so it will be tough to challenge them."

DIFFERENT VALUES

The new workers will bring different values. "Businessmen need to perceive the growing gap between themselves and young adults about what it takes to run a business," insists Harold S. Becker, vice-president of the Futures Group. One example: E.B. Weiss, a marketing consultant, warns clients that selling will have to change by 1985 because fewer good men will agree to be on the road as much—and their wives will be less willing to have them away.

The impact of more education and greater confidence is already apparent in the the labor movement. John Zalusky, collective bargaining expert for the AFL-CIO, says younger workers are more inclined to come to union meetings than members 10 or 20 years their senior, and they are a "better informed, more articulate membership."

With the number of teens down significantly, business will have less of an initial training burden. But companies expect to have a heavier load of mid-career training. And middle managers are likely to win promotions more quickly, to make up for the paucity of older executives.

Company treatment of workers in their 60s is poised for change, too. "With longer active lives, the pension benefits may require adjustment," says a Coca-Cola official. "And

more attention is being given to the transition from work to retirement."

THE INVESTMENT PROBLEM

For business in 1985 to obtain from individual investors the money it needs for risk capital, some basic savings patterns will have to be changed. The problem is there will be fewer persons in the high-earning, low-spending, late-middle-aged group that is the brokers' best selling target today. There also will be more young adults and retirees who traditionally spend most of what they make and bank what they do save.

Merrill Lynch hopes it can break some of those traditions. "There's an increase in liquid assets held by older people as a bulk," notes one official there, who singles out the tendency of retirees to sell large homes at inflated prices and move to smaller, less expensive units. While investors in their 60s generally buy Treasury bills or corporate bonds, Merrill Lynch plans to aim more sales pitches for high-yield, stable common stocks at this age group.

The Institute of Life Insurance is urging companies to think of more innovative policies to appeal to customers with a changing lifestyle. Among its ideas: policies that would stay in force during periods of up to two years without premium payments for those who want to take occasional breaks from work; life insurance coverage that converts to a health insurance policy when the holder reaches retirement age; and policies that in later years will pay out "alternative forms of financial security, such as rent subsidies, vacation and travel allowances."

The banks, too, are changing. The coming demographic changes were one reason Citibank pulled all its consumer financial services together into one group. The hope is that when a married couple takes out a mortgage or opens a credit card account, that contract can be used to sell other programs.

America's mix of changes—an older population, better educated, living in smaller family units—will be unique. "The bulk of the world population will still be young in median age and living in a different environment," one Coca-Cola executive reminds his company brass. But Harold Becker of the Futures Group believes that values are shared increasingly across national boundaries and by age groups rather than across age groups. "For example," says Becker, "the young in America have more of a language commonality with the young in Europe and Russia and China than they do with their parents." That means that when U.S. business learns to cope with the changes coming here, it will have a leg up in dealing with changing populations and attitudes worldwide.

48

MAN WHO BURNED CAR IS NOW FOLK HERO TO MANY

by Jay Sharbutt,
Associated Press

WHITTIER, CAL.—Eddie Campos was talking about the problems he's had with his car when the phone rang. The caller was a man in San Bernardino who wanted to talk about the problems he's had with his car.

Campos didn't know the caller, but listened anyway. Then he shrugged his shoulders and said: "Well, I feel sorry for you. I solved all my problems with one match."

Campos' problem was his new Lincoln Continental Mark III.

He got so fed up at the things he said went wrong with it he burned it to a crisp on August 31 with a great deal of ceremony and five gallons of gasoline. On the front lawn of a nearby Ford assembly plant.

Since then, Campos, married and the father of three, has become sort of a folk hero to some car-owners.

His car trouble started about seven miles after he bought the auto in October 1969: His wife, Carletta, says the entire ignition assembly fell out when she tried to start the car.

From then on, says Campos, it was back

From Jay Sharbutt, "Man Who Burned New Car is Now Folk Hero to Many," The Associated Press, carried in the Houston Chronicle September 26, 1971. Reprinted by permission of The Associated Press Newsfeatures.

and forth to the dealer with power windows that wouldn't go up or, if up, wouldn't go down, an air conditioner that wouldn't condition, a battery that wouldn't electrify, and more.

Campos, described by a deputy sheriff after the Great Car Burn as "perfectly sober, perfectly rational and completely disgusted," denies he's on a one-man vendetta against Ford.

"I don't think it's that," he says. "It's more of a service to the consumers to help them stand up and demand their rights. As long as they remain silent I'll remain active."

Campos, meanwhile, put the charred black and rust-brown hulk of his $10,300 Lincoln on display on the front lawn of his plastering business here. He's still making payments and has $1812 to go.

A five-foot lemon tree sprouts from a hole he chopped in the car's roof.

He also took the car, lemon tree and all, on a nighttime tour down a busy street "and before we knew it we had a line of cars nearly two miles behind us, with people cheering and blowing their horns."

Campos says he's at least saved another car maker, Chrysler, from an even gaudier display of consumer wrath.

"This lady called me up and said she'd been having trouble with a Barracuda she bought," he recalled. "She wanted to drive the car back to the dealer's showroom, set it on fire and burn the whole place down.

"Thank God I managed to talk her out of that."

49

SHE WAS WEARING ORANGE AND SHE WAS FRIENDLY

by Judy Lunn,
Houston Post

NEW YORK—"The plaid is reminiscent of school days, a more secure and safe period in the lives of most people. In times of stress, there is a return to plaid and a feeling of reminiscence related to that earlier safer time."—Dr. Joyce Brothers.

"In the mind of a man, the woman who sews is considered sexy. He relates sewing to creativity and sewing is one of the few feminine pastimes left to women."—Dr. Joyce Brothers.

"The knit fabric emotionally and physically fulfills the need for uninhibited freedom, ease and comfort demanded by today's youth. For freedom, it comes closest to being naked."—Dr. Joyce Brothers.

Dr. Joyce Brothers who has her psychologist-fingers in so many emotional pies is into something else.

She has turned her knowledge about the behavior and motivation of people and focused it on clothes.

Under the lofty label, "psychographic marketing," Dr. Brothers has become consultant to a major fiber firm dealing with

From Judy Lunn, "She Was Wearing Orange and She Was Friendly," Copyright 1972, Houston Post, November 11, 1972. Reprinted by permission of the publisher.

"feelings and opinions and the psychological profile of the consumer.

"In this way not only the immediate but the future needs are satisfied," she said.

Somehow one gets the feeling this is one huge gimmick to sell lots more trevira polyester. But Dr. Brothers does have many interesting things to say about what clothes do say about people.

"Clothing fulfills many needs, many functions . . . only part of that is modesty," she said.

Some cultures expose their genitals, while others cover them. The ancient Chinese thought the hobbled foot sensual: "It drove men out of their minds . . . the woman was an object, totally dependent."

The second function is that of protection—not only from the elements. In cold cultures some people wear nothing, in hot weather the Arabs wear woolens as a form of air-conditioning.

The third function is that of signaling or status. "One naked person has no status over another," stated Dr. Brothers.

"Clothing says 'I am more important, treat me with more respect,' or 'I am interested sexually, treat me with less,' " and she laughed.

Sloppy people say via clothing-talk: "Pay more attention to me . . . forget the cover . . . find me, my importance."

Hippie types or young people who dress "differently" say according to Dr. Brothers:

1. Too much attention is paid to unimportant things . . . if you are worthwhile you'll see me.
2. I am interested in you . . . don't take attention away from that . . . don't distract from real values.
3. I'm going to bug you, says the unkempt person to parents or those outside the circle, i.e., plastic young people as well as plastic old people.
4. I'm going to reject you by wearing clothes adults look absolutely ridiculous in.
5. Signaling statement: You and I will know each other . . . see eye to eye . . . talk and relate to each other.

But this signaling to one's own kind is universal.

"It's like older people at conventions. I'm with the Widget Company, too, say the 'Hi' badges," says Dr. Brothers.

This goes too with the status Gucci bag, the "BB" Bill Blass sweater, the "V" for Valentino belt.

"It proves your status . . . that you're different from the next man . . . oh this language," she said in mock exasperation. "I mean man or woman."

It works until everyone else has your status object and then it's out. It's only status if only "your" people have it.

Joyce Brothers herself was wearing an orange robe she had put on between tapings of her syndicated television show. Trevira fabric of course, surprisingly thick glasses in square tortoise frames, her blonde hair carefully combed. She was munching an apple and eating yoghurt though it didn't seem necessary to keep her small five foot frame in shape.

Dr. Brothers continued. Belonging to any given group of one's choice counts whether it's wearing the same hairdo or whatever it may be that "fits."

"You've seen 50-year-old Betty Co-ed," she said. "She's locked in time and space to how she fit as a teen."

It holds true for everyone that in their teen years they try on various personalities. Some will forever be locked in on the wan Ali MacGraw look. Once set, this personality will not change.

"Fashions will change with the times, but the wearer will not change that much," Dr. Brothers said.

"The one who wore the way-out padded

bra at 14 will wear the see-through blouse, the dress cut down to 'here', the first mini."

The leader of trends will remain constant within her own choices.

The exhibitionist by shock reaction says "look at me . . . I am real."

"Some never get beyond the normal three-year-old stage of primping before the mirror . . . look at me, how adorable I am. Or later, how sexy, how shocking."

Even color choices throw off signals in any number of studies, especially some done at the University of Toronto.

Dr. Brothers constantly quotes from studies and papers she receives from interested professional correspondents who keep her up to date about what's happening.

"They know I won't jump publication or distort or misquote," she interjected.

The favorite color yellow says you're intellectual, idealistic.

(Sort of like palm reading or numerology it seems, but this is proven scientifically.)

Green indicates you're likely to be a good neighbor—outgoing, helpful.

Blue people are sensitive and self-controlled. Oranges are friendly, purple people want admiration.

"Women who like pink tend to join clubs . . . their conclusion, not mine," she laughs.

People who prefer black, white, neutrals are far less emotional, more self-controlled. It can be a rejection of color . . . a rejection of many things. They possibly are people who won't take chances.

"Taking a chance means risking hurt but receiving great joy," she said.

50
JAPAN IS OPENING UP FOR GAIJIN WHO KNOW HOW

by Louis Kraar,
Fortune

From the flood of gloomy reports in American papers recently, U.S. businessmen might easily conclude that Japan's economy is tumbling into a crisis that will cripple opportunities for their companies in that promising market. But the impact of Arab oil cutbacks has been much exaggerated. The resilient economy has never been threatened with collapse. In fact, Japan has been receiving adequate energy supplies. Over the past few years a surprisingly wide range of U.S. companies have broken into the long-closed Japanese market, and nearly all of them are pushing ahead with expansion plans made before the Mideast erupted last fall.

U.S. executives on the scene plainly see rich prospects in Japan, though there are economic problems. The greatest is raging inflation. But one problem that used to be the most formidable—stubborn Japanese resistance to letting foreigners conduct business in their country—is rapidly receding.

The lopsided trade relationship that frustrated Americans for many years is no longer so lopsided. Not long ago, the Japanese were grabbing rich segments of the U.S. market (such as cameras, television sets, and

From Louis Kraar, "Japan is Opening Up for Gaijin Who Know How," Fortune *(March 1974). © 1974 Time Inc.*

compact cars), but American corporations couldn't gain equal access to Japan's consumers. Now that the country has opened its doors, many U.S. companies are making the most of it. A quarter of Coca-Cola's worldwide earnings flow from its subsidiary in Tokyo. And Brunswick Corp. receives 24 percent of its total net profits from a joint venture that sells bowling equipment in Japan.

"The Japanese market must be viewed as the largest overseas opportunity for U.S. business," says James Abegglen, president of the Boston Consulting Group, which advises corporate clients about how to sell in Japan. "Most of the old protectionist barriers are down, and the rest are fast disappearing."

TOWARD A WESTERN LIFE STYLE

Only in the last year and a half has the Japanese government, under relentless international pressure, eased the major restrictions against foreign enterprises. A voluntary 20 percent across-the-board tariff cut on manufactured items put Japan's import duties roughly on par with those in the U.S. and Europe. Import quotas on nonagricultural products were largely removed. And the government adopted a sweeping liberalization policy that allows foreign investment in nearly all industries. The few notable exceptions, such as computers and pharmaceuticals, will be opened before the end of 1976, according to a precise timetable.

Consumers in Japan, who have attained buying power comparable to those in Western Europe, are especially ready for U.S. goods. After long years of self-denial to speed economic growth, they want to improve the quality of their lives. The Japanese, in fact, are moving toward a life style somewhat closer to the Western pattern. They eat an increasingly varied diet, pursue leisure activities with frantic zest, and are

spending huge sums to improve and replace their generally shabby, cramped housing.

A SPIDER WEB THAT RESISTS OUTSIDERS

But the key to Japan's locked market was the ability of some U.S. corporations to perceive that doing business there requires considerably different techniques than in any other country. Companies that have accepted the unique environment and adjusted to it are doing well. They point the way for others to follow if they have the wit and patience to learn. The main business obstacle, often underestimated in the past, is the clannishness of the Japanese. In this homogeneous, tight-knit society, foreigners are not only called *gaijin*—outsiders—but are instinctively treated as such. The Japanese business system resembles an intricate spider web of personal and financial relationships. It is inherently difficult, though not impossible, for an outsider to enter.

U.S. businessmen face a costly, multilayered distribution system, bound together by credit arrangements and friendships, which is very difficult to crack. Salesmen since feudal days have enjoyed little status; even now they mainly take orders from wholesalers. Aggressive, hard-selling techniques clash with the overwhelming Japanese concern for harmony. Though competition is fierce, there is a tacit understanding that no company will abruptly take away too much of a rival's share of a market.

Ingrained corporate practices pose formidable difficulties. Japanese corporations recruit the best students right out of school, nurture them with paternalism and fat annual pay increases (20 percent last year), and keep them for life. As a result, foreign companies find it is so difficult to attract talented Japanese employees that few of them can operate independently. Though wholly foreign-owned ventures are now permitted in most fields, most companies find it necessary to take a Japanese partner.

SEARS MAKES A QUICK START

A new Sears, Roebuck venture illustrates the possibilities open to companies that adopt a deft approach. Without making any capital investment, the world's largest retailer offers virtually its entire U.S. line to Japanese consumers. The Siebu Group of Retail Enterprises, a family-controlled company with over $2 billion annual sales, serves as a sales agent on a commission basis. Already seventeen Siebu outlets have opened Sears mail-order centers. The Japanese have responded enthusiastically to the Sears way of merchandising and to Sears's prices. Though sales started only eight months ago, customers have snapped up 200,000 catalogues, and monthly volume in merchandise is about $1 million.

Sears owes its quick start mainly to the selection of an able local associate, which shares its aims. Seibu eagerly accepts the Sears policy of money-back guarantees on catalogue sales—far from the usual retailing practice in Japan. Robert Ingersoll, a Chicagoan and former business executive who helped arrange the Sears venture while he was ambassador to Japan, points out: "They're really taking a market survey, and it will lead to much more later—even though Sears top management doesn't fully realize it yet."

COKE'S GIFT TO THE COMPETITION

Few foreign businesses have had more success in Japan than Coca-Cola—or had more troubles because of it. From the start in late 1957, the company avoided the cumbersome local distribution system. Instead, Coke followed its normal practice of franchising bottlers. They are controlled by powerful Japanese corporations, such as Mitsubishi and Mitsui, which have sufficient influence to defy the system and sell directly to dealers for cash.

But as sales skyrocketed toward their present 40 percent of the country's soft-drink market, disgruntled Japanese competitors counterattacked. Small local soft-drink bottlers charged that a "foreign invasion" was driving them into bankruptcy. The press widely publicized claims that large Coke bottles mysteriously exploded. Although the company says it has had no such complaints in any other country, it brought out new bottles reinforced with a double coat of epoxy resin. Even the Coke slogan—"It's the real thing"—was forbidden by Japan's Fair Trade Commission on grounds that it implied other drinks were somehow not genuine.

Finally Coca-Cola turned to what was widely regarded as the major source of its trouble. The company appointed a Japanese as president; he arranged payment of $550,-000 to the protesting local bottlers as a conciliation gift, a traditional gesture. The moves have calmed criticism and protected the company's dominant market position.

A "SOFT TOUCH" THAT SELLS COPIERS

Xerox found an extraordinary way to bridge the gap between American business methods and Japanese culture. Its joint-venture partner, Fuji Photo Film, completely manages daily operations without a single Western senior executive or board member in residence. The solid local image has helped to attract bright, young employees who readily adopt—and adapt—Xerox sales techniques.

The company has held the lion's share of an expanding market for copying machines, despite intense competition recently. In the past seven years, sales have grown an average of about 40 percent annually to $200 million last year, and net profits have generally approached 10 percent of sales.

Fuji Xerox thrives by blending aggressive Western marketing with subtle Oriental touches. Signing up rental customers poses special problems in a land that has habitually looked down upon salesmen. So senior management not only advises new recruits that selling is the path to rapid promotion, but also rewards the best performers with prestige titles. "It means something socially, so we call them managers—even if there aren't many people reporting to them," says Yotaro Kobayashi, managing director and general manager for marketing.

At Xerox's urging, the company bucked custom by providing personal monetary incentives to salesmen. The difficulty is that Japanese regard group effort as more important than individual accomplishment. Moreover, most employees feel insecure working on a commission basis. "Our feeling at the beginning was that this was really against the Japanese grain," says Kobayashi, "but we really wanted better results." So Fuji Xerox set sales goals as team objectives. Salesmen collect regular salaries and benefits, but teams that exceed targets receive extra payments in the bonuses given all personnel twice annually. The system works.

One innovative Japanese approach to customers succeeded so well that Xerox is trying it in other countries. Fuji Xerox created a completely new job category, the customer-service officer (C.S.O.), and filled it mainly with attractive women college graduates. They regularly visit offices that already have the rented machines and offer advice about their use. The "soft touch from an intelligent woman," as Kobayashi puts it, helps to retain contacts and persuade customers to convert to more profitable newer models. The C.S.O.'s proved especially resourceful in countering a wave of cancellations two years ago, when rival machines were offered at lower prices. Nowadays many of its customers call Fuji Xerox with requests to arrange marriages with C.S.O. women, for matchmaking is an enduring Japanese custom.

The U.S. company initially considered the C.S.O. system unnecessary. But as an American executive of Xerox explains: "We're smart enough to realize that there are lots of things about doing business in Japan that we really don't comprehend."

LEARNING TO LIVE WITH GROUP DECISION MAKING

The joint venture started in 1962 as a compromise, for Fuji wanted a straight licensing agreement and Xerox sought majority ownership. Each settled for 50 percent of the joint company. Fuji insisted on managing the venture, but its executives rely heavily on Xerox for advice and technology. Almost all the machines rented in Japan are manufactured locally. Major decisions, including introduction of new products and annual budgets, must be approved by a board on which both partners are equally represented; neither can act alone.

A major advantage of the setup is that Japanese employees and customers regard the corporation as one of their own. Fuji preserves such venerable practices as group decision making; a proposed policy or action plan is circulated among all connected with the problem and discussed until a consensus is reached. By Western standards, it is a lengthy process and often appears to dilute the authority of top executives. But Kobayashi maintains, "Any plan has to be backed up by those who carry it out. People tend to stay with a company here, so you don't want to make enemies of those you'll be working with for many years."

Fierce competition is putting the Xerox arrangement to a severe test. Ten rivals are wooing its customers with lower-priced copying machines. This is a common tactic in Japan, where companies invest heavily to increase market share even at the sacrifice of immediate profits. Even though it is the industry leader, Fuji Xerox is vulnerable because rising operating costs and profit-consciousness rule out price cuts. So the company is responding in other ways that draw on resources of both joint-venture partners. For the first time, Japanese engineers are participating in the design of new product in the U.S. so that Fuji Xerox can introduce them simultaneously. Previously, there was a year or more of delay because American machines had to be adapted for the larger standard paper sizes used in Japan.

A LOSS OF FACE

By contrast, Caterpillar Tractor oversees its joint venture with a large team of Americans. The resulting clash of cultures has caused plenty of management problems. For the past ten years, Caterpillar has politely but firmly "advised" Japanese managers to do things its way—and often succeeded. Says a Caterpillar senior executive, "It's like working with independent U.S. dealers, who must be persuaded to do things but never forced." Half the company is owned by Mitsubishi Heavy Industries, which belongs to Japan's largest zaibatsu; it is known for strong-minded executives, too. Says one insider: "Mitsubishi people are very proud. When Caterpillar told them what to do, they felt a loss of face."

Initially, U.S. executives sharply questioned the relatively high salaries and fringe benefits of employees that Mitsubishi as-

signed to the joint venture from its other companies. But Caterpillar had to accept them. As startup costs mounted, it was Mitsubishi's turn to worry. Japanese companies plan ahead, but they don't make the highly detailed financial projections common in the U.S. Having carefully calculated the costs of building a huge plant outside Tokyo and establishing dealerships, Caterpillar expected a large cumulative deficit. Much to the consternation of Mitsubishi Group officials, the losses eventually reached some $38 million. It was early 1972—right on the Caterpillar timetable—before profits erased the red ink.

IT'S HARD TO SAY "NO"

Caterpillar guides the company by means of a tandem management setup that has become the talk of Tokyo. Twenty-two Americans sit close by Japanese executives who have precisely the same responsibilities; the Caterpillar men advise their counterparts, who give orders down the line. At every level, each official is supposedly coequal. But Caterpillar managers reinforce their influence by reporting to the chairman of the joint venture, an American. He takes the case to the president, a Japanese. "Above all, we avoid confrontations and adjust details to get results," insists E.J. Schlegel, who was chairman of Caterpillar Mitsubishi from 1970 through 1973 and is now a Caterpillar vice president in Peoria. "There are times that we say, 'Okay, we'll do it your way.' "

Getting the joint venture to adopt Caterpillar's manufacturing and sales methods demands long rounds of meetings that are often beset by snarled communication. Neither partner is completely fluent in the other's language. "Sometimes we come out with completely different impressions of what's been decided," says Schlegel. One reason is that in Japan both the ambiguities of the language and customary politeness make it difficult to express a blunt "no."

The most difficult task was persuading Mitsubishi to adopt the Caterpillar marketing system, which relies on sizable dealerships to provide customers with parts and servicing. Normally in Japan, there's a much greater division of labor: manufacturers sell to trading companies, which in turn finance dealers, who have little capital of their own. Maintenance and repairs are left to small independent shops. The Caterpillar-type dealerships have enabled the joint venture to snare about 30 percent of the country's annual sales of earthmoving equipment.

Though the business relationship seems to be working, it has to be conceded that personal relations at Caterpillar Mitsubishi are somewhat tense. In the managers' dining room, one sees Caterpillar people choose tables on one side, while all the Mitsubishi men sit on the opposite side of the room. Few of the Americans have close personal relations with their Japanese associates, and turnover among the Mitsubishi executives has been high, because they prefer to go back to other divisions of the zaibatsu where they feel the atmosphere is more congenial. Profits hold the joint venture together.

HOW HEINZ GOT OUT OF THE SOUP

One of the most inviting opportunities for U.S. companies is the processed-food industry, which is increasingly receptive to Western products. But, again, the convoluted distribution system poses an implacable barrier to most outsiders who tackle it alone. Selling any brand involves pushing it through a maze of intermediaries into thousands of tiny retail outlets. When H.J. Heinz tried to buck the system, the result was a fiasco. To enter Japan, Heinz hastily took a minority interest in a joint venture with Nichiro Fisheries, which lacked both capital and broad distribution channels. Heinz ketchup, canned goods, and baby foods reached the Japanese market in 1963—and flopped. One problem: Nichiro's name on the label gave many housewives the false impression that the contents were fish-flavored.

As losses mounted, the partners argued bitterly over what to do about them; Heinz finally bought 80 percent of the joint venture in 1967 and began using American-style marketing. It bypassed primary wholesalers and sold directly to smaller ones; then it began dealing directly with large retailers. The whole Japanese food network banded together in a boycott of Heinz products.

To repair the damage, Heinz turned in December, 1970, to a gentle Japanese executive, Kazuo Asai. He had marketing experience in both countries (having worked for a Japanese trading firm), a degree from the Wharton School of Finance, and a willingness to leave his last employer, Dow Corning. Asai also has what counts most in Japan—an acute sensitivity for human relationships and good personal connections through his wealthy family. In a year as president of Nichiro Heinz, he turned the chaos into profit.

"My predecessors didn't understand the delicate situation here," says Asai. He put Heinz back into normal distribution channels through the sort of personal effort that most impresses his countrymen: he visited every major wholesaler and profusely apologized for bypassing them: "At first, most of them wouldn't even listen and several said, 'Go to hell.' I kept going back until they were convinced we were sincere," he recalls. Asai purposely offered no additional monetary incentives to distributors. "No matter how much money you offer or how many big geisha parties you give, it makes no difference if people don't trust you. That was our problem." Within the company,

Asai conducted a similar campaign of persuasion to restore morale, which had been shattered by high turnover of personnel.

Once harmony was restored between Heinz and Japan, the company's products gained increasing acceptance. Its market share of canned soups, for instance, has doubled, to 60 percent. In addition to regular retail outlets, Asai has developed substantial business with hotels and restaurants by carefully cultivating a relatively small group of specialized wholesalers. Heinz has also broadened its appeal by making products in Japan (among them curry-flavored ketchup) that cater to long-standing local tastes.

Since the Japanese president took over, sales have risen by an average of 30 percent annually, to nearly $4 million last year. Asai expects they will climb 50 percent this year and next because of a shift to an even more traditional distribution channel. Mitsubishi Corp., Japan's largest trading firm, now handles all Heinz products. The trader's extensive contacts and credit facilities will greatly increase outlets for Heinz.

DOING "THINGS WE NEVER DREAMED OF"

Unlike Heinz, Brunswick Corp. bet on the right strategy immediately when it came into Japan in 1961. It formed a joint venture to sell bowling equipment—and then shrewdly used its presence to develop ever widening business in other lines, ranging from boat motors to medical supplies. Each activity has enhanced Brunswick's ability to move into another.

Taking a long-range view of the potential returns, Brunswick asked for no royalties when it teamed up with Mitsui & Co., a major trading house. Instead, the company waited for profits from the fifty-fifty joint venture, called Nippon Brunswick. It over-

came a sluggish start when the new Japanse bent for leisure brought on a bowling boom. The company has provided a third of the country's 130,000 lanes—and profited immensely. Among corporations with substantial foreign capital, its pretax earnings of $58.6 million were second only to I.B.M.'s according to Japanese tax returns published last year.

From the start, Brunswick itself has also been expanding its activities through an independent Tokyo branch. One big reason the company has been able to do so successfully is that, unlike most American corporations, Brunswick keeps U.S. executives in Japan for long periods and expects them to learn the language. Garrett M. Flint, managing director of the Tokyo branch for nine years, speaks Japanese fluently. "Just because you're here leads to all sorts of other things—things we never dreamed of at first," says Flint. The Japanese mania for golf opened the way for MacGregor clubs and bags, which bring Brunswick $10 million in annual sales. In status-conscious Japan, golf is now the prestige game and name-brand clubs bestow extra cachet. By being on the scene, Brunswick spotted the trend early and built up volume gradually. The clubs are exported from America; the bags are manufactured in Japan by a licensee. Initially, the U.S. company sold through normal wholesale channels. But Flint saw that he could cut prices and raise margins by selling directly to retailers. That's a risky step in Japan, but the company made the switch in 1970 without stumbling.

"You can do things differently here if you know what you're doing and proceed in the right way," says Flint. He bypassed distributors by working through Brunswick's Japanese staff. The staff concluded that the shift was feasible, recruited a larger sales force, and—most delicately—broke the news to wholesalers. Brunswick now provides credit to 300 mostly small retailers who were previously financed by wholesalers.

Brunswick uses its association with large corporations to good advantage too. In 1968 its own sales force started promoting products for Sherwood Medical Industries, a U.S. subsidiary that makes disposable hypodermic needles and syringes. But Flint found that he needed better contacts with Japanese hospitals. So Brunswick turned to Mitsui, which is in touch with every major industry through its own teams of specialists. Last year Brunswick and Mitsui formed a new company, Nippon Sherwood, to manufacture and sell the medical items.

"There's certainly a synergistic effect," observes Flint. "The more contacts you have, the more power you have to get things done. I don't mean dictating, but skill in finding your way through the labyrinth of negotiations and achieving results."

THE SALESLADY HAS TO BE FORMALLY INTRODUCED

Business contacts normally begin with formal introductions through mutual friends and rarely occur in Japanese homes. In the face of these strong traditions, Avon has launched door-to-door sales of cosmetics. But the system it uses in seventeen other countries had to be modified to suit the sensitivities of Japan—as did many of its products.

Under its well-tested system, the company has found 20,000 housewives willing to become sales representatives on a commission basis. As elsewhere, each is called an "Avon lady." But the similarity ends there. In Western countries, Avon sales representatives routinely call on people they don't know and often obtain an order on the first visit. Japanese, on the other hand, regard their homes as sacrosanct, and any sales relationship is fraught with fear that one of the parties—buyer or seller—may lose face. Not surprisingly, as George E. Gustin, Avon general manager in Japan reports, "the Avon lady here is not as aggressive and outgoing as her counterpart in the West."

After much hand wringing and experimentation, Avon started adapting its approach to meet these special challenges. Through friends and relatives, area managers around the country arrange formal introductions of Avon ladies to prospective customers. To help overcome the innate shyness of its sales force, the company appeals to Japanese group-consciousness; as it does nowhere else, Avon holds large "beauty class" meetings, where it dispenses product data and pep talks.

Even though Avon offers up to 33 percent commission on sales in Japan, the company has discovered it can't be too blunt about monetary rewards alone; working only for money seems crass to most Japanese. Thus Avon inspires its Oriental ladies by discussing things of value they can buy with earnings, such as a TV set or refrigerator, and stressing what Gustin calls "pleasant objectives," such as helping make customers look better.

Average sales of a Japanese Avon lady still lag behind those in most other countries where the company operates. But each Japanese customer buys more. So far, Avon has garnered about 2 percent of Japan's cosmetics market, which has reached a wholesale volume of $1.2 billion a year (the world's second largest after the U.S.). If the company continues to overcome the social barriers, it expects to earn profits in Japan starting next year. It is showing its confidence by investing $5 million to build a plant near Tokyo to meet anticipated demand for the next decade.

Both the successes and the failures of American companies in Japan demonstrate that the only way to operate there is to accept the country's ways and adapt to them.

Once the Japanese are met on their own terms, there is a lot of latitude for introducing fresh techniques in sales and management.

Above all, things get done through personal contacts, not just formal business transactions. Cultivating the essential friendships requires more time than the usual two- or three-year executive assignment. Most corporations would be better served by keeping men in Japan for five or even ten years. Top executives need not speak Japanese fluently, but some knowledge of the language not only smooths social relations but also affords valuable insights into the Japanese way of thinking.

Patience, grace, and the ability to communicate are especially important in Japan. Even a seemingly relaxed evening of entertainment, for instance, may be a crucial test to a Japanese of an American's compatibility. Smart U.S. executives never talk business at such gatherings.

When they do get down to business, alway in the office, Japanese executives are just as interested in harmonious relations as in profits. Brisk Americans eager to sign contracts are likely to run into delays; the Japanese move deliberately and prefer to rely on overall understanding rather than legal contracts. There are few business secrets in Japan. As many U.S. companies have learned, anyone who discusses investment plans with a government ministry can expect the whole local industry to know about it, too. Thus it is usually best to meet Japanese competitors and tell them directly, for their acceptance is also vital. Avon, among others, did this before entering Japan.

NEW HELP FOR U.S. EXPORTERS

The Japanese themselves have belatedly recognized that their cohesive business system and insular customs remain formidable barriers. To prove that the old protectionism has ended, several of the nation's leading exporters have assumed a new role—helping U.S. companies sell in Japan. Sony is distributing through its own facilities about fifty products, including Shick electric razors, Heathkit amplifiers, and Whirlpool refrigerators.

Still, the best starting point for many U.S. export items is a Japanese trading company. Some of the giant traders are already so busy handling rival products that they may give newcomers insufficient attention, but hundreds of smaller, specialized firms are eager to exploit Japanese enthusiasm for international name brands and unusual products. Some fifty companies expressed interest in teaming up with Sears for catalogue sales. "There are still a lot more opportunities here than American companies are aware of," says former U.S. Ambassador Ingersoll, "but first they must know more about Japan."

51

ONWARD AND UPWARD FOR ONE MORE YEAR

by Warren R. Ross,
Harper's

What is your most ardent wish for 1976?

If you don't know, you are obviously not a corporate marketing manager. The executives who rule the destinies of the nation's corporations, large, small, or in between, know precisely what they want for '76. It is the same thing they want for '75, are working for in '74, and will want again each year for as long as they hold their jobs: an increase in sales.

It doesn't matter whether the executive is in charge of selling toothpaste to the millions, asphalt to the state highway department, drugs to doctors, or fragmentation antipersonnel bombs to the Pentagon. His primary corporate responsibility is to boost sales, and his career rides on whether he can do better this year than he did last.

The reason is obvious. All but a few corporations are publicly owned, and stockholders care only that their stock go up. So all they want to hear from the president at annual-report time is that sales and profits have improved. Which means that all the president wants to hear from his VP-sales is

From Warren R. Ross, "Onward and Upward for One More Year." Copyright © 1973, by Minneapolis Star and Tribune Co. Inc. Reprinted from the May, 1973, issue of Harper's *Magazine by special permission.*

how he proposes to make sales go up . . . ditto for what the VP wants to hear from his regional managers . . . down to the salesman in the field. Yes, sir, chief, we'll make those sales go up! Yes, indeed, can do!

It's odd that this basic fact of our economic life seems never to be taken into account by those who want to reform the system's flaws. Yet it's at the bottom of so much that's wrong. Take just a few examples.

POLITICAL

Since few companies can increase product sales indefinitely, the surest way to grow is through mergers and acquisitions. Until this basic motive is removed, no antitrust law will ever be enforceable, and such laws as we have, *vide* ITT, merely provide incentives for corruption.

ECONOMIC

On the record, possibly in all sincerity, corporate executives are all for the sound dollar. But every time a choice has to be made —whether or not to raise prices, whether to borrow, whether to keep production going by giving in to what the union wants—they cast a vote for inflation. Thus there is a large and influential, even if unintentional, lobby for easy money.

ECOLOGIC

Barry Commoner has clearly shown that it is neither growth nor efficiency but the search for greater profits that has fueled the pollution explosion of the past two decades. Almost as a corollary, more and more experts are telling us that the key to preserving our resources and cleaning up the environment is economic stability. Yet how can the national product be maintained at zero growth if all the national producers are working overtime and weekends to make *their* portion of it grow?

ETHICAL

If the one thing you can never tell your boss is why business didn't grow this year, you will often be tempted to resort to price-fixing, quality-cutting, or dubious selling tactics. Conscience and common sense may tell you that in the long run your company might profit more from quality products fairly priced and sold. But you also know that in the long run you simply aren't going to be around if you don't achieve this year's sales goals. However, if you do attain them, they immediately become the record that you have to improve on next year. Which brings us to the:

PERSONAL

For a few years, Sisyphus [the mythical character who pushed a heavy stone uphill] probably loved his job, and, as he learned to roll that stone faster and faster, experienced a sense of great achievement. But after a while, he sometimes felt as if a crushing weight were threatening him, and more and more often there were days when he felt he was between the rock and the hard place. But as with so many executives, the one thing that seemed riskier than to keep pushing was to let go.

Is there an answer? In an economy as intricate and creaky as ours, it would be a bold man who would claim to know. But the first step, surely, is to face up to the fact that many of our societal and individual ills will never be cured until a product manager can file a marketing plan that says: business is good, we're making a nice profit; let's aim at doing equally well next year. And still keep his job.

WHAT ELSE AFFECTS MARKETING?

Marketing plans must at some stage involve forecasts of what will happen if:

—Our firm tries this

—Competitors try that

—Buyer needs change, or don't

—Ability to buy changes, or doesn't . . .

—And so forth, for a long, long list.

The trick is to figure out the most important IF's for a particular marketing plan, then develop alternatives when the changes that will drastically affect that plan either happen, or don't, or some of each. To discover the crucial IF's, we'd recommend reading not only these articles in this section, but as many newspapers, trade magazines, and current events publications as possible. Questions to ask while reading (these articles, for a start) are the following:

1. Suppose I view this article as describing a trend line. Exactly *what* is going up or down—and which way is it going?

2. What happens to the marketing of X (you pick the product) if the trend keeps going in the same direction? What happens if we're really looking at part of a cycle—so the trend will change after a while?

3. Which is more likely—continuous trend or cycle? We might be evaluating the increasing number of required product recalls, the increasing proportion of one-person households, the increasing proportion of U.S. firms marketing overseas—or whatever.

4. What should the marketers of X do in case the trend continues? What should they do differently if it reverses?

5. What will help them to forecast which is more likely in the case of: use of natural materials in clothing? demographic diversity among motorcycle buyers? emphasis on growth in large corporations?

⑧ MARKETERS YOU DIDN'T KNOW WERE MARKETING

Besides the butcher, the baker, and candlestick maker, who is marketing these days? Can you imagine—hospitals? An organization called Religion In American Life? Museums? Lawyers? Universities?

Cities are marketing police careers to black and Mexican-American "prospects." Obstetrics? Good works? They're all products, too—because Marketing is Everybody's Business.

52

ATTRACTING MINORITY POLICEMEN

The billboard proclaims, "MACHO! Join the LAPD. 485-4051." Los Angeles is recruiting Mexican-American police officers. But elsewhere in the same city, another billboard shows a black policeman on a motorcycle, with the simple slogan "Right on." Los Angeles is also recruiting black police officers, and with a marketing effort sophisticated enough to aim different messages at its two target groups.

Recruiting policemen from minority communities has gained nationwide recognition; increasingly it is viewed as a marketing problem. As in any marketing problem, competition is a factor: an Associated Press survey shows that stiff competition from industry in the hiring of minorities has been a major factor in the low percentage of minority-group policemen. To meet competition, cities have turned to a marketing approach: examination of the "product" from the perspective of the desired customer, and a campaign to enhance the product's "price," "promotion," and "distribution."

Examining the product from the point of view of the "buyer"—for example, a black policeman—has led departments to realize that one of the byproducts of a police career may be social ostracism. An Associated Press story about a black officer in Santa Ana, California, for example, quotes him as saying that once he joined the force his social life with black friends was curtailed. "You and your wife go to a party which is merry and gay—until you enter . . . the music dims, the laughter slowly melts, the faces looking at you become hostile or grim." The product also includes working conditions, hours, degree of danger, chance for promotion, and other components that become, once the marketing viewpoint is adopted, subject to scrutiny by those marketing police careers.

Price? The inverse of a price: a salary. Promotion? Not only by billboards but through "direct sales" by high school guidance counselors. Here, however, the common requirement that police be 19 or older complicates the marketing effort. The high school guidance counselor can hardly be effective as a salesperson if the potential buyer must wait a year until he or she is eligible to buy the product. As is often the case, a rule, or "product specification" established for a non-marketing purpose has significant marketing implications.

Those marketing police careers recognize that they are in competitipon not only with industry, but also with fire departments, the armed forces, and even criminal careers. This last alternative career is of special interest, since it may preclude qualification for a later police job. A more conventional marketing parallel would be the competition between marketers of mobile campers and marketers of vacation homes. The man who purchases the latter very likely removes himself from the market for the former because he is no longer interested, and because he is no longer financially qualified. Aware of this threat, the marketer of campers does not advertise, "Don't buy vacation homes," but he does vigorously promote his vehicles on billboards near vacation home developments, in the hope of pointing out the alternative before it is too late. Similarly, cities that undertake the vigorous promotion of police careers to young people in minority-group communities hope that they provide a more effective form of competition with crime than do signs saying "Shoplifters will be prosecuted."

"Distribution" of police careers is usually through only one channel; the prospective "buyer" applies in writing at City Hall. It may develop, however, that neighborhood offices and mobile "police information centers," or booths in the malls of shopping centers, will become a more effective channel in minority communities. Taking the product to the customer is an ancient marketing strategy, and as cities recognize that they are, in fact, marketing in minority communities, they may reinstate the equivalent of the peddler: selling shields and blue uniforms.

SOURCES

1. "Police Department Is Having Trouble Recruiting Blacks." Houston *Chronicle*, April 8, 1973, Section 4, p. 4.
2. "Social Pressures Hinder Police Minority Recruiting." Associated Press, carried in the Houston *Post*, February 22, 1973, Section C, p. 5.

53
BRITISH DOCTORATES FOR SALE

advertisement

So far as we know, 1973 was the first year in which anybody ran a full-page ad in *Business Week* selling doctorates, and one might suspect that the advertisers enjoyed hurling their tongue-in-cheek barbs at universities— almost as much as they enjoyed opening the envelopes containing $100 checks.

Everyone, of course, was not amused. The New York state attorney general's office brought suit under the state's consumer protection law against Diners Club, asking that the Diners Club card not be used as a credit card with which to buy the honorary degrees. The suit was successful: Diners Club agreed in the state supreme court to stop letting card holders charge the degrees.

The New York *Times*, in a news story on the London Institute for Applied Research, reported that 808 of the honorary degrees had been purchased with Diners Club cards. The "Institute," whose initials are LIAR, lists a mailing address in London, but the *Times* reported that mail is actually forwarded from London to an American named John Bear, living on the Isle of Wight. The newspaper said that Bear "is presumably the same John Bear who back in 1971 gained some small fame in this country as the promoter of spoof degrees (Doctor of Pinochle Sciences, for example), purportedly from the Millard Fillmore Institute."

BRITISH DOCTORATES FOR SALE

Aha, you are thinking, another one of those phony diploma mills, out to make a fast buck (or pound). Not so. Permit us to explain who we are and what we are up to. Perhaps we will be able to convince you that exchanging a $100 gift for one of our lovely diplomas may be a good thing to do.

Who we are.

We are a large group of university faculty and other academic types who have gotten together to form a most unusual new kind of school: a correspondence school with no pre-packaged courses; a school whose main activity is setting up one-to-one postal relationships between students and faculty. A 'course' may consist of anything from a long series of telephone calls to several years of directed studies in a variety of fields. When a predetermined number of faculty have been satisfied, we award a legitimate earned bachelor's degree. We accepted our first students in the Spring of 1973. If you would like to know more, please tick the appropriate box on the coupon and we'll send you our catalogue.

The honorary doctorates.

In order to finance the development of our school, and so we can charge our students less and pay our faculty more, we are selling honorary doctorates for $100. Isn't this illegal or immoral or something? We think not. A significant proportion of honorary doctorates given each year by major American and British universities go to people who donate large sums of money to the school. A famous American comedian, for instance, gave $800,000 to a large university and 'happened' to receive an honorary doctorate from them the same year. Coincidence? It happens all the time. Oxford and Cambridge

both recently renamed an entire college after the same major donor the only man other than Jesus to be so honoured. In selling our honorary doctorate for $100, we are merely doing openly (and comparatively inexpensively) what many other reputable schools have been doing covertly.

What good are honorary degrees?

Whether from us or anyone else, they have no legitimacy in the academic world. As Mark Twain said on receiving his first honorary doctorate (from Oxford), 'What a glorious piece of wallpaper!' We have tried to make our diploma as decorative as possible, as you can see from the small illustration.

The actual size is 13 by 17 inches, and we use the same good imitation parchment used by major British universities. We offer ten 'traditional' degree titles, each of them in use as honorary titles at least 100 universities. We imprint your name in gold, using professional diploma printing equipment, affix our embossed seal, and send you your order by air mail in a strong mailing tube.

The ten degrees offered.

1. Doctor of Laws.
2. Doctor of Science.
3. Doctor of Letters.
4. Doctor of Music.
5. Doctor of Divinity.
6. Doctor of Commercial Science.
7. Doctor of Humane Letters.
8. Doctor of Literature.
9. Doctor of Humanities.
10. Doctor of Fine Arts.

How to order.

Send us $100 by cheque or money order, or authorise us to charge your credit card for this sum. Tell us which title you want. All diplomas are dated 30 June in the year of issue. We cannot print titles (Dr., Rev., Ph.D., etc.) before or after your name.

Regarding postage and timing.

Air mail letters from the US to England cost 21c and take about a week. We ship only by air. It will probably be faster, but please allow 45 days for receipt of your order before you begin to grow alarmed. Thank you.

London Institute for Applied Research
Suite 50, 29/30 Warwick Street
London W1R 5FA, England

London Institute for Applied Research 29/30 Warwick St., Suite 50, London W1R 5FA, England.

Please send me _____ *honorary doctorate(s) at* $100 *each (or equivalent in any currency)*

☐ *Personal cheque or money order enclosed. (Cheques payable to 'London Institutes' please.)*

☐ *Charge to my credit card; I have filled in the credit card ordering information at the right.*

Name _____

Address _____
Number & street   City & state or province   Postal Code   Country

For credit card orders, please fill in the following information:
☐ *Diners Club*   ☐ *American Express*   ☐ *Master Charge*

Card number _____
All raised numbers & letters please. Please be very legible.

Expiration date _____

Authorised signature _____

NAME ON DIPLOMA PLEASE WRITE CLEARLY!!! DEGREE ON DIPLOMA	

☐ *Please send further information about the undergraduate programme.*

("British Doctorates for Sale," advertisement in Business Week, May 26, 1973, by London Institute for Applied Research. Reprinted by permission of the publisher and the advertiser.)

54
BEAUTIFUL OLD SIWASH

by Allan J. Mayer,
Wall Street Journal

Berkeley advertises the "California summer" with its "perfect weather." The University of Maine says its "recreational opportunities are endless." The University of New Hampshire boasts "room to spread out, quiet lakes, the ocean, mountains and clean air." The University of Colorado offers a "vacation in a beautiful mountain setting."

No, the schools aren't filling in for their local Chambers of Commerce. They're simply trying to survive in what Martin W. Sampson, dean of Cornell University's summer school, calls "the fierce competition" for the more than a million students who use their summer vacations to continue their education.

"Universities are all trying to make maximum use of their brick and mortar because of the financial emergency currently gripping American higher education," says a spokesman for the Association of American Colleges, "and that means keeping open in the summer."

While university enrollments and income have increased in the last decade, they haven't kept pace with sharply rising costs. And many universities fear that any further

From Allan J. Mayer, "Beautiful Old Siwash: Schools Wax Eloquent in Vying for Students," Wall Street Journal, July 6, 1972. Reprinted with permission of The Wall Street Journal © 1972 Dow Jones & Company, Inc. All Rights Reserved.

increases in tuition will result in pricing themselves right out of the market. Thus the emergency.

FIGHTING FOR FEES

"The universities are desperately fighting for fees," says Charles E. Noyes, director of the University of Mississippi's summer session and president of the National Association of Summer Sessions. "And so they advertise, they go on radio, they send out letters—in fact, they do almost anything they can."

The University of Arizona numbers among its attractions a series of weekend tours, including visits to Las Vegas and the Grand Canyon. "They just eat that stuff up," says Pendleton Gaines, dean of the summer session.

But Dean Gaines isn't exactly enthusiastic about advertising. "It's like football scholarships," he says. "You wish nobody gave them but since everybody does, you have to also." The sentiment reflects the feelings of many educators, who are uncomfortable over the prospect of hard-sell advertising as a means of raising summer enrollments.

"I hope we don't come to that," says Robert A. Plane, Cornell's provost. But though he draws the line at ads containing pictures of sunbathing coeds, he says "there's nothing wrong with a picture of a sailboat on Lake Cayuga."

"That," he insists, "isn't hard sell. It's simply truth in advertising."

CRUSADERS PROVE PROFITABLE

Like many universities, Cornell offers a number of noncredit summer programs (last year it had 52 of them), some prepackaged by outside groups who provide the students and the teachers. In return for the use of its facilities, a school can make a tidy sum. Last summer, for example, the Campus Crusade for Christ brought some 500 adherents to Cornell for a five-and-a-half-week Bible-study course. Including dormitory rent, the program added more than $55,600 to the Cornell coffers.

Noncredit courses, attended simply for enjoyment, perhaps, or under company orders, can be a big help to hard-pressed universities. A series of noncredit engineering seminars at Cornell "made a bundle of money for us," says Dean Sampson; most of the students were "professional engineers brushing up whose companies paid their way."

Another popular noncredit course is one in mountain climbing offered by the University of Colorado, which calls it "a natural development because of Boulder's proximity" to the Rockies.

But designing summer programs with an eye to popularity doesn't sit well with many educators. "If you run a summer session on a self-sustaining basis, it's very easy to let commercialism creep in," says Frederic Morrissey, director of summer sessions at the University of California at Berkeley.

"You have to maintain academic standards," he insists, "since it's very easy to let them deteriorate in the pressure to get students." And though he feels "there's nothing wrong with advertising the summer session," he was unhappy with an ad Berkeley ran in college newspapers. It featured a curvaceous coed in a bikini who beckoned to prospective students: "Enjoy summer this school."

Such competition is intensified by the fact that the nation's colleges running summer schools—most experts put the number over 500—are competing for a pool of students that isn't growing right now. After a decade of 5 percent to 10 percent annual

growth, the summers of 1970 and 1971 saw a leveling off in the number of students attending summer schools, says Dr. Noyes of the association of summer sessions.

"It had to do with the economic recession." he says. "You can't say summer school is a luxury, but it is something close to it."

Dr. Noyes explains that a large number of students attend summer school "because frankly, things in the old home town can be a bit dull in the summer." These students, Dr. Noyes says, never made up the bulk of summer enrollees but did account for much of the growth in the 1950s. When the economic decline made it harder to send young people to summer school, more and more of such students stayed home. . . .

New York University, one of the largest private universities and currently in deep financial trouble, is trying a variety of inducements, including the offer of a free room for the summer to any student who signs up for more than six credits at its University Heights campus.

Perhaps NYU's greatest disadvantage in trying to attract summer students is one shared by all the universities in New York City. "One of the strongest things against us," says William Owens, dean of Columbia University's summer session, "is that we're Columbia University in the city of New York."

MUGGINGS AND ROBBERIES

What that means, he says, is that "we have our share of muggings and robberies; there are many people, I think, who would have come here in the past but don't now because of the situation in the city." He suggests they are perhaps not so fearful that they would shy away from Columbia during the regular academic year but fearful enough to stay out of hot New York in the summertime.

Dean Owens says that this fear is partly responsible for the decline in summer enrollment at Columbia from 5,300 in 1965 to 3,500 last year.

So what does an urban school do? It offers to send its summer students not only out of the city but out of the country as well. NYU is sponsoring a graduate study abroad program for teachers of humanities, which offers three successive summers of courses in Paris, Kyoto and New York leading to a master of arts degree in English education, a program that some call of dubious value.

"It's a meaningless degree, created solely to attract high-school teachers because they're paying customers," charges one NYU professor. A New York City high-school teacher says, "The only reason I applied was that it seemed a good excuse to go around the world and pick up some graduate credit at the same time."

55
DOCTORS, LAWYERS, INDIAN CHIEFS

The office of the neighborhood dentist moves into a department store. The neighborhood lawyer buys TV time and advises clients by telephone. The neighborhood clinical psychologist tests two different approaches for advertising copy. The neighborhood M.D. offers "easy credit terms for cosmetic surgery."

Ten years ago any of these professionals could have expected that the appropriate state association would react. Depending on the circumstances, an action up to and including the suspension of license to practice could have been the penalty for marketing activity.

But there is new recognition that a convenient location is one way to encourage preventive care, and that a "bargain" category of service may be useful for some legal problems. And in a series of decisions from 1975 through 1977, the U.S. Supreme Court gradually extended constitutional protection to "commercial speech" by professionals —in other words, advertising. Most significant was a 1977 ruling, *Bates vs. O'Steen,* that lawyers cannot be barred from advertising their fees for routine legal services such as simple wills and uncontested divorces. Then in 1978, the Federal Trade Commission, in an antitrust action against the American Medical Association, sought to end the ban on advertising by doctors.

NEW STATE LAWS

In response to these legal developments, several states changed laws that had prohibited advertising by doctors, lawyers, engineers, druggists, and optometrists. While most of these professionals did not begin advertising, some tested the marketing waters in a variety of ways. Others are affected by Federal Trade Commission rulings, some of which are being appealed.

—A number of physicians have watched with interest the move by dentists into Sears, Roebuck & Company stores in California. Meanwhile, a spokesman for Montgomery Ward & Company reports, "It's conceivable that we could eventually have as many as 100 of our stores with leased dental units." One factor in predicting expansion of the dentist/department store relationship is cost: chain leasing of space can cut expenses by 25%, principally through larger wholesale purchases of supplies. Sears is also studying the idea of adding franchised legal services to its current customer service "mix."

—Supplementing advertising by legal firms, a California group has begun the TV Law Forum, which teaches people how to write their own wills and contracts and even to plead their own cases in court. Another law practice, with a storefront location, sells kits of information and legal forms to buyers who want to handle simple legal procedures on their own. Still other clients are charged less than $20 to pick up a telephone at a location called the Law Store and consult with an attorney. For an additional small amount, the attorney will write a simple letter or make a routine phone call—for example, to suggest to someone who owes the client money that the bill should be paid promptly.

—The Federal Trade Commission has issued a trade regulation rule affecting opthalmic goods and services. The rule prohibits state codes from banning advertising. It also requires that consumers be provided with copies of prescriptions after eye examinations, so that they can "shop" for eyeglasses or contact lenses on their own.

—The American Medical Association is appealing another FTC ruling, one which seeks to permit enough advertising to give patients "a decisional basis for selecting one doctor as opposed to another." The FTC says such advertising would lead to wiser choices in the purchase of medical services. The AMA says it would lead to "hucksterism."

—Proposed guidelines by the American Psychological Association permit a description of the service provided, level of certification of the psychologist, and such issues as "third-party payment policy." Degrees held, fee information, and a brief listing of the type of services offered is already permitted. Research on the kinds of ads that "sell" appeared in a newsletter sent to APA members. A researcher had showed several hundred college students 40 mock ads, ranging from the stodgy to one that began: "My name is Lane, anxiety and depression relief is my game." Free trial offers proved popular, but a refund idea— "Personal distress and suffering relieved or money back"—was favored least often.

Like other professional associations, the APA does restrict "unethical advertising," and has examples to cite. One was a full-page ad in a national newspaper, featuring caricatures of two well-known psychologists dressed up as a legendary gun-slinging twosome. The ad referred to them as the "Butch Cassidy and Sundance Kid of Psychology," and promoted a book they had co-authored. The APA sent a "cease and desist" warning; the psychologists stopped the ad.

HOW MUCH CHICKEN?

Equally picturesque was the advertising by Dr. Richard J. Talsky, a Chicago-area chiropractor who, as he later declared in court, felt the need to "express a vitally important message of great potential interest to consumers of health services." His ad in a suburban newspaper called Berwin *Life* advertised:

> Free Chicken, Free Refreshments, Free Spinal X-Ray.
>
> Chiropractic open house. So that we may know how much chicken to order, please call and tell us how many will be in your group. How about a chiropractic back-to-school checkup?

The Illinois Department of Registration and Education suspended Dr. Talsky's license to practice chiropracty for 90 days. The Illinois Supreme Court concurred, and on later appeal, so did the U.S. Supreme Court. Clearly, not all advertising by professionals will be permitted. As of 1979, several issues had been left unresolved:

—Can professionals be prohibited from using "trade names"? Early in 1979, that case was under review by the U.S. Supreme Court. An optometrist and a consumer organization challenged a Texas law that prohibits optometrists from using any trade or corporate name.
—Can professionals make claims in advertising about the quality of their work? One Chicago lawyer, for example,

placed advertising that showed a man behind bars and a police officer in front of the cell. "Busted?" it asked, and offered the lawyer's phone number. Opponents of the ad said it implied that the lawyer could help win release from jail.
—Can a state or a professional organization regulate the style of ads? The Supreme Court has said that authorities retain the right to regulate the "time, place, and manner" of ads. But an Ohio judge has ruled that the state's dental board has no right to enforce rules barring dentists from using "large displays" of "glittering light signs" or showing pictures of teeth.

So far, no doctor has bought a "glittering sign" showing a diseased appendix. Furthermore, there is no evidence that advertising by doctors will bring down fees, as the Federal Trade Commission hopes. One medical economist doubts that even price advertising would have much effect, simply because the insurance company, not the patient, is so likely to be paying the bill. Staff members at the FTC disagree, though. It remains to be seen whether they will try to win converts to their point of view—and whether their strategy for doing so will be to take out ads.

SOURCES

1. Cohen, Dorothy, "FTC Preempts States in Rule on Eyeglasses." *Marketing News,* November 3, 1978, p. 4.
2. "FTC Judge Orders AMA to Drop Doctor Ad Ban." Houston *Post,* November 30, 1978, Section A, p. 23.
3. "Lawyer Pitchmen Find It Pays to Advertise on TV." New York *Times* News Service, published in the Springfield, Illinois, *Journal-Register,* September 10, 1978, p. 9.
4. Lazarus, George, " 'Department Store Dentistry' May be Coming." Chicago *Tribune,*

December 17, 1978, Section 5, p. 6.

5. Mann, Jim, "Nation's Courts Are Regulating How Professions May Advertise." Los Angeles *Times*-Washington *Post* News Service, published in the Houston *Chronicle*, January 1, 1979, Section 1, p. 22.

6. Massow, Rosalind, "Should Doctors Advertise?" *Parade,* June 11, 1978, pp. 19–20.

7. Nicholson, Tom, "Doctor's Dilemma." *Newsweek,* January 5, 1976.

8. Pendleton, Jennifer, "Sears, Roebuck May Give Legal Clinics a Trial Run." *Advertising Age,* January 22, 1979, p. 2.

9. Schaar, Karen. In the newsletter of the American Psychological Association, November 1978.

10. "Supermarketing Legal Services." *Time,* October 9, 1978, p. 116.

MUSEUMS MERCHANDISE MORE SHOWS AND WARES TO BROADEN PATRONAGE

by Roger Ricklefs,
The Wall Street Journal

NEW YORK—These days, the world remembers Richard II for precious little besides his follies, his intrigues and his decidedly antisocial decapitations of unfriendly subjects. Despised by multitudes, the 14th Century English king was forced out of his job and plunked into Pontefract Castle. He apparently died of starvation, possibly because he wouldn't eat.

But if New York's Metropolitan Museum has its way, King Richard will soon be remembered for something else: his dinner parties. For $5.95 plus tax, the museum will send you "To the King's Taste," the recipe book for Richard's kitchen, adapted for modern use. Illustrated with medieval woodcuts, this offbeat cookbook is based on a manuscript in the museum.

To make your own "Perrey of Person"

From Roger Ricklefs, "Museums Merchandise More Shows and Wares To Broaden Patronage," Wall Street Journal (August 14, 1975). Reprinted with permission of the Wall Street Journal. © 1975 Dow Jones & Co. All rights reserved.

(medieval pea soup) or "Sawse Madame" (stuffed goose), you will naturally need medieval spices and herbs. If the local A&P doesn't happen to stock elderflower, powdered galingale and the like, the museum will ship you your own special kit of six medieval herbs and spices—for $4 extra.

The mail-order medieval herb and spice biz is a far cry from Rembrandt etchings and other traditional museum fare. But these days, art museums are becoming hot merchandisers. Besides pushing cookbooks and similar wares, they are promoting art as never before and attracting crowds an old-time curator could scarcely believe.

MEXICAN ART IN OAKLAND

The Met here and the National Gallery of Art in Washington, two of the world's most prestigious museums, are leaders in the trend. But they certainly aren't alone. In California, the Oakland Museum says its "festivals" celebrating the cultural heritage of Chinese, Mexicans, Africans, Greeks and other ethnic groups in the area commonly attract 30,000 to 50,000 visitors apiece—including large numbers who had never set foot in the museum before. The J.B. Speed Art Museum in Louisville says its lectures on photography have attracted "thousands" who wouldn't come otherwise. Often, the photo fans get interested in the museum's paintings, too, says an official. Two years ago, the museum also opened a special permanent gallery for the blind filled with statues the visitors can touch, and several other museums have started similar programs.

The Art Institute of Chicago says it has doubled the size of its museum store in the last five years and now sells goods ranging from decorative Philippine baskets to antique English paperweights. An official says one patron tiled her bathroom with repro-

duction 17th Century Mexican tiles bought from the institute.

Indeed, museums across the country are stepping up promotion and merchandising efforts, says Joseph Veach Noble, president of the American Association of Museums and director of the Museum of the City of New York. "Some museums with the better traffic patterns have been able to double their shop sales in the last few years," he says. Shop sales aren't a panacea, but "literally, you look for everything" to help ease the current financial burdens, Mr. Noble says.

Museums also are seeking a wider audience because the museums want to "spread the gospel," Mr. Noble says. But the increased interest also helps to attract more museum admissions and more philanthropic and government support, he adds. In the long run, he says, the audience expansion and diversification are the most important things museums are doing to help their financial situation.

Whatever their motivation, the museums are certainly succeeding in reaching new audiences. The National Gallery says it now sends its free slide shows to the Kansas City Royals baseball academy in Florida, a nuclear submarine that makes six-month voyages, a prison in Alaska and the public schools of Bullhead City, Ariz. The museum says the shows reach 3.5 million Americans a year, five times the figure a decade ago.

NEWFOUND AUDIENCES

In New York, the Metropolitan says it now attracts over three million visitors a year, a 50 percent rise from four years ago. A single recent exhibition of Impressionist paintings drew 577,000 visitors in 10 weeks. "There's no question about it, the potential audience is far greater than anybody ever imagined," says Thomas Hoving, the Met's director.

Indeed, Hilton Kramer, art critic of the New York Times, believes museums are "on their way to rivaling the universities as major centers of culture, scholarship and education." The museums benefit not only from their own promotions, but also from the generally growing public interest in art. "We now are a society intent upon availing itself of cultural goods and services to an extent never before known to the history of civilization," Mr. Kramer contends. This has helped move museums from the sideline of the cultural scene to its "nerve center" and given them an "unmistakable air of ambition and exhilaration," he adds.

Ironically, art museums find that much of their new success indirectly stems from their financial plight. Between soaring costs and sagging endowment income, many museums now find balanced budgets are as elusive as stolen Botticellis. Ten years ago, endowment income and grants from New York City covered 89 percent of the Met's $5.5 million budget. Today, the budget is three times as large, and these traditional sources of income pay only 61 percent of the bills.

To try to make ends meet, the Met started promoting its cookbooks, charging admission and depending on crowds lining up to see its shows. "Without these new sources of income, the Met would be in grave financial circumstances," says Daniel Herrick, vice director for finance. As another reason to court crowds, museum directors say they are under rising political pressure to serve the broadest possible share of the taxpaying public.

While the promotional trend has developed gradually over a number of years, the growing pressures on museums are accelerating the process rapidly. Many critics and museum officials are worried that merchandising and box-office popularity may soon take precedence over scholarship and art—if it hasn't already in some cases.

But the public isn't worried. A Daniel Yankelovich Inc. survey showed New Yorkers consider the Met their city's No. 1 tourist attraction.

The mounting and merchandising of special shows are clearly attracting much of the public interest. In the year ended last June 30, the Met staged 32 special exhibits, eight times the figure eight years earlier.

Along with other museums, the Met has transformed the museum exhibition from a flock of related objects slapped on the wall to a multimedia spectacular. The Met has added popular, informative sideshows, called "orientation galleries," that usually demonstrate the art form being exhibited. Halfway through a recent smash-hit tapestry show, vistors came upon a room with a woman weaving a tapestry. They also had a chance to see a film on tapestries. "By the time you had seen it all, you had had a real tapestry experience," the museum's Mr. Herrick says.

NATIONAL GALLERY

Four years ago, Washington's National Gallery started a separate exhibition-design department with a full-time architect. To provide rustic background for a show of Alaskan native art, the department acquired weathered boards from a man who made his living tearing down old barns. Stone statues were placed on deer hides. The lights were arranged to simulate the Arctic sunlight. "In the old days, we just hung things on the wall," an official says.

Museums are also stepping up efforts to promote shows. Until five years ago, the Met never used any television promotions, even though stations will show them without charge as part of their public-service requirements, officials say. Today, the museum regularly films TV spots—in Spanish as well as English.

CHILDREN'S HOUR

While museums are seeking more adult visitors, they are hardly neglecting the next generation. Indeed, the National Gallery reports a sharp rise in visits from preschoolers. The Met holds special weekend sessions of art work and gallery visits for children as young as 2½.

More significantly, the Met arranges tours for 120,000 school children a year and must turn down as many groups as it accepts, says Louis Condit, who is in charge of education. The Met's popular Junior Museum has all sorts of gadgets to show children how art is created. Push a button and a movie shows prehistoric Frenchmen painting their caves. Pick up an earphone and a "medieval scribe" tells with a groan how hard it is to produce scrolls. One tour designed for elementary-school students even arranges for every child to try on 15th Century steel armor.

IMPRESSIONIST KIT

For use outside the museum, the Met has developed elaborate classroom materials for sale or rent that in effect are miniature art courses. For instance, the new Impressionist kit includes 12 slides of paintings, biographies of the artists, texts on the movement and suggested questions for discussion. It also has a large, almost indestructible reproduction of a Degas painting laminated onto construction board and billed as suitable for classroom handling. As a "related activity for the teacher," the kit also includes Renoir's wife's chicken recipe.

Color slides and a washable Degas are a big step from the traditional idea of educational materials from museums, of course. "When I went to school, 85 percent of the slides were black and white and had a thumb print in the middle," the Met's Mr. Hoving says.

REACHING OUT

On a larger scale than the Met's program, the National Gallery's slide shows are introducing art to literally millions of Americans in 3,200 towns. Oma Middleton, librarian of the Leachville, Ark., public schools, figures only 5 percent of the town's children have ever set foot in an art museum. So she orders several dozen films and slide shows from the National Gallery every year. "For most of our students, this is the first exposure to art except in a book," she says. In Bullhead City, Ariz., fifth-grade teacher Vona Mink, who recently used National Gallery sculpture slides, says, "Many of the kids weren't even aware that sculpture existed."

The museums are also trying to broaden their adult audience. In the Met's senior-citizen program, started a few years ago, retired volunteers take courses in art history, then show slides in nursing homes. And the Met worked with New York's Puerto Rican museum, El Museo del Barrio, to organize a show titled "The Art Heritage of Puerto Rico."

While the Met's services grow, so do its sales of merchandise. The museum now sells 6,000 items ranging in price to $1,850. Such sales have soared to more than $7 million a year from $3.2 million four years ago, according to the museum's Mr. Herrick. He says the museum now plans to mail catalogs several times a year, instead of only at Christmas. And the traditional Christmas catalog has grown to 116 pages from 48 pages five years ago.

The museum's search for production ideas ranges farther than ever. For the recent exhibition of gold works and other Scythian art from the Soviet Union, the Met commissioned a special Hermes scarf from

Paris portraying the jewelry. The Met sold up to 100 of the scarves a week—at $50 each, Mr. Herrick says.

MET T-SHIRT

Sensitive to market trends, the museum now offers writing paper with art nouveau designs. For the kitchen fashion market, it sells an apron decorated with woodcuts of 16th Century pots and pans—all taken from the cookbook of Pope Pius V's private chef. Lately, it has added the official Metropolitan Museum of Art T-shirt. It features a picture of the museum's mascot, a 4,000-year-old figure of a loveable Egyptian hippopotamus named William.

Moving into new areas, the museum now licenses Spring Mills Inc. to adapt sheet designs from the Met's 18th and 19th Century textile collections. In exchange, the sheet maker pays the Met royalties of more than $200,000 a year, Mr. Herrick says.

In addition to all this, the Met is getting into the computer business. The museum installed a computer in the basement to handle mail orders and the like and will also sell computer time to other cultural organizations in the area, Mr. Herrick says.

Such measures helped the museum pare its significant deficits of the early 1970s and practically break even lately. But in recent months, soaring costs and a cut in New York City grants resulting from the city's financial crisis made officials fear larger deficits again. They closed the museum on Tuesdays and cut guard services. They also raised to $1.75 from $1.50 the suggested "voluntary" admission fee. (While the amount is voluntary, no one is admitted without paying something, and the average actual payment under the $1.50 voluntary fee was 88 cents.)

Until 1970, the museum didn't ask any admission fee at all. But today, it says it couldn't get by without the $1 million or so a year that the fees provide.

This dependence worries critics. "Box-office considerations now hold sway over all other priorities in the (Metropolitan) museum's exhibition policy," charges Mr. Kramer, the New York Times critic. Along with others, he contends that the museum's recent show of French paintings from 1774 to 1830 was slashed to 150 paintings from 206 in order to make it quicker-paced, more "readable," and thus more popular. While the show was still a triumph, the cuts reduced its educational and scholarly value, Mr. Kramer says.

Robert Rosenblum, New York University professor of fine arts and one of that show's organizers, contends that hit shows like the Impressionist exhibit often don't add to knowledge or expand the public taste because they merely "repackage" familiar works. "It's like playing 'The Sound of Music' over and over again. But Hoving sees box office as his real triumph," Prof. Rosenblum charges.

Not surprisingly, Mr. Hoving denies that he is selling art down the river. "The critics say we're marketing our Monets like slabs of beef. But we don't put on exhibitions to have socko box office," he says. He claims many shows still cater mainly to scholarly interest. As he sees it, many critics want to return to the days when museums were quiet retreats for an educated elite. "They want to go back to the club, and they mask it with talk of scholarship," he says. "But museums have begun to realize that the real world is also important. Museums are no longer clubs."

57
PLEASE GET SICK

Imagine a store with some unusual patterns surrounding its marketing efforts:

1. The customers often are not the people who choose the store; somebody else sends them in and decides what they will buy.
2. Neither the customer nor the person who chooses the store pays for what's purchased. A third party has that responsibility.

The "store" described is of course a hospital. Doctors tell a patient which institution he or she will patronize. Insurance companies are responsible for most of the payments, or else that "third party" payer is the U.S. government.

Despite the fact that the patient may neither choose the hospital nor pay the bill, the hospital administration still wants to have the kind of institution patients will like. Doctors choose the hospitals at which they'll have staff privileges, and they don't want to antagonize patients by choosing hospitals their patients will despise. Consequently, while doctors are one market segment of greatest interest to hospital administrators, patients are certainly another segment to consider.

As shows up most vividly in the proprietary (profit-making) hospital, promotion to patients takes the hospital basically into the hotel business. According to a spokesman for the Hyatt chain, which owns both kinds of institutions:

There are a lot of similarities between putting up hotels and hospitals. The big difference is that where they have a bar we have a surgical suite. Operating-wise they also have a lot in common. Both are basically service oriented. Face it, you go into a hospital and the surgery could be terrible, but you'll probably never know. But what you do know and care about are the same things that matter to a hotel guest: good food, clean floors, and a big color TV.

Research by faculty members at the University of Pennsylvania has shown that, if given a choice, patients rate hospitals by type, location, appearance, and quality of nursing service. Only then do they consider the quality of physician services.

MARKETING OPPORTUNITIES

If we continue to focus on the marketing efforts to patients, a listing of a hospital's marketing opportunities may, at the extreme, sound somewhat bizarre. Interviewing the administrator of a fictional "Palm Harbor" Hospital in Southern California, writer Roger Rapoport depicts him pointing at the roadway outside the hospital and commenting:

You know, we're kind of lucky to be in this sort of a community. The people are behind us. We've got Disneyland generating a lot of emergency business for us, as well as the Garden Grove, Santa Ana, and Newport freeways. Man, there are a lot of wrecks out here. We lose on the emergency, but it's a good loss leader for us, just like obstetrics.

Obstetrics—the maternity service—is not a profit-maker. Still, the administrator looks at the department as a way of introducing families to the hospital. "During pregnancy mothers learn about the hospital through our Stork Club teas. After the baby is born they tend to think of Palm Harbor as their medical home away from home. You just know the mothers will bring these kids back to us when it's time for the old tonsils to come out. Then we'll make it all back and probably come out ahead."

Marketing to doctors, however, is the hospital's critical effort. According to a physician writing in *MBA* magazine, investor-owned hospitals are far ahead of most community and university hospitals (the non-profit institutions) in seeking to satisfy the physician-user.

KEEPING DOCTORS HAPPY

What do they do? Convenient parking, dictating, and lounge facilities help keep doctors happy. A well-run admitting office eliminates embarrassing breakdowns in communication. And it helps to have one administrator responsible for dealing with all the doctors' problems and complaints— someone with the "clout" necessary to resolve difficulties quickly.

Furthermore, the very fact of being an investor-owned (private) hospital can be a marketing tool directed to the physical segment, since one key to profits is giving doctors a financial stake in the hospital. Many chains achieve that objective by buying doctor-owned hospitals with stock. Others have encouraged physicians to buy shares in their corporations. Either way, the doctors end up with a clear financial interest in the hospital. Physicians at Beverly Enterprises' Encino, California, hospital keep a television set in a lounge adjacent to their surgical suite tuned to a UHF business news channel. Administrator Max Weinberg explains, "They like to see how their stock is doing. I

usually come down every morning to find out myself."

ANOTHER SEGMENT

Patients and even doctors need not be the whole marketing target area for a hospital, however. For sophisticated institutions, another segment to consider as customers may be other hospitals. A large-city hospital might, for example, decide to sell some services as a "tertiary care" institution to smaller hospitals in the area who are not themselves providing those services.

A Midwest hospital taking this approach surveyed surrounding hospitals and found several opportunities. For example, a 70-bed rural hospital could not afford to staff a critical-care unit full time, but its patients could be monitored remotely by nurses at the large hospital. Portable nuclear-medicine equipment and traveling personnel allowed high-quality diagnostic studies at the small hospitals. Eventually, regular referral patterns developed, an effort helped by the fact that the large hospital began to refer to itself internally as a "wholesaler" of these services.

Another institution, a specialized children's hospital, was already a tertiary care center, and therefore depended on physician referrals. To reach potential referring doctors staff physicians wrote articles that appeared in well-read medical journals, according to *MBA*. The community, which represented potential patients and supporters, was reached through tours, special health-related programs, and health-education radio spots.

With such sound use of marketing, it seems unfair to picture the hospital as a heartless promotor. Proprietary hospital corporations have brought health care to communities which otherwise could not muster the necessary capital, and marketing techniques have kept institutions solvent by keeping their beds in use. Still, there may be somewhere a counterpart to the "Palm Harbor" administrator who muses: "Sure you don't see smallpox anymore, but we've got new things going for us today. Thanks to all the smog, our inhalation-therapy business is picking up beautifully. Inhalation-therapy—now there's a moneymaker."

SOURCES

1. Fink, Daniel J., "Marketing the Hospital." *MBA,* Dec. 1978/Jan. 1979, pp. 50–56.
2. Rapoport, Roger, "A Candle for St. Greed's." *Harper's,* April 1974.
3. Seaver, Douglass J., "Hospital Revises Role, Reaches Out to Cultivate and Capture Markets." *Hospitals,* June 1, 1977, pp. 59–63.

58
THE SELLING OF THE DEITY

by Edward B. Fiske
Saturday Review

NEW YORK—Western religion has always been at home in the market place. Saint Paul used to preach in the agoras, or markets, of the Mediterranean world. Traders would arrive by ship, hear his message, and take it back home with them. Market places were the mass media of the day.

The folks at Religion in American Life, Inc., like to think of themselves as spreading their message in somewhat the same way. For 23 years this nonprofit organization has been peppering the landscape with billboards urging us to "worship together this week" or reminding us, with John F. Kennedy, that "God's work must truly be our own." Last month Religion in American Life launched a new campaign.

To give a fitting sendoff to what one might call The Selling of the Deity, 1973, RIAL threw a party at the Time-Life Building's Tower Suite, which overlooks the Newsweek Building in midtown Manhattan. Guests found two tables with lavish assortments of cheeses, a selection of red wines, and two large punch bowls filled with ice and bottles of chablis and *rosé*. At one end of the room, near a large plate glass window, was a

From Edward B. Fiske, "The Selling of the Deity, 1973." Copyright 1972 by Saturday Review Co. First appeared in Saturday Review *December 9, 1972. Used with permission of the publisher and the author.*

machine with a small screen that played RIAL's new musical television spots ("Sisters and brothers, loving each other we're gonna make a better day"), while at the other end a tape recorder recited the radio spots ("Activate your membership in the community of man and help reverse moral pollution"). In between, journalists, media representatives, businessmen, and multidenominational volunteers chatted informally.

On the way in, each of us had been handed a bulky kit containing copies of the new ads and background material on RIAL. It was evident at first glance that selling religious belief is big business in this country. Founded in 1949 and backed by 40 religious groups, including Protestants, Roman and Eastern Orthodox Catholics, and Jews, RIAL has an annual budget of about $200,000. Last year this money—most of which is spent in the development of television and radio spots, magazine and newspaper ads, and posters for subway and train stations—generated the equivalent of $27 million worth of donated time and space in the mass media. The ads are prepared by a "volunteer agency," Lieberman-Harrison, Inc., and placed through the Advertising Council, the arbiter of which public service ads are fitting and proper for the country to see and hear.

Curious as to how one goes about developing advertisements for the Almighty, I sought out some of the creative people who had put it all together. It was clear from just a few moments of conversation that they are divided into two camps. Charles Harrison, president of Lieberman-Harrison, asserted that one had to tackle religion like any commercial product. (He acknowledged, though, that there are distinct advantages in having such an eternal client. "You have the luxury of integrity," he said, "and you don't have the problem of product failure.") On the other hand, Paul V. Higgins, the senior vice-president who supervised the account said

that he prefers to think of the task in its own terms. "Since nobody's buying anything, I don't like to use the word 'commercial,'" he stated. "I prefer to call our spots 'message units.'"

I asked about this year's theme, which, summed up in RIAL's posters for transit stations, is "The community of man—God's club." Mr. Higgins said that the RIAL board had come up with the "community of man" idea and that the creative people had jazzed it up with the "God's club" part. "We had to bring a quite theological idea down an octave to the level of the average person," he explained. "It's actually quite an accomplishment to compress a religious idea into 30 or 60 seconds and do it with artistic validity."

The "God's club" slogan, however, caused some problems within the RIAL fold. As one official explained, "The Episcopalians and Presbyterians are touchy about accusations that they are elitist and exclusive." The problem seems to be solved by the way the slogan is presented in TV and radio ads. Reference to "God's club" is swiftly followed by the comforting reminder: "It's not exclusive. It includes you and me." Lois Anderson, the new head of RIAL's mass media committee, said that irony is part of the ads' effectiveness. "We are giving the exclusive idea a new twist and making it clear that the community of man, not the churches, is God's club," she said. . . .

Between sips of wine RIAL leaders indicated that they are trying to get away from their in-group reputation. For one thing, they have steered away from the get-people-to-church approach of the fifties in favor of themes that have broader appeal. "40 percent of adult Americans attend worship in an average week," said Jerald Hatfield, RIAL's fulltime program director, "but what about the other 60 percent? We want to reach them, too."

This year's campaign indicates a shift away from the old preoccupation with sectarian faith and toward social issues. The big business world view lingers on—shoplifting is singled out as one of our urgent national problems—but the kits also showed ads dealing with open housing and urban blight. Two of them bring up the question of business morality and suggest that concepts of personal morality must be applied to the business world.

The creative people said that they intended quite frankly to raise in people's minds questions about the responsibility of corporations in such areas as housing, pollution, and minority employment. Arthur Davies, the outgoing head of the media committee, suggested that this approach took a bit of courage because "it sounds like we are talking about the very businesses behind RIAL." Ian MacGregor, the new national chairman of RIAL, assured me, however, that the basic thrust is still personal. Mr. MacGregor, who is chairman of American Metal Climax, Inc., and has been involved in a running battle with the Episcopal church over the ecological and social damage allegedly caused by some of his company's mining operations in Puerto Rico, said that RIAL's ads are aimed at alerting people to major problems and getting them to "take some interest in their faith." . . .

What good does all the advertising do? RIAL officials are not sure, and some are even a bit reluctant to try to measure effectiveness. "You can't quantify a qualifying effort," said Mr. Higgins. Mr. Hatfield, though, said that the Compton agency is going to try to measure the impact of RIAL's promotion efforts as part of its regular research studies in California. He said further that even if the campaigns do nothing but reinforce people's faith and their belief in brotherhood, they can be considered worthwhile.

The materials for this year's campaign being set, all that remains to be done is to get them placed. One network balked at a TV spot because it was too explicit about belief in God; but officials expressed confidence that this snag could be worked out. I asked some of the media public-service people what they thought of the spots; they were universally pleased. "They're something we can really use," said a man from one New York radio station. "They're not at all controversial."

This didn't sound much like Saint Paul. But then he didn't have an interfaith board, and he got his money from making tents.

SECTION FOLLOW-UP
MARKETERS YOU DIDN'T KNOW . . .

Colleges have learned that recruiting students, keeping them, and raising money are three interrelated activities; if they fit together, the college is practicing marketing. More money raised can be put into scholarships to help attract and keep more students; attracting and keeping more students makes the college appear successful to foundations and individual donors; therefore it raises more money. Similarly, any successfully marketed product brings in revenue that can be put to work in even more successful marketing. The museum can buy more merchandise; the psychologist can take time out to appear on a call-in radio talk show and thereby publicize his or her clinical practice. The successful police force that lowers the crime rate can make a stronger case to city council for higher pay. They then may attract even better applicants, hire a better force, and bring the crime rate down further.

Those "safer streets" are the product the police offer to the city, while they offer careers to recruits. Like any marketing organization, they need to identify the "product" from the viewpoint of different market segments. When colleges market to students, for example, the "product" is future status and advantage in the job market. When the college development officer visits a community donor, the college's product is redefined as "well-educated graduates."

For each marketing organization in this group of readings, it may be intriguing to ask:

1. What is the product, as defined to what segments?
2. Are there potentially profitable segments that most marketers of this kind are not serving? Should lawyers and psychologists, for example, arrange with businesses for a retainer that would make their services available free every Wednesday to the business's employees?
3. What buyer attitudes limit the marketing strategies available to each of these marketing organizations? How likely are those attitudes to change—and in what direction?

INDEX